Empowering AI Applications in Smart Life and Environment

Nour Eldeen Mahmoud Khalifa •
Mohamed Hamed N. Taha
Editors

Empowering AI Applications in Smart Life and Environment

Springer

Editors

Nour Eldeen Mahmoud Khalifa
Faculty of Computers and Artificial Intelligence
Cairo University
Giza, Egypt

Mohamed Hamed N. Taha
Faculty of Computers and Artificial Intelligence
Cairo University
Giza, Egypt

ISBN 978-3-031-78037-0 ISBN 978-3-031-78038-7 (eBook)
https://doi.org/10.1007/978-3-031-78038-7

This Springer imprint is published by the registered company Springer Nature Switzerland AG
The registered company address is: Gewerbestrasse 11, 6330 Cham, Switzerland

Dedicated to the memory of my father
(Mahmoud Khalifa Ali)

Dedicated to my father, mother, sister, and
my children (Abdelrahman, Nelly)

Preface

Artificial intelligence (AI) is the simulation of intelligent behavior in computers in a way that we, as humans, would consider this behavior is intelligent or humanlike. AI is considered one of the most breakthrough advances nowadays. The integration of AI with visual, audio, and haptic devices will lead to the rise of smart sustainable environment transformation. This book's primary objective is to comprehend the influence of various AI applications on smart environments and life. This includes studying the impact of AI on smart environments, encompassing areas such as energy optimization in smart city systems, intelligent transportation, healthcare management, smart farming, and smart homes. This book is aimed to introduce the state of the art in research on Artificial Intelligence with respect to applications on smart life and environment. The included chapters are covered in the following two parts:

- Part I—Artificial Intelligence in Smart Systems, Environments and Security
- Part II—Artificial Intelligence in Smart Healthcare and Sustainability

Part I includes chapters on AI-driven energy efficiency in smart homes, advanced object detection in intelligent environments, deep learning techniques for pipeline defect detection, AI-enabled IoT data platforms, the use of YOLO model for automated mango quality assessment, and machine/deep learning strategies for cybersecurity in smart environments. Part II covers topics such as deep learning in multi-class skin disease diagnosis, AI integration in elderly care, and AI's role in enhancing the recycling of post-consumer plastics. Together, these parts illustrate the diverse and impactful ways AI is being used to create smarter, more sustainable, and secure environments.

We extend our sincere gratitude and acknowledgment to everyone involved in the publication of this book—authors, reviewers, and the publishing team. Their dedication and support have been influential in bringing "Empowering AI

Applications in Smart Life and Environment" to realization. We hope that readers will find the chapters insightful and appreciate the effort invested in this collective work.

Giza, Egypt

Nour Eldeen Mahmoud Khalifa
Mohamed Hamed N. Taha

Contents

Editors and Contributors

Editors

Nour Eldeen Mahmoud Khalifa received his B.Sc., M.Sc., and Ph.D. degrees in 2006, 2009, and 2013, respectively, all from Cairo University, Faculty of Computers and Artificial Intelligence, Cairo, Egypt. He also has a Professional M.Sc. Degree in Cloud Computing in 2018. He authored/coauthored more than 50 publications and 3 edited books. He has more than 3500 citations. His name is included in the Stanford list for the top 2% percent scholars around the world. He is an associate editor for *PLOS ONE* journal. He reviewed several papers for international journals and conferences including (*Scientific Reports*, *IEEE IoT*, *Neural Computing*, *Artificial Intelligence Review*). Currently, he is an Associate Professor at Faculty of Computers and Artificial Intelligence, Cairo University. His research interests include wireless sensor networks, cryptography, multimedia, network security, machine, and deep learning. https://scholar.cu.edu.eg/nourmahmoud

Mohamed Hamed N. Taha received his B.Sc., M.Sc., and Ph.D. degrees from the Faculty of Computers and Artificial Intelligence, Cairo University, in 2006, 2009, and 2013, respectively. He has been an Associate Professor with the Information Technology Department, Faculty of Computers and Artificial Intelligence, Cairo University, since 2016. He is a reviewer of the *IEEE Internet of Things* journal. Deep learning, machine learning, the Internet of Things, wireless sensor networks, and blockchain are his research interests.

Contributors

Hady Abdalla School of Computer Science, Canadian International College (CIC), Cairo, Egypt

Wafaa Abdelgawad School of Computer Science, Canadian International College (CIC), Cairo, Egypt

Ramazan Aksoy Department of Software Engineering, Faculty of Engineering and Architecture, Istanbul Beykent University, Istanbul, Turkey

Mohammed Alameri College of Engineering, UAE University, Al Ain, UAE

Doris Aschenbrenner Hochschule Aalen – Technik und Wirtschaft, Aalen, Germany

Natalie Basedow Hochschule Aalen – Technik und Wirtschaft, Aalen, Germany

Gulay Cicek Department of Biomedical Engineering, Faculty of Engineering and Architecture, Istanbul Beykent University, Istanbul, Turkey

Cecilia Colloseus Aalen University, Aalen, Germany

Esraa Darwish School of Computer Science, Canadian International College (CIC), Cairo, Egypt

Mohammed Hassan El-tohamy School of Computer Science, Canadian International College (CIC), Cairo, Egypt

Nicole Fangerow Hochschule Aalen – Technik und Wirtschaft, Aalen, Germany

Kathrin Hadasch Hochschule Aalen – Technik und Wirtschaft, Aalen, Germany

Sena Karaoglu Department of Software Engineering, Faculty of Engineering and Architecture, Istanbul Beykent University, Istanbul, Turkey

Amir Sohail Khan Jiangxi University of Science and Technology, Ganzhou, China

Zeashan Hameed Khan IRC-IMR, King Fahd University of Petroleum & Minerals, Dhahran, Saudi Arabia

Arun Sri Krishna The Math Company, AI and Analytics, Bengaluru, India

Marwan Makhlouf School of Computer Science, Canadian International College (CIC), Cairo, Egypt

N. Manohar Department of Computer Science, School of Computing, Amrita Vishwa, Vidyapeetham, Tamil Nadu, India

Qurban Memon College of Engineering, UAE University, Al Ain, UAE

Dietmar P. F. Möller Clausthal University of Technology (TUC), Clausthal-Zellerfeld, Germany

Ata Jahangir Moshayedi Jiangxi University of Science and Technology, Ganzhou, China

Youssef M. Nassar School of Computer Science, Canadian International College (CIC), Cairo, Egypt

Akshatha Prabhu Department of Computer Science, School of Computing, Amrita Vishwa, Vidyapeetham, Tamil Nadu, India

N. Shobha Rani Department of Artificial Intelligence and Data Science, GITAM School of Technology, GITAM (Deemed to be University), Bengaluru, India

Gehad Ismail Sayed School of Computer Science, Canadian International College (CIC), Cairo, Egypt

Andrea Sell Aalen University, Aalen, Germany

Mohamed Sohail Dell Technologies, Cairo, Egypt

Said Tabet Dell Technologies, Cairo, Egypt

Zhenglin Wang School of Engineering and Technology | Tertiary Education Division, Institute for Future Farming Systems, CQ University Australia, Sydney, Australia

Ergin Yuzak Department of Software Engineering, Faculty of Engineering and Architecture, Istanbul Beykent University, Istanbul, Turkey

Xiaohong Zhang Jiangxi University of Science and Technology, Ganzhou, China

Part I
AI in Smart Systems, Environments and Security

Chapter 1
Smart Home Systems and Energy Efficiency in Daily Lives

Ramazan Aksoy, Sena Karaoglu, Ergin Yuzak, and Gulay Cicek

Abstract This chapter examines the differences between the energy efficiency and environmental impacts of traditional houses and smart home systems in daily life. Compared to classical arrangements in traditional homes, the advantages of automation and energy management provided by using smart home systems are discussed. This chapter evaluates and compares the effects of both concepts on daily life, focusing on criteria such as comfort, security and energy saving between a traditional house and a house furnished with a smart system. The chapter also addresses the environmental sustainability of smart home systems. The potential of smart home systems to provide energy efficiency has the potential to reduce the environmental impact of this technology. The chapter addresses how smart home systems can be optimized, especially in terms of energy saving, to understand their environmental impact and discusses how this technology can contribute to a sustainable lifestyle. In this context, it evaluates the environmental sustainability and user convenience of future home designs by evaluating the environmental impacts of smart home systems compared to traditional homes. This study also aims to evaluate the performance of commonly used classification algorithms such as Neural Network, Support Vector Machines Rbf Kernel, Logistic Regression, Decision Trees, K Nearest Neighbor Algorithm, Support Vector Machines and Random Forest on smart home systems and traditional home energy consumption dataset. The effectiveness of each algorithm in energy consumption classification is analyzed using various performance metrics, and the results allow inferences to be made to support important decisions on the energy efficiency of smart home systems. This study provides valuable insights into identifying optimal classification algorithms for future smart home systems design to support energy saving and sustainability goals.

R. Aksoy · S. Karaoglu · E. Yuzak
Department of Software Engineering, Faculty of Engineering and Architecture, Istanbul Beykent University, Istanbul, Turkey

G. Cicek (✉)
Department of Biomedical Engineering, Faculty of Engineering and Architecture, Istanbul Beykent University, Istanbul, Turkey
e-mail: gulaycicek@beykent.edu.tr

N. E. M. Khalifa, M. H. N. Taha (eds.), *Empowering AI Applications in Smart Life and Environment*, https://doi.org/10.1007/978-3-031-78038-7_1

Acronyms

AI	Artificial Intelligence
AB	Ada Boost
CV	Cross Validation
DT	Decision Tree
GB	Gradient Boosting
GNB	Gaussian Naive Bayes
kW	kiloWatt
KNN	K Nearest Neighbor
LSTM	Long Short Term Memory
LR	Logistic Regression
MAE	Mean Absolute Error
MSE	Mean Square Error
PIR	Passive Infrared
RBF	Radial Basis Function
RMSE	Root Mean Square Error
RF	Random Forest
SVM	Support Vector Machine
SHTs	Smart Home Technologies
TP	True Positive
FP	False Positive

1.1 Introduction

Smart homes are systems that allow users to remotely control devices and systems in their homes using artificial intelligence (AI) and other automation technologies. Today, with the innovations that technology brings to home life, an important turning point is experienced in energy consumption and environmental sustainability. Detailed comparisons and meticulous analysis clearly reveal that smart home systems are both more efficient and environmentally friendly than traditional home designs. We owe the fact that smart systems contain such useful features to their well-designed architectures. Smart home systems consist of different components such as sensors, microprocessors, transducers and antennas. Sensors optimize the condition of the house with the data they collect. For example, when the temperature level rises, temperature sensors transmit this situation to the relevant support units and ensure that the overheated air returns to normal levels. Actuators, which consist of many mechanical components such as gears and shafts, It controls lights, heating and devices. Controllers installed at the central point of the house have an integrated system with sensors and actuators and play a role in the management of devices. Screens and interfaces used in smart home systems are used to provide feedback and interact with smart home systems.

Smart homes have many advantages such as energy saving, security and energy efficiency, thanks to their integrated technology systems. By integrating energy-saving devices and lighting systems into these houses, electricity bill costs and carbon footprints are reduced and time and energy are saved. For example; Energy consumption can be prevented with a smart bulb. With the smart thermostat, the air conditioner that is left on is detected, energy waste is prevented and energy is saved. When smart door locks are used, residents do not have to carry their door keys with them at all times. Beverages such as coffee and tea can be prepared at the desired time with the smart plug-in wifi application, thus preventing individuals from wasting time on such tasks. Smart homes are also preferred for advanced security. Modern sensor systems use a passive infrared (PIR) system. While indoor and outdoor motion sensors save energy by using them for lighting, outdoor motion sensors, especially when used with security cameras, provide a significant benefit in terms of security. For example, when someone enters the house without permission, it is detected with smart devices and the situation is immediately notified to the residents via smart phones. Residents ensure that their homes are safe by watching from anywhere with real-time video providers. Smart door locks and video doorbells, using different communication systems such as Bluethoot and Wi-fi, have a very positive impact on the security level of homes. With wireless alarm systems, for example, a break sensor you place in your home can easily detect different inputs and further increase the security of the home. Smart homes also offer a healthy and comfortable life to their residents. Smart air purifiers can purify indoor air and further improve air quality. Changes in temperature and humidity are detected by the relevant sensors and necessary changes are made. The demand for smart home systems, which have many advantages compared to traditional homes, is increasing day by day. Many smart home technologies, such as smart sprinkler systems, pool pumps and faucet technologies, can operate with the minimum level of energy they require. Robotic vehicles used in smart home systems meet the health, safety and independence needs of sick and elderly people and provide them with a better quality of life with support technologies such as remote control systems and communication tools.

The aim of the work was to ensure efficiency in every aspect. Topics that will ensure efficiency: Energy Saving, Increased Security, Comfort and Convenience, Remote Access and Control, Environmental Sustainability, Cost Effectiveness, Data Security, Automation and Smart Scenarios, Home Health and Comfort, Compatibility and Integration, Use of Advanced Technology, Customizability , Home Automation and Coordination Across Smart Devices, Updatability and Flexibility, Advanced Analytics and Data Collection. When past research is examined in detail, it is clear that energy use and savings are at the forefront in the development of smart home systems. With the advancement of technology, the need for energy has increased significantly and the efforts made to meet this need have led us first to energy saving and then to renewable energy sources. Energy saving is the ability of devices to operate in the most efficient way, thus meeting their needs by consuming less energy. Research examining the effects of smart home systems on energy efficiency shows that these systems can make a significant difference.

For example, a study revealed that homes using smart home systems consume 10–20 percent less energy than traditional homes. Additionally, there are still some gaps regarding the environmental impacts of smart home systems. For example, the environmental impacts of the production and installation of smart home systems are not fully understood. This article aims to give ideas on creating new systems by examining the extent to which energy savings are achieved and to what extent these changes the environmental impacts. The potential benefits that arise from the use of smart homes in a specific region will make a significant contribution to demonstrating the positive features of smart homes. In this context, the following basic questions are at the center of the chapter: Talking about the potential benefits of smart homes, what are the results of the research conducted in the USA on energy consumption? Do these systems affect users' energy expenditures? Also, are smart home systems more advantageous in terms of environmental sustainability? Different types of devices used in these homes have automated many aspects of the home, such as lighting and security. The most important result of this automation is to save energy by preventing energy waste. In smart homes, energy costs are reduced by ensuring energy efficiency. Energy-saving devices such as lighting, heating and cooling reduce energy costs by consuming less energy, and these results are directly reflected in electricity bills. The US Department of Energy has stated that energy-saving smart homes save up to 30% in energy costs compared to traditional homes. Environmental impact is among the important features of smart homes. Energy-efficient smart homes reduce carbon footprint because they reduce greenhouse gas emissions. In the USA, homes are responsible for 20% of the country's greenhouse gases. Therefore, as the demand for smart homes increases, it will have a direct impact on reducing the environmental impact as the emission of greenhouse gases will decrease. In the country, half of the energy use in a conventional home comes from heating and cooling. Energy-saving devices used in smart homes reduce the environmental impact. One of the important statements made by the US Department of Energy is that LED lighting consumes 75% less energy than traditional lighting and lasts 25 times longer. One of the important tools that reduce energy consumption is the use of smart plugs and power strips. According to the report of the International Energy Agency, these devices reduce energy consumption by up to 30%.

This chapter also includes the classification of the data set containing smart and traditional home energy consumption data set with machine learning algorithms and statistical models and the performance evaluation of the algorithms. Modeling was carried out using Neural Network, Support Vector Machine with Rbf Kernel (SVM with RBF Kernel), Logistic Regression, Decision Trees, k-Nearest Neighbors Algorithm (KNN), Support Vector Machine classification algorithms. More detailed explanations are detailed in the methods section. Machine learning and statistical models provide powerful tools to improve the energy efficiency of smart home systems and compare them with traditional home systems. The use of these models can guide homeowners in developing energy-saving strategies and promoting sustainable energy use.

The following sections of the article are organized as follows; Latest studies on energy efficiency and energy saving in smart home systems and studies on smart home systems with machine learning are explained in the "Related Studies Section" (Sect. 1.2). Recommended Methods are described in the "Method Part" (Sect. 1.3). The experimental and graphical results of the proposed approaches and the discussion of these results are explained in the "Experimental Results Part" (Sect. 1.4) and the "Discussion Part" (Sect. 1.5), respectively, and in the last part of the chapter, the "Conclusion Part" (Part Completed with Sect. 1.6).

1.2 Literature Studies

Research has been conducted on energy efficiency and energy saving in smart home systems, and it has been seen that many studies have been conducted providing experimental data on this subject. As examples of these; In the study of Hargreaves and his team, it was emphasized that smart technologies, which offer new possibilities for automatically and remotely controlling home environments, have the potential to significantly improve home energy management. According to the research, it is suggested that users can simplify their lives by delegating control aspects such as energy management, security and entertainment to automatic smart home systems [1]. The key factor in smart home energy management is efficient home appliance design as well as improved customer awareness. Since users who are not aware of energy use cannot ensure efficient use, even if a good technology is developed and designed, it will not achieve its purpose. In their study of device design, Koomey and colleagues addressed delays in replacing old, less efficient electronic devices with new, more efficient ones and customers' failure to remember energy consumption when purchasing a device. According to the research, this reveals that the overall energy efficiency of the devices falls below best practice standards [2]. According to the work of Saad al-sumaiti, Ahmed, Salama and their team, more stringent standards are recommended to increase energy efficiency; However, it is emphasized that customers still play an important role in energy savings. According to the research discussed, increased awareness of energy use and therefore electricity prices can allow users to make more informed decisions about suitable devices and gain more effective control over electricity consumption. One of the reasons for this lack of awareness is that analog meters are not based on real-time measurements, and it has been stated that this situation creates an obstacle to instant feedback on invoices [3]. Learn more According to research by Jentsch, Prause, Pramudianto, Al-Akkad, and Reiners, meters are commonly used to measure hourly consumption in most Canadian homes, although customers may often be unaware of how much energy a watt represents. To clarify this concept to customers, it is necessary to provide the cost in equivalent dollars; However, even the (dollar)/KWh value published on the electricity provider's website may not encourage all customers to regularly monitor their actual consumption. Although solution suggestions include methods such as transmitting hourly consumptions directly to mobile phones, a more effective solution is a fixed monitoring device that is connected to all equipment and displays information about all equipment along with the current electricity price. The authors do not believe that even this proposal would result in an energy-efficient smart home, given the dual requirements for complex technology and user interface transparency. Lack of customer awareness of home content and communication methods requires prior review of smart home design and optimal positioning of existing devices. These steps can be included in a long-term plan; However, addressing the current situation should include transforming existing homes and determining how smart devices are identified. Many studies have been conducted on these issues [4]. In addition, user-friendly designs should be created to save energy. These products, which are based on both convenience and efficient use of time, should also provide business efficiency in human life. According to the research of Fatih and his team, the use of technology to facilitate home and work life is increasingly increasing today. As a product of rapid technological advances, the concept of smart home was born. The smart form of houses has provided serious convenience in the field of remote control and security, providing convenience in areas where security, time control and comfort increase in our lives. In order to prevent energy waste and increase security while away from home in the fast pace of life, remote control of AC lamps and garden cameras was provided via Telegram in this study. In addition, face detection systems detect the face of the person entering the house and this information is transmitted to the homeowner as a message via Telegram. Thus, security is ensured at home entrances. This study has presented us with a model proposal [5]. In the research conducted together by Li, Hathaipontaluk and Luo, smart home ovens, which are generally defined by manufacturers as faster cooking ability, were discussed in detail. However, a prominent feature of this study was the suggestion of a different characterization. The smart oven has been defined by focusing on the capacity of a family member to prepare healthier food according to pre-determined healthy recipes, rather than just focusing on the ability to cook faster. Research has shown that the smart oven has functionality that not only speeds up the cooking process but also focuses on healthy eating. In this context, the device's ability to allow users to cook meals according to pre-determined healthy recipes has captured the value offered by the smart oven from a broader perspective [6]. Additionally, it was pointed out that the smart oven is not limited only to its internal functionality. The device's ability to communicate with other home devices such as mobile phones, fire alarms and smart refrigerators is highlighted. In this way, the smart oven can determine whether the materials are available at home and interact with the integrated smart system in the home by sharing this data with other devices. This is an approach that supports the integration and communication features in the smart home definition determined by Intertek [7]. This research has made a significant contribution to how smart home technology can transform a wide range of in-home experiences, starting from cooking processes. Machine learning is one of the topics addressed during the production of smart home systems. In the study conducted by Azizoğlu and Ünsal, data sets produced by the water neutralization system of Sivas Numune Hospital, which converts medical waste into domestic waste, were used. Medical liquid waste in hospitals is subjected to chemical neutralization by being processed with neutralization devices before being discharged into the sewer. In this process, real-time monitoring of pH levels in the medical waste neutralization system is of great importance for environmental protection. Within the scope of the study, linear regression (LR), support vector machines (SVM), support vector machines (SVM), k-Nearest Neighbors Algorithm (KNN), random forest (RF), and decision tree (DT) machine learning algorithms were used. As performance measurements, mean absolute error (MAE), mean square error (MSE), and root mean square error (RMSE) were evaluated. According to the analysis results, especially the support vector machines (SVM) algorithm showed a more effective performance on two different data sets. This evaluation shows that machine learning algorithms can be used successfully to predict missing pH data In addition, in Metin et al.'s research, systems in which data obtained from accelerometer and gyroscope sensors in smartphones are used to classify and recognize the activities of individuals are used in various applications such as developing disease diagnosis processes in the field of health and smart home projects. In studies like this, artificial neural network models generally focus on processing time series and cannot analyze higher level attributes and the relationships between these attributes. In this context, the long-short-term memory (LSTM) model is used as a recurrent neural network to better analyze the relationships on time bundles. It attracts attention with its ability to understand and offer a flexible structure in layers.

This study shows that a deep learning-based approach used to classify individuals' activities can offer an effective research area on energy saving, especially in smart home systems. Such information obtained through accelerometer and gyroscope data can be important data sources in terms of energy management and automation, which can contribute to making smart home systems more effective and energy efficient [8]. It is possible to create intrusion detection and selective systems using machine learning. In this context; In the work of Semih ÇAKIR, Nesibe YALÇIN, and Sinan TOKLU, Internet of Things (IoT) devices have a rapidly increasing usage rate with advances in wireless sensor networks. Heterogeneous networks where IoT devices are connected to each other are highly susceptible to external attacks. Many routing protocol attacks have occurred so far, and these attacks continue to increase over time. However, the proposed detection and prevention methods need to be updated in accordance with today's conditions [9]. Fake identity attacks occur in the routing protocol (Routing Protocol for Low-Power and Lossy Network, RPL) in lossy networks at the network layer in IoT. Among these types of attacks, attack detection based on the signal strength of nodes is among the most common and recommended methods. However, resource constraints such as energy conservation and low processing load are important issues in IoT devices. Attack detection, especially with classical methods, may be insufficient to effectively detect and prevent attacks. In this study, the packet distribution rates of nodes and the detection of fake identity attacks with Naive-Bayes, Random Forest and Logistic Regression, which are machine learning approaches, are proposed. Fake identity attacks have been detected with a higher success rate (accuracy rate of 99.51%) compared to classical methods [10]. In the research conducted by Harun DOLCEL, Mahmut DURGUN, and Levent GÖKREM, competition on water resources is expected to increase due to factors such as population growth, urbanization and climate change. The fact that the annual amount of usable water per capita in our country is around 1500 m3 shows that we are a country experiencing water shortage. For this reason, it is necessary to use the available limited water resources economically and to be careful and careful in water usage. This study aims to create a special irrigation reform for each product in accordance with the diversity of products planted in the soil in gardens where various products are grown, and to use water resources effectively and correctly. It aims to increase production efficiency by using An internet-of-things-based, remote-controlled and artificial intelligence-supported multi-layered system was designed for 8 different products. The multilayer system manages information from wireless sensor networks for information discovery and decision-making in rural environments. The proposed system aims to minimize water use and get the best efficiency by analyzing the data collected by sensors. Since water is a scarce natural resource, the proposed system offers the opportunity to irrigate according to product type, track live data, and monitor and control this data from anywhere via mobile devices or computers. In addition, all energy needs to be used are provided through renewable energy sources (Solar Photovoltaic) [11]. The purpose of giving examples of these studies is to indicate how successful machine learning is in detecting problems. Based on these, we can choose the machine learning that best suits our work. Human harmony is very important in this field. When research on people's approach to smart home systems is examined, according to the research conducted by Wilson, Hargreaves and Hauxwell-Baldwin, a representative national survey conducted on homeowners in the United Kingdom (n = 1025) revealed that potential users It shows a positive perception about Home Technologies (HHTs), especially those with multiple functions such as energy management. SHTs are a set of technologies that include the automation of sensors, monitors, interfaces, devices and equipment to enable localized and remote control of the home environment. This technological system includes controllable devices such as heating and hot water systems, lighting, windows, curtains, garage doors, refrigerators, televisions and washing machines [12]. Finally, in research on the effects of smart home systems on the environment, the following was said about the preferences of choosing smart home systems: According to Civan's [13] research, energy efficiency is of increasing importance today. In this era where resources are rapidly depleting and the environment is under threat from various aspects, special attention should be paid to the use of recycled materials, the integration of renewable energy sources and environmental harmony when designing smart home systems and building structures. These methods can contribute to the goal of leaving a more livable world to future generations by not only saving energy but also increasing environmental sustainability [13]. According to the work of Herrero and his team, tackling global energy challenges requires a large-scale transformation in societies' energy use to address interconnected issues such as energy emissions and accessibility. This transformation aims to significantly reduce the carbon footprints of final energy use, while also confronting the deep roots of energy injustices and deprivation. During this period of major change, households are at the center of these efforts, playing an important role in effectively managing and reducing energy use. Smart home technologies (SHTs) are among the new tools emerging as part of this transformation. In addition to providing solutions for residential emissions reductions, SHTs have the potential to provide associated benefits for households experiencing energy poverty. These technologies can contribute to a sustainable energy future by providing households with a powerful set of tools to manage energy use more consciously and reduce environmental impacts [14].

1.3 Method

This research, which was conducted to compare the energy consumed during the use of smart home systems and the energy data sets consumed by a house configured with traditional methods, evaluates the differences in energy consumption. In the chapter, various classification methods will be used to understand the effects of smart home systems on energy efficiency. Various pre-processing steps and data augmentation techniques will be applied on the data sets, then various models will be trained and the results will be examined.

1.3.1 Dataset Description

The data sets used in the article include home systems with and without smart home systems. These data sets contain data collected over specific measurement periods. There are a total of 5598 measurement lines under two main categories (Table 1.1). In detail: Smart Home Systems: This category contains a total of 2799 measurement examples of 19 different home systems. Each line contains information about specific features and measurements of smart home systems. Smart Non-Home Systems: This category covers a total of 2799 measurement samples from 9 different home systems. Similarly, each line reflects the features and dimensions of non-smart home systems. The data set named PartialDataSmart contains the attributes of smart home systems. The attributes and their descriptions in this data set are as follows, respectively. Duration refers to reading times within a 1-minute interval. Usage [kw] refers to the total energy consumption, household [kw] refers to the overall household energy consumption, dishwasher [kw] refers to

Table 1.1 Datasets

Data types	Type	Data row
Smart home systems	19	2799
Non-smart home systems	9	2799

the amount of energy produced by a particular appliance, oven 1 [kw], oven 2 [kw], household office [kw], refrigerator [kw] indicates the amount of energy consumed by a particular appliance, and living room [kw] indicates the energy consumed in the living room. The data set named PartialDataNormal contains the features of traditional houses. Global_reactive_power is the total active power consumed by the household in kilowatts(kw), global_reactive_power is the total reactive power consumed by the household in voltage, average voltage is the global_intensity, voltage is the average current density, Sub_metering_1 is the energy produced for the kitchen in watt-hours (wh). Submetering refers to the amount of active energy produced for the laundry. These data sets were used to compare energy consumption patterns between smart home systems and traditional home systems and formed the basis of the analyzes in the article.

1.3.1.1 Data Preprocessing

The aim of this chap is to understand the effects of smart home systems, which are widely used in daily life, on energy efficiency. In this context, various data preprocessing techniques have been used to improve the quality of the used dataset and increase its practical applicability (Fig. 1.1). First, to reduce noise in the dataset, noise removal steps were applied to clean data points containing unwanted or meaningless information. Thus, more reliable results were obtained by minimizing the effect of unexpected breaks in energy consumption data. Then, by eliminating unnecessary and low-information features in the data set, the training process of the model was accelerated and more effective learning was enabled. In this way, attributes that cannot be more directly associated with energy efficiency or have low variance are filtered out, allowing the model to focus on more meaningful attributes and improving performance.

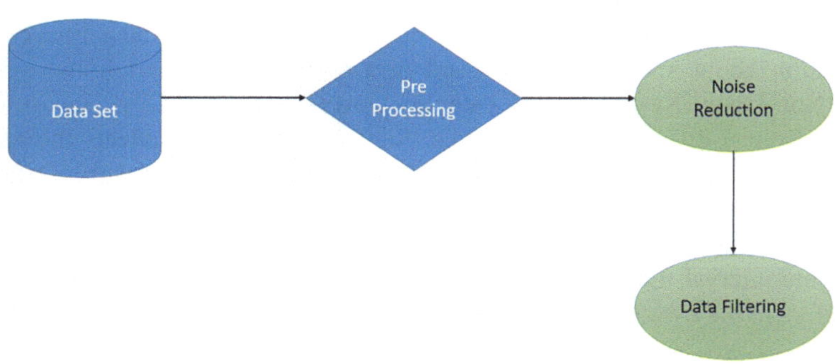

Fig. 1.1 Main steps of pre-processing

Noise Elimination

Each data set may contain some measurement errors and technical glitches depending on the environment in which it was collected and its sources. Some measurements in this data set could not be recorded due to such technical problems. This could have negatively affected the accurate and reliable learning process of the model. By identifying and removing invalid values in this data set, it was aimed to optimize the training process of the model. Cleaning up invalid or corrupt measurements helped the model produce more consistent and reliable results. While this step made the data set clearer and easier to understand, it also contributed to the model creating a noise-free, more accurate representation. Denoising improved the model's generalization ability, allowing it to better cope with real-world data. In this way, the model was made more powerful and reliable by minimizing the effects of data errors caused by technical problems.

Data Filtering

In the data analysis process, one important step encountered is managing the size and complexity of the data set. Significant differences in the measurement times of the house with a smart home system and the traditional house prevented it from processing this data set effectively. It contained 503,910 lines of data for the smart home system and 2,071,527 lines for the traditional house, and in both cases, measurements were made at one-minute intervals. The size of these data sets required significant computing power during the model training process. However, considering that existing physical hardware is not capable of dealing with large datasets, data minimization has become inevitable. At this point, it was decided to keep measurements at 3-hour intervals instead of storing data at minute intervals in order to analyze energy consumption more accurately. This approach allowed having a more comprehensive data set with measurements obtained from every time period of the year. 3-hour measurements obtained by expanding the measurement intervals allowed energy consumption to be evaluated from a more general perspective. Additionally, by reducing the dataset to a smaller and manageable size with this method, the computational cost in the model training process was significantly reduced. This data filtering process contributed to faster and more effective training of machine learning models.

1.3.2 Classification

1.3.2.1 Neural Network

Neural network is a model that touches the essence of the world of artificial intelligence and imitates the working principles of the human brain. This network

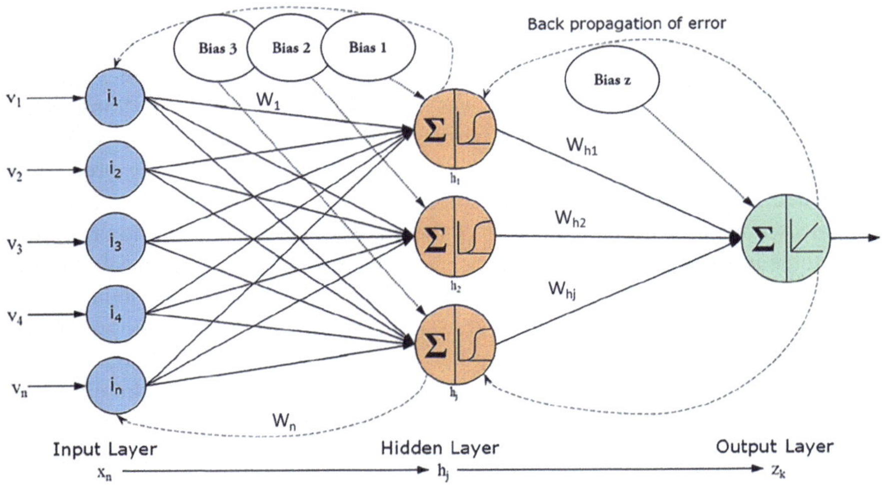

Fig. 1.2 Neural network classification algorithm

consists of mathematical neurons and stands out for its ability to understand and learn complex relationships in the data set. Neural networks, which are generally used in large data sets, gain the ability to generalize the results by learning from this data during the training process. It is especially successfully applied in areas such as image recognition, sound processing and language understanding. For example, a neural network can recognize objects in images, understand voice commands, or analyze tone in a language. However, the use of this technology requires large computational resources and large training datasets. Additionally, a balanced education is important as there is a risk of overlearning. Neural networks (Fig. 1.2) become stronger with experience and repetition. Their ability to continuously learn allows them to become more precise and effective over time. However, it is important to pay attention to ethical and safety issues when using it. As a result, neural networks are an important component of artificial intelligence with their ability to solve complex problems and learn.

1.3.2.2 k-Nearest Neighbors Algorithm (KNN)

k-Nearest Neighbors Algorithm (KNN) algorithm is a simple but effective method used to solve classification and regression problems. Its basic principle is based on the majority or average of its surrounding k nearest neighbors to classify a data point or predict a value. KNN assumes that data points with similar characteristics tend to be close to each other. Therefore, the classification of a data point is determined by the majority of its surrounding neighbors. This simple approach can be especially effective on small and medium-sized data sets and simple classification

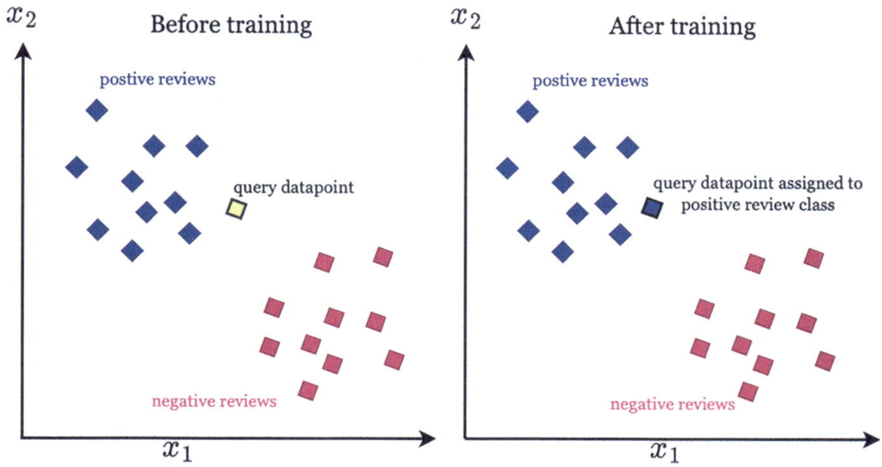

Fig. 1.3 k-nearest neighbors algorithm

problems. However, the disadvantages of KNN include its high computational cost and difficulty in dealing with the size of the dataset. Additionally, issues such as choosing the optimal k value and sensitivity to noise in the data set should be taken into account. KNN (Fig. 1.3) provides an effective solution, especially in cases where samples with similar properties tend to belong to similar classes. However, it is important to evaluate performance in situations such as large and complex data sets or high-dimensional feature spaces. In conclusion, KNN is an algorithm known for its simplicity and understandability. However, it is important to carefully consider the characteristics and requirements of the dataset before use.

1.3.2.3 Logistic Regression

Logistic regression is a statistical method used to estimate the probability that an item in a data set is in a particular state. This method is an effective tool for making binary (two-class) predictions, especially in classification problems. Logistic regression (Fig. 1.4) is a variant of linear regression. However, an advantage of logistic regression is that it compresses the results using a transition function across bounds. This ensures that the resulting estimate is probability based. For example, predicting whether an email is spam is a common application area where logistic regression is used. Logistic regression is preferred in many applications because it is simple and understandable. However, it models linear relationships, so it has some limitations in expressing more complex relationships. In this case, more complex models, such as neural networks or support vector machines, may be more effective. In conclusion, logistic regression is a basic and common statistical method used in classification problems. It is especially effective in binary classification

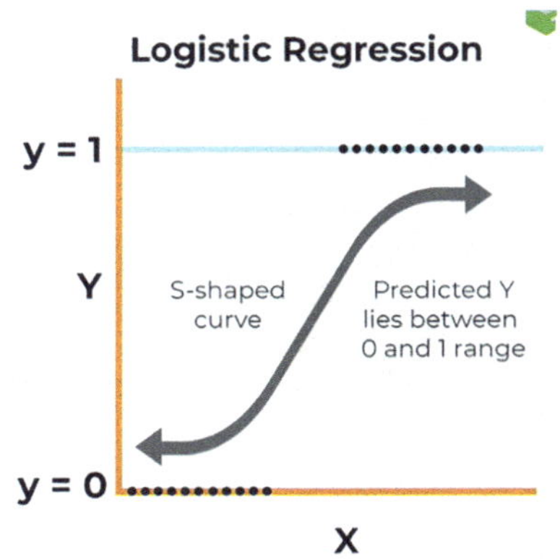

Fig. 1.4 Logistic regression classification algorithm

problems, and its understandability provides ease of application. However, the nature of the data set and the complexity of the relationships must be taken into account.

1.3.2.4 Decision Tree

A decision tree (DT) is a model that provides a step-by-step roadmap for deciding on a solution to a problem. Imagine that a friend of yours starts asking you questions about something. The first question is usually about a general topic, and your answer determines whether your friend asks the next question. The decision tree works in a similar way. Initially, it asks a question about the most important feature and determines the next question based on the answer to that question. At each stage, the branches of the tree draw a path along which questions and answers follow each other. This simple and understandable structure makes decision trees especially explainable to humans. Decisions are explained step by step, so there is no major difficulty in understanding a concept. At the same time, as the tree deepens, you can turn to more complex and specialized questions. However, the risk of a decision tree (Fig. 1.5) is that it tends to overfit the data set. That is, the model can be fitted very closely to the training data, but this can make it difficult to generalize with new data. As a result, a decision tree mimics the concept of finding a step-by-step solution to an issue. Similar to asking step-by-step questions while talking to a friend about a topic, a decision tree tries to find the correct classification by asking questions based on the features in the data set.

1.3.2.5 Random Forest

Random Forest (RF) is a learning model where a forest is created by bringing together various trees. Each tree is trained independently using different subsets

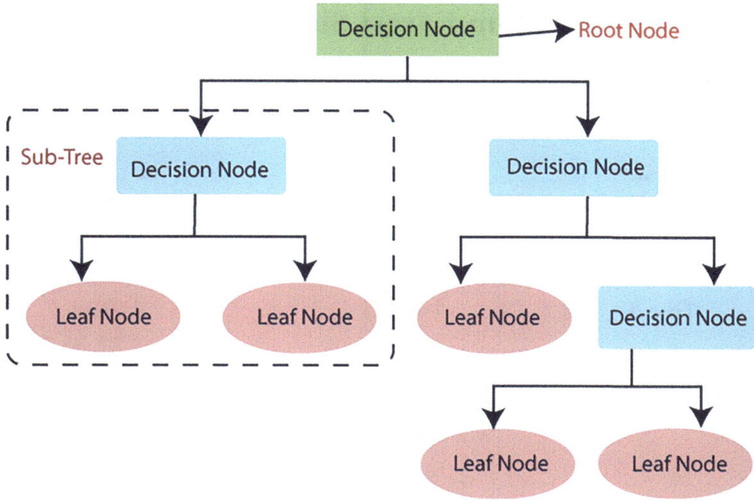

Fig. 1.5 Decision tree classification algorithm

of the dataset. The random nature of this forest allows each tree to focus on different characteristics. This multi-tree structure can be thought of as getting different perspectives from various people while listening to one individual's opinion. Random Forest (Fig. 1.4) aims to make the overall model more robust and reliable by ensuring that each tree provides its own "view." Random Forest is resilient to overlearning and offers a wide range of applications on various datasets. It resists noisy data and missing values. It is very effective in feature selection and the generalization ability of the model, especially in large and complex data sets. This algorithm is used in many fields, especially image recognition, biomedical engineering and financial analysis. Each tree focuses on different features, allowing the model to use a wide set of features. As a result, Random Forest offers a learning model empowered by combined multiple perspectives. The variety of different trees makes the model generally more reliable and durable. However, the complexity of the model and the high computational cost must be taken into account (Fig. 1.6).

1.3.2.6 Support Vector Machines (SVM with RBF Kernel)

Support Vector Machines (SVM) is a powerful algorithm used to classify data points and solve regression problems. SVM performs effectively by focusing specifically on maximizing the separation between classes. The Rbf (Radial Basis Function) kernel makes SVM particularly effective on complex and irregular data sets. This kernel function moves data points into a higher dimensional space, allowing them to better describe complex relationships between classes. This allows SVM to perform better on more general and complex data sets. SVM with Rbf Kernel is used in

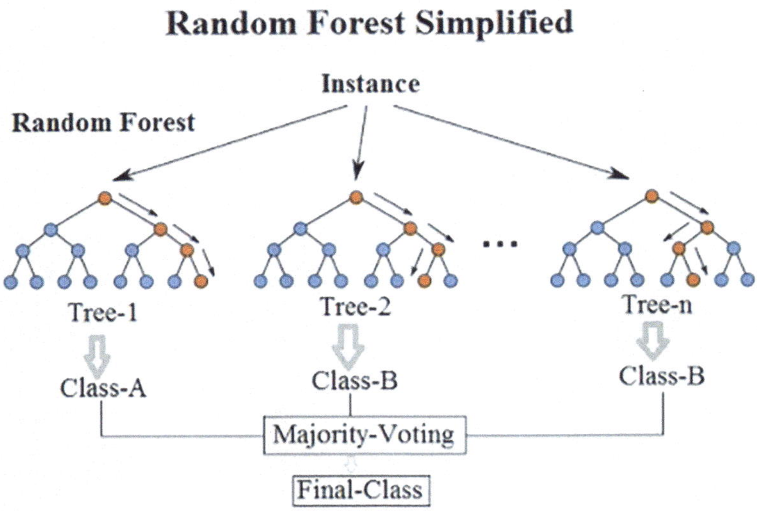

Fig. 1.6 Random forest classification algorithm

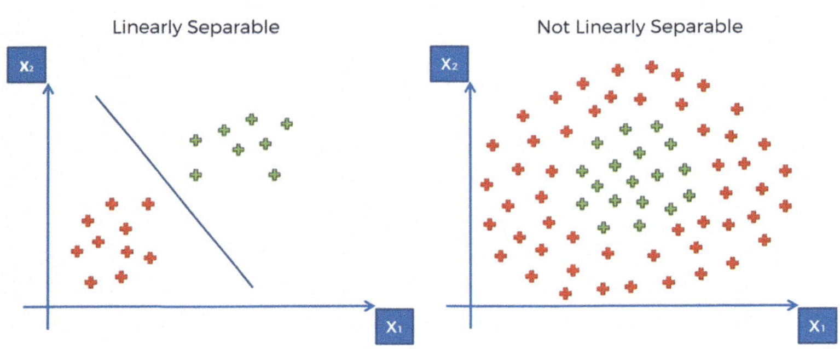

Fig. 1.7 Support vector machines with Rbf kernel

many application areas, especially image recognition, biomedical engineering and financial analysis. However, it is important that this powerful algorithm is tuned and trained correctly. Additionally, it may require large data sets and computational resources. As a result, with the Support Vector Machines Rbf Kernel (Fig. 1.7), a powerful algorithm is obtained that can effectively solve classification and regression problems on complex data sets. However, its use and adjustment must be done carefully. The SVM model was used to classify linear and nonlinear data using kernel functions.

1.3.2.7 Support Vector Machines

Support Vector Machines (SVM) represent an approach to solving a problem. It aims to find the best hyperlevel that separates a point from others. This hyperlevel tries to separate class points accurately while trying to maximize the margin between classes. Imagine that there is a piece of paper between you and a friend and you draw a series of dots on it. SVM tries to find a gap that is widest between these points. This space represents the hyperlevel that best separates the classes from each other. This makes it more reliable when classifying new points in the future. An interesting feature of SVM is its kernel functions. These functions allow the creation of more complex boundaries in low-dimensional data sets by moving data to higher dimensional spaces. Kernel functions help SVM (Fig. 1.8) better understand the dataset, as if evaluating a topic from different perspectives. However, a disadvantage of SVM is that its computational cost is high in cases with large data sets or large numbers of features. Additionally, optimal parameter tuning may be required, which affects the success of the model. In conclusion, SVM is a powerful tool used to solve classification and regression problems. Similar to trying to understand a topic with a friend and finding the best solution from different perspectives, SVM tries to provide the best separation in the data set.

1.3.3 Evaluation Metrics

1.3.3.1 Cross-Validation

Cross-validation (CV) is a technique used to objectively evaluate a model's performance and measure its generalization ability. It is especially important to understand how well the model adapts to new and unseen data, as well as its performance on

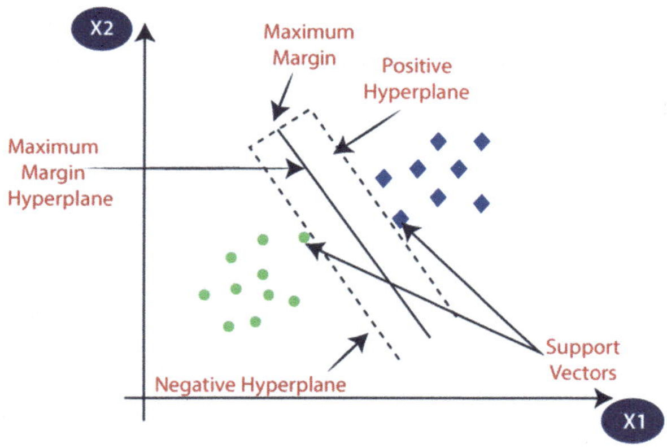

Fig. 1.8 Support vector machine

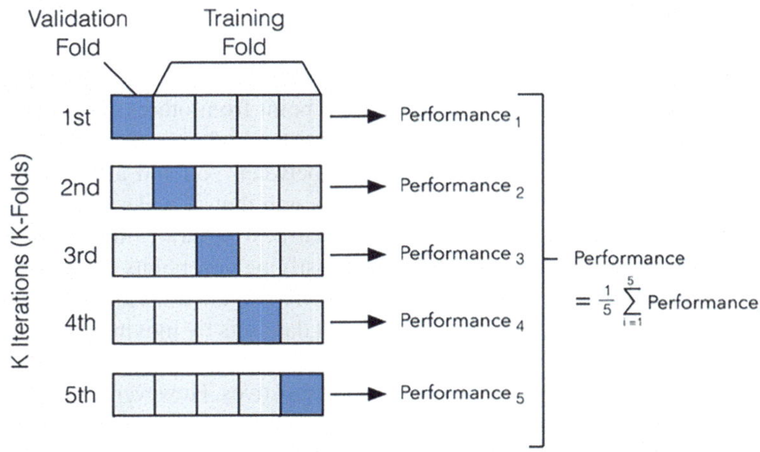

Fig. 1.9 Cross validation

the dataset on which it was trained. This process involves dividing the data set into random pieces and training the model on some of these pieces and testing it on the other. One of the most commonly used cross-validation methods (Fig. 1.9) is k-fold cross-validation. In this method, the data set is divided into k pieces and each piece is used as the test set in turn, while the remaining k-1 pieces are used as the training set. Cross-validation reduces the model's tendency to overfit and evaluates its overall performance more reliably. It is also used to increase the reliability of the model in limited data sets. However, cross-validation also has some disadvantages. The computational cost can be high, especially with large data sets. Additionally, given the structure and characteristics of the data set, choosing the right number of k-folds can be difficult. Consequently, cross-validation is an important tool to assess the generalization ability of the model and protect against overfitting. Various cross-validation methods can be used to deal with new data and reliably evaluate the performance of the model. The K-Fold used in this article is intended to obtain a more reliable performance evaluation and better analyze real-world data.

1.3.3.2 Model Plotting

Model drawing is a technique used to visually understand the internal structure or functioning of a machine learning model. This is the process of graphically representing the layers, connections, and outputs of the model. Model drawing is an extremely valuable tool for understanding the complexity and internal relationships of the model. A drawing of a model is usually just a graphic composed of layers and connections. This graph contains all layers of the model, starting from the input layer to the output layer, and the connections between them. Additionally, the number of nodes in each layer, the activation functions used, and other important parameters can also be displayed. Model drawing is used to evaluate a model's generalization ability and to detect potential overfitting situations. It can also provide guidance to reduce or optimize the complexity of the model. These visualizations can be used both to evaluate the performance of the model from a technical perspective and to make the operating principles of these models more understandable. It is also useful for understanding how the model evolves throughout the training process. In conclusion, model drawing is a powerful tool for visualizing and understanding the internal structure of a model. Using these visualizations to better understand and debug your model can increase your success in your machine learning projects. "Confusion Matrix", a model drawing type used in this article, visualizes evaluation metrics. These visuals show the number of "True Positive", "True Negative", "False Positive" and "False Negative" predictions. These numbers are represented by the table and heat map. These plots are important tools for understanding and evaluating the performance of machine learning models.

1.4 Experimental Results

Two separate data sets containing the energy consumption of smart homes and traditional homes were used in the research. One of the parameters that enable the creation of a robust model is to ensure that the number of samples between classes is selected close and equal. Therefore, in our chapter, a balanced dataset was created by taking equal numbers of samples from the smart dataset and the traditional dataset. Open source Python libraries such as Matplotlib, Scikit-Learn, Pandas, Seaborn and Tensorflow were used in this study. Tensorflow and Scikit-Learn have played an important role in training models used with various classification algorithms in the field of machine learning. In order to facilitate the analysis of the trained models, visualization was made using Matplotlib. Numpy library was used to facilitate the calculation of mathematical operations. Numpy is a powerful library used for mathematical operations in many fields, especially scientific calculations and statistics. Thanks to the Pandas library, operating on data sets has become easier. This library helped read dataset files with ".csv" extension and the read data was processed through Scikit-Learn and Tensorflow. The data set was modeled with Rbf Kernel Support Vector Machine (RBF Kernel SVM), Logistic Regression, Decision Trees, k-Nearest Neighbors Algorithm (KNN), Support Vector Machine classification algorithms. In the chapter, by applying cross validation (K=5), accuracy, Sensitivity Specificity TP Rate FP Rate Precision recall values were calculated for detailed performance evaluation of each model. Detailed results of the classification results are given in Table 1.2.

Table 1.2 Datasets

Metrics	Accuracy	Sensitivity	Specificity	TP rate	FP rate	Precision	Recall
LR	0.91	0.94	0.87	0.94	0.12	0.90	0.94
RF	0.93	0.93	0.92	0.93	0.07	0.94	0.93
GB	0.93	0.94	0.92	0.07	0.94	0.94	0.95
SVM	0.92	0.94	0.88	0.94	0.11	0.91	0.94
KNN	0.92	0.94	0.90	0.94	0.09	0.92	0.94
GNB	0.90	0.94	0.85	0.94	0.14	0.89	0.94
DT	0.88	0.88	0.87	0.88	0.12	0.90	0.88
MLP	0.93	0.93	0.91	0.94	0.08	0.93	0.94
AB	0.93	0.94	0.92	0.94	0.07	0.94	0.94

1.5 Discussion

This research addresses the significant differences between smart home systems and traditional home designs in terms of energy consumption. It has been observed that traditional houses have higher energy consumption than houses using smart home systems. This situation reveals how effective the choices made regarding energy efficiency and technological adaptation are on the energy use in our daily lives. Smart home systems are equipped with automation and energy management features, and these features offer users the potential to save energy. Intelligent management of energy-intensive systems of homes such as lighting, heating and cooling results in lower energy consumption compared to traditional homes. This not only reduces individuals' energy costs, but also represents an important step in minimizing environmental impacts (Fig. 1.10).

Factors such as energy use, industrialization, waste materials and transportation increase the carbon footprint. Burning electricity, natural gas and energy sources causes significant amounts of CO2 emissions. Energy consumption is reduced by using energy-saving devices. One of the most important benefits of smart home systems is energy saving. For example, energy-saving bulbs and devices used in smart homes make a significant contribution to reducing energy consumption. A simulation tool was developed a few years ago to measure electricity consumption in detached houses. The results showed that automation has a positive impact on the environment by reducing electricity consumption. For example, a significant reduction in energy consumption has been observed by shifting the operation of some electrical devices from day to night. Automatic shutters reduce the use of air conditioners by adjusting them according to sunlight during the hottest hours of the day. As a result, the devices used in the smart home system reduce energy consumption and reduce the carbon footprint. Since there are no devices in traditional home systems that will directly affect energy consumption in this way, it is not possible to talk about reducing the carbon footprint for these homes. More sustainable and more efficient products are used in smart home systems rather than traditional home systems. Home automation and smart devices prevent significant

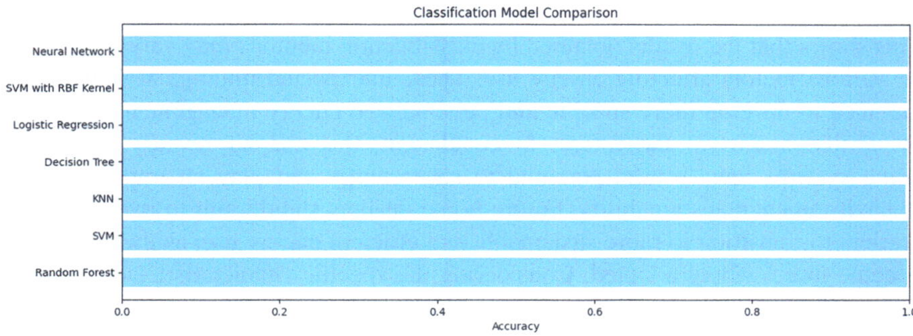

Fig. 1.10 Accuracy results of classification algorithms

energy waste. The system was analyzed by comparing traditional hood, smart hood and smart filtering kitchen hood with smart additional suction system. The results show that when the smart kitchen hood is compared to traditional hoods, CO2 emissions are reduced due to the optimization of the energy consumption of smart devices. It has been seen how effective these direct, smart devices are in reducing the carbon footprint

Higher energy consumption in traditional homes is often based on manual control systems and traditional lighting and heating arrangements. Lack of automation can lead to ineffective management of energy consumption and unnecessary energy expenditure. Lack of technological innovations can lead to limitations in energy efficiency. This research shows that smart home systems are more advantageous in terms of environmental sustainability. Low energy consumption can contribute to a more effective use of natural resources and reduce the environmental impact of energy production. This shows that smart home systems can not only save energy but also stand out as a means of transitioning to a sustainable lifestyle. This research highlights the importance of more widespread adoption of smart home systems to achieve the energy savings goals of future home designs. By increasing the use of smart home systems, a significant reduction in total energy consumption can be achieved, which can increase environmental sustainability. This chapter revealed that the values obtained by classification methods may vary with customers' knowledge and experience of energy management. This situation reveals the impact of dynamic changes in data sets on classification results. Compared to the energy consumption of traditional houses, it is clearly seen that smart home systems are more advantageous in terms of energy saving and environmental impacts. Smart home systems, along with the advantages offered by technological innovations, play an important role in optimizing energy consumption. Equipping future home designs with smart technologies will allow important steps to be taken in terms of energy efficiency. These steps will not only help individuals save energy in their daily lives, but will also be effective in achieving environmental sustainability goals with reductions in total energy consumption. Unexpected Findings and Changing Data Dynamics: This research also reveals that customers' knowledge and experience with energy management leads to dynamic changes in data sets. This shows that the results obtained by classification methods may vary depending on various factors affecting energy use. These unexpected findings also highlight the need to develop more specific and personalized energy management strategies in similar studies in the future. In conclusion, this chapter reveals that smart home systems have a high potential to save energy and play an important role in environmental sustainability. Future home designs should aim to overcome the barriers to transition to more sustainable and efficient energy use, as these systems become more widely adopted. Considering the specific characteristics of the data set, the success of the "SVM" model against the "RBF kernel" is due to the values being closer to each other. This is an important factor that affects the evaluation and preference of the performance of two different "SVM" models. The use of "SVM" with "RBF kernel" is known for its ability to handle non-linear and complex data sets. However, if the values in the data set are close to each other and have a regular structure, the use of "RBF kernel" made incorrect predictions instead of improving performance (Figs. 1.11 and 1.12). Linear SVM tends to make better use of more regular and linearly separable features in the data set. This means that the distinction between classes can be made more effectively with a linear hyperplane. In this case, the linear form of the SVM model allowed for more effective classification of regular and close values in the data set.

In this data model, RandomForestClassifier (Figs. 1.13 and 1.14), Gradient-BoostingClassifier (Figs. 1.15 and 1.16) and AdaBoostClassifier (Fig. 1.14) are used because they are more suitable for ensemble learning principles. Three models such as Figs. 1.17 and 1.18 tend to achieve higher hit rates. These models have been

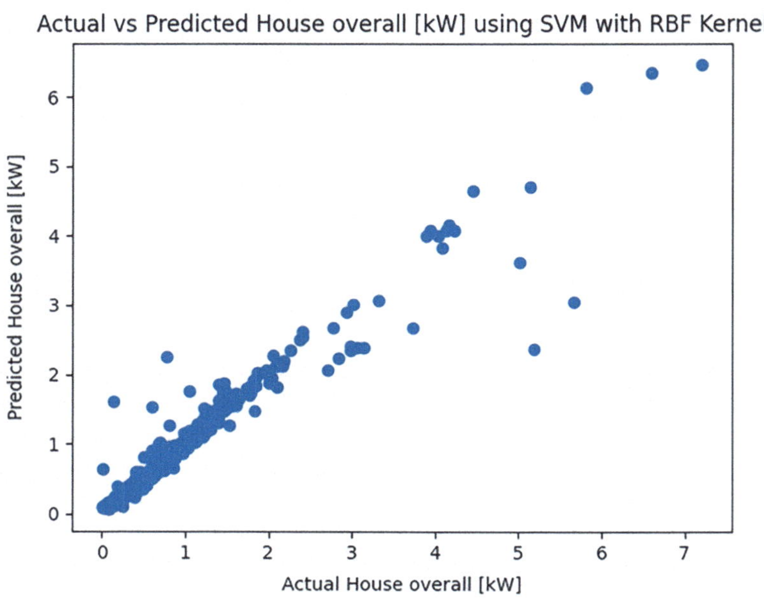

Fig. 1.11 SVM-kernel smart system home

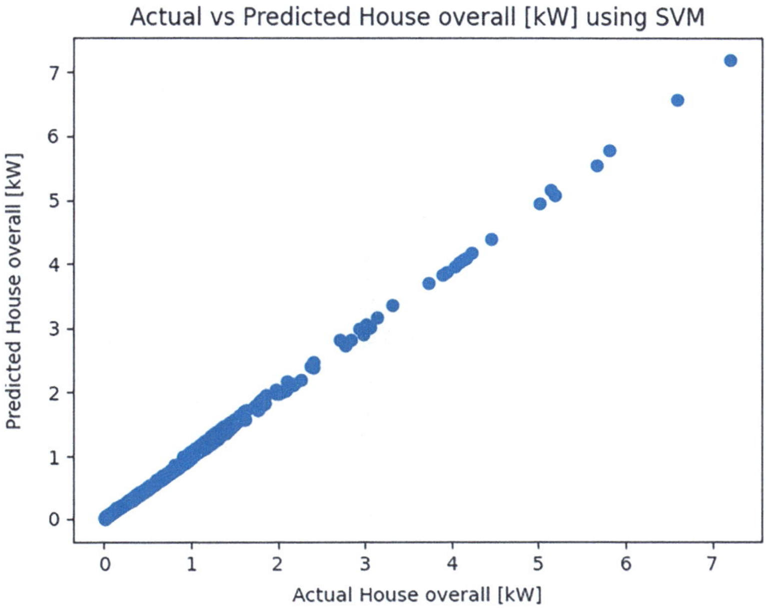

Fig. 1.12 SVM smart system home

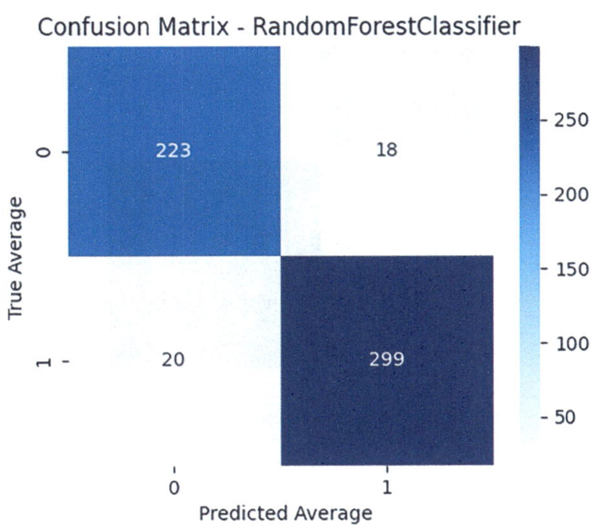

Fig. 1.13 Random forest traditional house confusion matrix

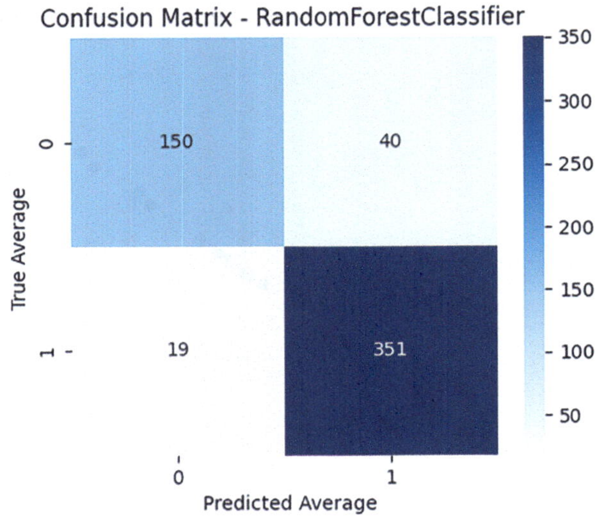

Fig. 1.14 Random forest smart home confusion matrix

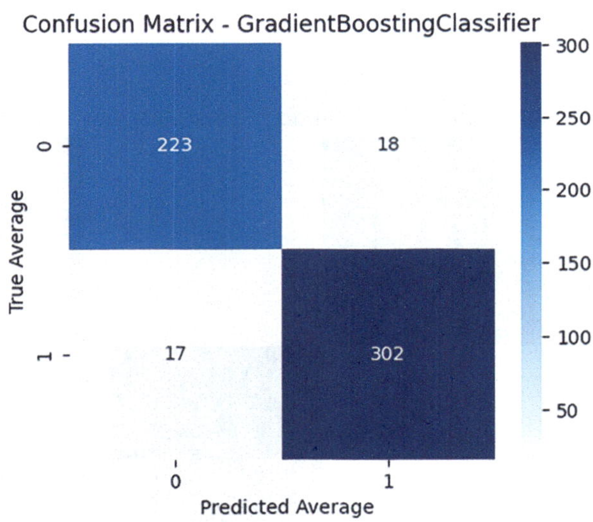

Fig. 1.15 Gradient traditional house confusion matrix

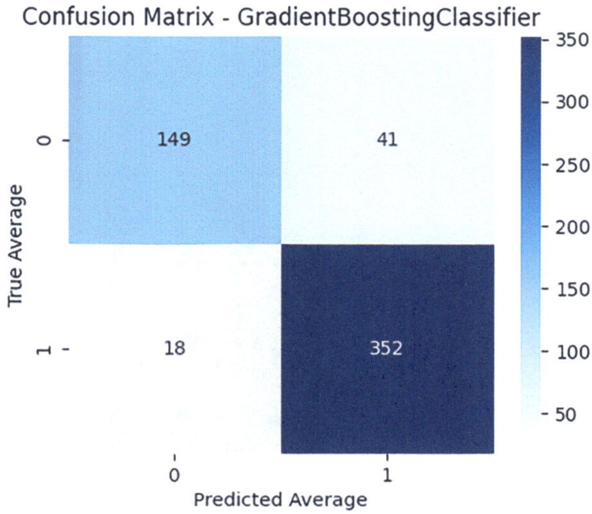

Fig. 1.16 Gradient smart home confusion matrix

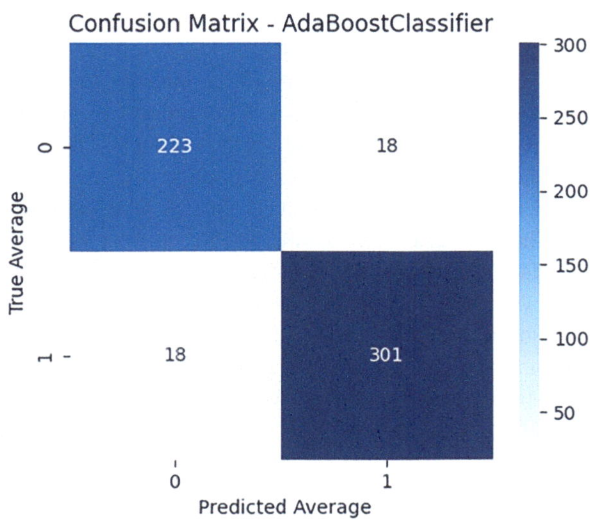

Fig. 1.17 AdaBoost traditional house confusion matrix

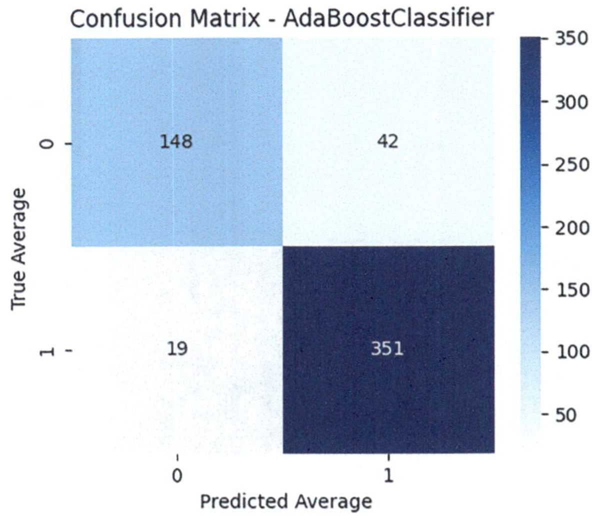

Fig. 1.18 AdaBoost smart home confusion matrix

meticulously managed to minimize the risk of overfitting during the training phase. Because RandomForestClassifier, GradientBoostingClassifier, and AdaBoostClassifier work by building decision trees in classification tasks, these models are often better able to learn complex data structures. This reflects the power of ensemble learning obtained from the combination of various models. Overfitting prevention strategies during the training process were applied to ensure that the model can generalize better with real-world data. In this way, RandomForestClassifier, GradientBoostingClassifier and AdaBoostClassifier models have become able to successfully apply the learned patterns to a larger data set. These three models can perform effectively on complex data sets, thanks to their ability to achieve high hit rates in classification tasks. This increases the reliability of the model and helps us achieve more robust results in classification processes.

In addition to Machine Learning models, statistical testing was performed to detect significant differences between the two groups. Mann-Whitney U test was used to detect a significant difference between two groups that did not have a normal distribution. Data sets named smartDataset and nonSmartDataSet were given as parameters to the ranksum method and p value ($p = 0$) was obtained. Since the obtained p value is less than 0.05, the null hypothesis is rejected. Therefore, it has been observed that there is a significant difference between smart home system energy consumption data and traditional home system energy consumption data. Matlab software (Fig. 1.19) was used for the Mann-Whitney U statistical test. The hypotheses are as follows.

- Null Hypothesis (H0): There is no significant difference between the two data sets.
- Alternative Hypothesis (H1): There is a significant difference between the two data sets.

```
[p, h, stats] = ranksum(smartDataset, nonSmartDataSet);

% Printing the hypothesis test result to the screen
disp(['Mann-Whitney U test result, can H0 be rejected? ', num2str(h)]);
disp(['p-value: ', num2str(p)]);
```

Fig. 1.19 Mann-Whitney U test in Matlab

1.6 Conclusion

Today, with the innovations that technology brings to home life, an important turning point is experienced in energy consumption and environmental sustainability. Detailed comparisons and meticulous analysis clearly reveal that smart home systems are both more efficient and environmentally friendly than traditional home designs. These systems that make homes smarter are not just an aesthetic touch; At the same time, changes that can change energy management are also made by managers. Automation transforms a structure that can adapt to the instant needs of home systems and minimize energy waste, providing ease of use and maximizing energy savings. The results of the research show that smart home benefits are effective not only in saving energy but also in reducing energy costs. These savings not only offer individuals an environmentally friendly solution, but also enable them to switch to economical energy use. Smart home systems increase user comfort as well as energy saving and efficiency effects. The structure and comfort features of automation offer homeowners a more comfortable, practical and personalized lifestyle. This research highlights that wider adoption of smart home outcomes in permanent home designs can play a critical role in supporting a sustainable and energy-efficient lifestyle. Smart home systems make homes smarter, more efficient and environmentally friendly through technological innovations, making the energy savings of the future accessible.

These systems that make homes smarter are not just an aesthetic touch; It is also pioneering revolutionary changes in energy management. Automation transforms home systems into a structure that can adapt to instant needs and minimize energy waste, providing ease of use and maximizing energy savings. Energy management, an important feature of smart homes, has increased comfort, security and energy efficiency in these homes. Energy efficiency is achieved by optimizing production, distribution and consumption in homes using advanced technologies. Solutions are produced that minimize energy efficiency by reducing environmental impact. Here are the trends that promise to shape the future in the smart home energy sector:

- Integrating renewable energy sources:Solar energy, one of the most popular renewable energy sources, is increasingly used in the installation of smart homes through solar panels sold at more affordable and accessible prices. Wind energy, another type of renewable energy, is used to produce clean electricity in smart homes built in regions where wind conditions are suitable.
- Energy storage solutions (Storage solutions of smart homes) The goal in smart homes is to increase energy sustainability. It is necessary to produce its own energy and at the same time store the produced energy in order to be used when necessary. For example; Battery storage solutions can be used to store excess energy produced by solar energy. This stored battery power can be used during periods when demand is high or when renewable resources are not producing.
- Energy monitoring and management Smart home technology allows devices to be monitored and managed remotely. Smart meters used in smart homes reduce consumption and measure real-time energy usage, allowing smart decisions to be made. By measuring usage, these meters provide consumers with important information that can help them reduce usage, in addition, real-time usage data is transmitted to utility companies to enable more efficient resource management, which provides the necessary load control in smart meters. With the advancement of technologies, expectations from smart meters may increase. These devices are expected to have more connectivity and also this connection is expected to be uninterrupted. Another expectation is to include artificial intelligence methods in smart devices to make them smarter and more efficient.
- Artificial Intelligence The sustainability of energy will increase with the inclusion of artificial intelligence, which plays an important role in solving problems in almost many areas, in smart devices. In addition, it will be possible to make predictive analytical decisions, renewable energy forecasting and more, and adapt smart devices with artificial intelligence methods.
- Smart devices: Smart devices will allow remote devices to be managed and controlled when connected to smartphones and tablets. For example; The temperature can be adjusted by optimizing energy with smart thermostats. These devices can be controlled remotely, enabling them to operate and shut down. Smart lighting systems prevent unnecessary energy use by providing lighting when necessary. Devices such as smart washing machines, dryers, and dishwashers can be designed to operate during periods when electricity prices are lower. With smart ventilation systems, energy waste is prevented by ventilating the areas of the house that need to be ventilated. With smart curtains, indoor temperature is adjusted by taking into account parameters such as the amount of sunlight and outside air temperature.
- Working together in the smart home energy sector: A recent trend in the smart home energy sector is to create interoperable systems. It refers to the ability of smart devices to work together, regardless of brand. Today, the lack of full interoperability of smart devices is a major deficiency in the energy sector.

Conflict of Interest Declaration

All authors; They declare that they have no conflict of interest. Conflict of Interest Declaration is true.

References

1. Hargreaves, T., Hauxwell-Baldwin, R., Coleman, M., Wilson, C., Stankovic, L., Stankovic, V., Liao, J., Murray, D., Kane, T., Hassan, T., et al. (2015). Smart homes, control and energy management: How do smart home technologies influence control over energy use and domestic life? In *ECEEE-2015, 2015*.
2. Koomey, J. G., Mahler, S. A., Webber, C. A., & McMahon, J. E. (1999). Projected regional impacts of appliance efficiency standards for the us residential sector. *Energy, 24*(1), 69–84.
3. al sumaiti, A. S., Ahmed, M. H., & Salama, M. M. A. (2014). Smart home activities: A literature review. *Electric Power Components and Systems, 42*(3–4), 294–305.
4. Jahn, M., et al. (2010). The energy aware smart home. In *The IEEE 5th International Conference on Future Information Technology, 21–23 May, Busan*.
5. İlkbahar, F., Şeyma, Ü., Karakaya, A. T., & Bayram, E. (2021). Akıllı ev sistemleri üzerine bir model önerisi. *AJIT-e: Academic Journal of Information Technology, 12*(45), 90–105.
6. Li, B., Hathaipontaluk, P., & Luo, S. (2009). Intelligent oven in smart home environment. In *2009 International Conference on Research Challenges in Computer Science* (pp. 247–250). IEEE.
7. Jiang, L., Liu, D. Y., & Yang, B. (2004). Smart home research. In *Proceedings of 2004 International Conference on Machine Learning and Cybernetics (IEEE Cat. No. 04EX826)* (vol. 2, pp. 659–663). IEEE.
8. Metin, İ. A., & Karasulu, B. (2019). İnsan aktivitelerinin sınıflandırılmasında tekrarlayan sinir ağı kullanan derin öğrenme tabanlı yaklaşım. *Veri Bilimi, 2*(2), 1–10.
9. çakir, S., Yalçin, N., & Toklu, S. (2020). Nesnelerin internetinde sahte kimlik saldırılarının makine öğrenme yöntemleri ile tespiti. *Avrupa Bilim ve Teknoloji Dergisi*, pp. 530–536.
10. Tahsien, S. M., Karimipour, H., & Spachos, P. (2020). Machine learning based solutions for security of internet of things (IoT): A survey. *Journal of Network and Computer Applications, 161*, 102630.
11. Dolcel, H., Durgun, M., & Gökrem, L. (2021). IoT tabanlı ve makine öğrenmesine dayalı seçici sulama sistemi. *Avrupa Bilim ve Teknoloji Dergisi, 28*, 395–401.
12. Wilson, C., Hargreaves, T., & Hauxwell-Baldwin, R. (2017). Benefits and risks of smart home technologies. *Energy Policy, 103*, 72–83.
13. Civan, U. (2006). *Akıllı binaların çevresel sürdürülebilirlik açısından değerlendirilmesi*. Ph.D. Thesis, Fen Bilimleri Enstitüsü.
14. Herrero, S. T., Nicholls, L., & Strengers, Y. (2018). Smart home technologies in everyday life: Do they address key energy challenges in households? *Current Opinion in Environmental Sustainability, 31*, 65–70.

Chapter 2
Advanced Object Tracking for Empowering Smart Environments: A Comparative Review

Mohammed Alameri and Qurban Memon

Abstract Object detection and tracking is a vital area of computer vision that has several applications. Despite considerable progress in this field, real-time and platform-dependent difficulties remain unresolved. This includes recording temporal information of the target and background clutter. As of today, numerous deep learning-based detection and tracking algorithms have been reported in the literature, with substantial gains. To fully exploit the promise of present research in this area, object detection, tracking, and associated problems, are explained first in this chapter, followed by a relevant literature review covering the background of this interesting field. This is followed by a description of modern models, benchmark datasets, and performance metrics. Based on these benchmarks, the comparative results of well-known tracking algorithms found in the literature are presented. Finally, this chapter concludes with future research directions in this field.

Keywords Object tracking · Deep learning · Machine learning · Benchmarks

2.1 Introduction

Many human-robot interactions need object detection and tracking. The primary focus in the military industry has been on constructing object trackers for well-known types or specific instances, such as boxes, persons, hands, and cars. This option offers the benefit of allowing item-specific trackers to be developed or trained offline, as well as the availability of object shape models. However, it is not always possible to specify which types of objects must be tracked. Drone-based surveillance involves an operator or remote user designating an object of interest by clicking on a single image frame. Similarly, in learning from demonstration, a user handles an unidentified object, requiring the robot to track the object throughout the

M. Alameri · Q. Memon (✉)
College of Engineering, UAE University, Al Ain, UAE
e-mail: qurban.memon@uaeu.ac.ae

N. E. M. Khalifa, M. H. N. Taha (eds.), *Empowering AI Applications in Smart Life and Environment*, https://doi.org/10.1007/978-3-031-78038-7_2

demonstration. In both scenarios, the robot must swiftly create an internal model of the relevant object and continuously update it to reflect changes in the object's pose, shape, scale, and appearance. This model must also remain robust against external factors like occlusions and variations in lighting conditions. However, several minor changes in the appearance of the object may cause the model to be unsure if this is the desired selected target or not. These difficulties could be overcome with adequate training and good data augmentations, as well as selecting the best hyperparameter to modify the pre-training operation.

If we want a quick tracker, we need a faster training session, but this is also crucial for accuracy because training time and accuracy are trade-off characteristics. Furthermore, the algorithm must be developed to reliably recognize and pinpoint objects of interest in the shortest period possible. Improving tracking speed is critical for real-time object tracking models, as the speed or frame per second (FPS) should be high to avoid any delays to other integrated systems, such as ROS for robots or gimbal for military jets and weaponry. To manage time, the model must be tailored or carefully selected in terms of a variety of criteria such as accuracy, size of the model, and so on.

Instead of relying on a known object model, generic object tracking in a real-time RGB video can be summarized as follows: given a bounding box around an arbitrary object at a specific moment, generate bounding boxes for that object in all subsequent frames. This requirement can be seen in many robotics and military applications, where detection is often employed in conjunction with another technique, such as trajectory prediction. Sort [4], DeepSort [46], StrongSort [10], Kalman filter [22], and various correlation filters are examples of tracking algorithms. As illustrated in Fig. 2.1, all of these approaches can be classified based on the approach employed for object tracking.

Including photogrammetry in the tracking and detection process would allow for the addition of extra layers of filters to differentiate between real and false detected items. More data may be obtained from photogrammetry, such as translation vector parameters in both the 2D picture plane and the 3D world coordinates reference and rotational vectors that can be represented by Euler angles to obtain roll, yaw, and pitch. However, distance measure by combining three separate translation vectors may also be utilized to provide relevant data.

There is a requirement for the development of a detector and tracker algorithm that delivers rapid and accurate detections to all required applications, including industrial, where a robot must act swiftly to decide whether the target in front of the camera is the desired and selected target or not. Furthermore, high-confidence object trackers are significant in the defense industry because high confidence leads to high resolution in hitting the target, and speed is also vital because delays in choices or operations lead to failures.

Unmanned aerial vehicles (UAVs) have been extensively employed for object tracking algorithms as an important resource in rescue operations, in which the field is scanned through a camera with or without a gimbal and thus potential dangers in the field are recognized. When we need to recognize and track small things, such as vehicles and people, the detection and tracking jobs become even more difficult.

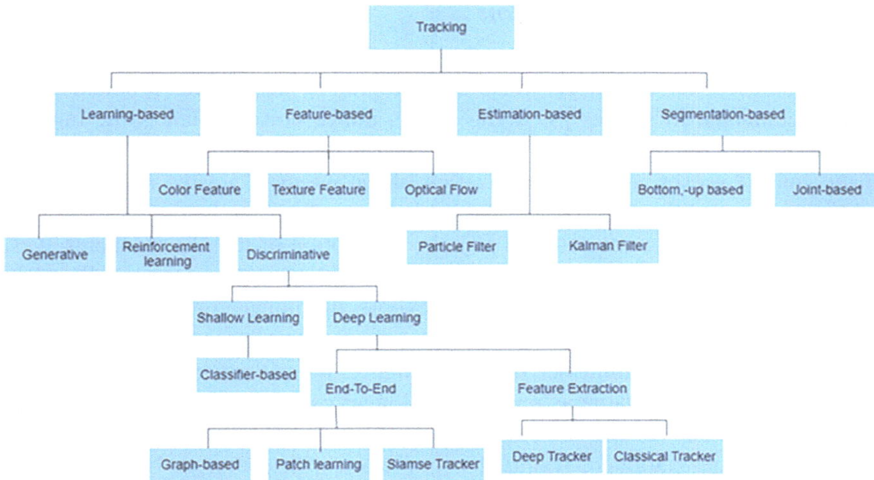

Fig. 2.1 Classification of object tracking methods

Because the objects appear small from a high height, we have fewer features to extract. The VisDrone dataset has a large number of objects of ten distinct kinds, including pedestrians, cars, trucks, and other types of vehicles [54]. As a result, great accuracy can be gained with the model's ability to generalize, allowing it to detect items outside of the dataset accurately. Furthermore, another milestone must be established for accelerating the inference speed by either quantization, which reduces the bit length from 64 to 16 (Float - Half) or even to 8 bit, while considering the accuracy metrics and F1 scores of the model's findings. Using various optimizers might improve accuracy, but there is a trade-off that must be made such that the model is accurate while also being fast enough. During some operations in the robotics or defense industries, the distance between a camera and an object must be determined; however, there are other constraints such as a limited budget, the need for multiple cameras but only a single camera is available, and a data pipeline from other sources such as lidar is not available.

The objective of this chapter is to benefit readers who are interested in updating their knowledge of object tracking in terms of state of art methods, benchmark datasets, evaluation metrics, and corresponding performance analysis of different trackers.

2.2 Literature Review

In this section, a literature survey is presented that is relevant with contributions published on the same topic.

2.2.1 Challenges to Detection

During the detection of objects in aerial photographs, tremendous problems have been documented in studies [39]. The first is image noise, which is the random change in pixel intensity values. The statistical quantum fluctuations, the physics of the camera sensor, and the quantization of the intensity are the most essential aspects. Another difficulty to overcome is blurring, which can be produced by several sources, including out-of-focus objects, the motion of the objects themselves, and camera motion or tremor. Furthermore, motion blur can occur, especially when the lighting is low and the camera must expose the image for a longer amount of time. When an image blurs, both the contrast and sharpness diminish. The illumination has a huge influence on image quality. When there is not enough light, such as around sunset, cameras must utilize longer exposure periods, which might induce motion blur or increase image noise. Intense light can cause the camera sensor to become saturated, resulting in a picture with excessive brightness and a reduced amount of image details. Finally, the smaller object size is caused by the low spatial resolution caused by the greater distances between the camera and the ground. The fact that objects contained within a range of only a few pixels carry minimal information about their look and shape complicates detection and classification. When the image resolution is altered, the proportions of the objects change, which can result in inaccurate classification.

For the object and scene variation tasks, four different types of variations are used. High intra-class variance, low inter-class variance, rich backdrops, partial occlusion, and shadows are examples of these differences. The rationale for why learning a reliable feature representation capable of distinguishing between cars and non-vehicles becomes more challenging when intra-class variance is significant. This is due to the wide range of vehicle colors, sizes, and shapes. The unpredictable vehicle orientations caused by the camera's perspective contribute to an increase in intra-class variance in aerial photographs. This problem makes distinguishing between the many sorts of items difficult because of the extremely low inter-class variance. Because of the angle at which the video was shot, various objects, such as vehicles and vans, may appear to be the same size and shape. As a result, objects may be misclassified. For example, in urban or industrial areas, various objects have a substantial resemblance in scale and form to automobiles, resulting in only minor variations in feature representations. Partial occlusion, which can be caused by things like trees or traffic lights, causes objects to appear different. Because there are fewer visible pieces, it is more difficult to differentiate the foreground objects from the background objects. In most circumstances, shadows are cast when an object blocks some or all of the direct light falling on the surface. Sunlight is an example of this. Shadows cast on an object can cause the contour of the object to be distorted and can also result in low-contrast areas.

Real-time criteria must be met to ensure online processing, which is required for a range of applications. If the frame rate is 25 hertz, for example, there will be around 40 milliseconds available to extract and analyze the information contained

Table 2.1 Challenges to detection and tracking

	Challenge	Meaning		Challenge	Meaning
1	Illumination variation	A significant change in illumination	5	Variation in scale	The ratio of bounding boxes of the first frame to those of the current frame is out of range.
2	Background clutter	The near target in the background is similar in texture or color.	6	Occlusion	The target is occluded, fully or partially.
3	Low Resolution	Fewer pixels in ground truth bounding box	7	Target position changes	The target gets deformed or rotated, etc., during movement.
4	Fast motion	Ground truth motion is high.			

in the current image. It is vital to remember that working with larger image sizes often makes it more difficult to meet real-time requirements due to the increased processing effort [39].

Airborne platforms have a limited payload capacity, which limits the hardware and computations. These limits have an impact on computing power. Low-power onboard computation for deep learning and other vision applications is enabled by embedded systems such as NVIDIA Jetson platforms, which incorporate a strong GPU as well as a powerful processor. However, GPU memory is typically shared with random access memory (RAM), and the number of parallel processing units is reduced when contrasted to server installations that may include multiple GPUs. Deep learning models' size and complexity are thus limited [34]. In summary, the most important challenges to object tracking are tabulated in Table 2.1.

2.2.2 *Detection and Tracking Algorithms*

The surveyed literature shows that there has been much progress in the development of object detectors in speed up and accuracy over time. As shown in Fig. 2.1, a timeline is presented that shows well-known object detectors from 2001 until 2020 (Fig. 2.2). A similar timeline is also presented for object trackers in Fig. 2.3. Below, well-known research works are briefly discussed.

2.2.2.1 Tracking Learning Detection

The tracking of unseen objects in video is a research topic for tracking learning detection (TLD) trackers. All that matters in a single still photograph is where and how big the thing is. The following frame needs you to either pinpoint the

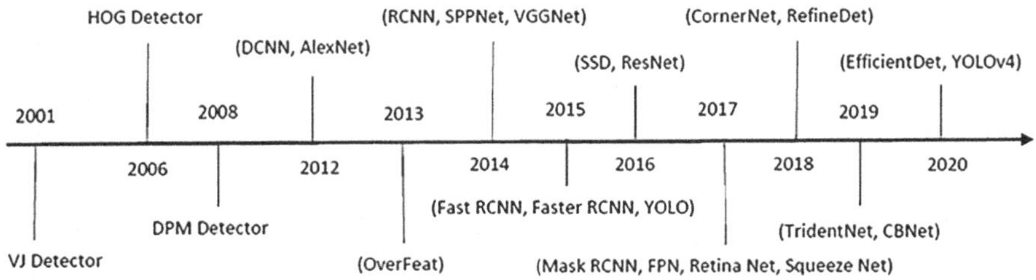

Fig. 2.2 Evolution of object detectors [38]

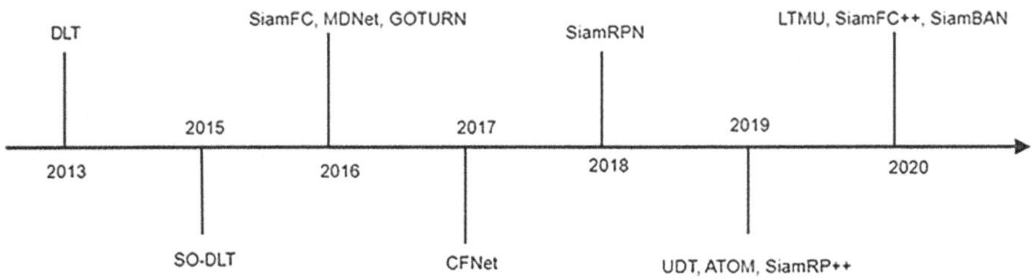

Fig. 2.3 Evolution of deep learning-based trackers [38]

location and size of the object or prove that it is not present. A tracking framework (TLD) divides the tracking task into three independent phases: tracking, learning, and detection. The tracker follows the object in each, then the detector identifies previously observed appearances and modifies the tracker accordingly. Next, the learning process estimates the detector errors and makes corrections so that they do not occur again.

2.2.2.2 Visual Object Tracking

A unique method of spatially supervised recurrent convolutional neural networks, (known as recurrent YOLO—ROLO) has been developed for object tracking [33]. In addition to the deep neural networks' distinctive visual properties, the recurrent convolutional network makes use of location history. The authors [33] proposed combining numerous high-level features provided by convolutional neural networks with regional information, a strategy inspired by current object identification bounding box regression algorithms. As opposed to existing learning-based trackers that employ binary classification, this approach uses regression at both the recurrent unit and the convolutional layer to directly predict tracking locations. Extensive experimental results and performance comparisons with novel tracking algorithms on benchmark video tracking datasets show that the ROLO tracker is accurate and robust while keeping a low computing cost.

2.2.2.3 Tracking Based on Sparse Subspace Representation

The researchers [44] have suggested an online tracking technique that integrates incremental subspace learning and sparse representation. The authors apply Gaussian random sampling in the framework of the particle filter and filter the data using subsampling. An incremental PCA approach is applied to bring the training set's state up to date, and then the training set's eigenvectors are used to develop a sparse subspace model. Before including the result in the training set, an approach for occlusion detection is utilized for estimation. A real-time tracking system is used in a range of settings, including light change, rotation, occlusion, and deformation. Meanwhile, the tracking box can adapt to changes in scale as well as rotation.

2.2.2.4 Tracking Based on Prior Knowledge

The focus of the study [47] is on tracking and categorization of several image objects in a sequence at the same time. The method starts by tracking all of the scene objects without using any prior knowledge of objects. The tracked objects are subsequently classified using a learning-based image classifier using a shallow convolutional neural architecture. It is demonstrated that object recognition increases when this information is paired with algorithm information about the object's state. Based on this, the approach shifts the usage of prior information from the detection and tracking to the classification stage, resulting in a reliable system capable of detecting and tracking a variety of types of objects. An experimental assessment shows that this method is competitive to cutting-edge recognition systems that employ object-specific previous information in tracking.

2.2.2.5 Tracker Based on Sparse Deformable Template Models

Using an SVM-trained active basis model [37], a sparse deformable template is generated and applied to objects. The active basis model is a sparse model, where each image is represented by a small number of bases drawn from a Gabor dictionary. If the bounding box of the item in the first frame is known, the model can then be trained with the (positive) image patch contained within the bounding box and the (negative) images located outside of the bounding box. The tracking is then completed by detecting the item in successive frames using the trained model. The model then updates using new positive and negative images after a few frames.

2.2.2.6 Improved TLD Tracker

Zdenka Kalal [36] introduced a novel tracking architecture that divides the task of object tracking into three subtasks: tracking, learning, and detection. In each subsequent frame, the tracker and detector independently determine the object's location, while learning facilitates information exchange between them. The detector is constructed using a local binary pattern (LBP) feature, which enhances the framework's robustness [36]. Initially, the LBP descriptor for each scanning window is identified to generate the LBP feature vector. Next, a new LBP feature vector is created based on the histogram statistics of the LBP feature vector. This process is applied simultaneously to both positive and negative samples (known as image patches). Then, the newly created LBP statistics feature vector for the scanning window is matched with the positive and negative sample sets using normalized cross-correlation. Finally, the results from detection and tracking are combined, and the detector is updated online. Trials conducted on a publicly available dataset demonstrate that this approach yields superior tracking performance and robustness.

2.2.2.7 Multiple Targets Tracking

The researchers [25] present a novel learning framework for tracking multiple objects based on their detection. Rather than heuristically developing a tracking algorithm, they use a discriminative structure prediction model trained on labeled video data to capture the interdependence of various influencing factors. This model uses data to predict the structure of the data. By considering the joint targets' states from the previous time step and the current frame's observation, the current joint targets' state can be inferred by maximizing the joint probability score. Additionally, tracking cues enhance detection accuracy. The method integrates indicators for both detecting and tracking targets, reducing the risk of errors in post-processing, and improving tracking performance. The researchers then transform the entire model training process into a convex optimization problem and estimate its parameters using cutting-plane optimization. Experiments demonstrate its effectiveness in various scenarios, including tracking pedestrians in crowded environments and vehicles in heavy traffic.

2.2.2.8 GOTURN Tracker

The "GOTURN" approach mentioned in [18] solves the challenge of single target tracking by using a bounding box label of an object in the initial frame of a video, subsequently tracking that object throughout the remaining frames. The tracker can handle data at a reasonable rate. The GOTURN tracker is built on a simple network that does not require any prior online training. By learning a general relationship between object motion and appearance, the tracker is capable of tracking new objects not included in the training set. A commonly used tracking benchmark is utilized to evaluate the approach's success. Furthermore, their performance improves when more videos are added to their offline training set. Additionally, this approach can also withstand shifts in perspective, deformations, and illumination quite well.

2.2.2.9 Part-to-Target Tracking

Part-to-part (P2P) trackers typically have two distinct processes, namely part matching and target localization. The authors [13] provide a unified strategy that directly infers the position of the target from parts. This method differs from the ones already in use. Convolutional neural networks are used for P2T regression in an end-to-end architecture to achieve this task. The suggested model is designed to learn part reliability to emphasize part importance as well as to employ part context information to maintain the spatial layout structure. The built tracker was tested on difficult benchmark sequences, and the results show that the approach outperforms the well-known trackers.

2.2.2.10 Memory and Regression-Based Tracker

Many tracking-by-detection systems have recently achieved state-of-the-art performance. However, most of these trackers overlook the temporal information available from target sequences. In response to this limitation, the authors [8] developed a memory network that utilizes both the history of object placements and distinctive visual features. By employing discrete visual cues and the history of object positions, this network serves as an area predictor for the current frame. The vast majority of existing trackers rely on binary classification to assess candidates for regions drawn around the target. The Memory and Regression-based Tracker (MRT) in particular is made up of a CNN-based architecture for extraction of features, a stacked Long Short-Term Memory network (LSTM) for memory update, and a series of regression layers for refinement. This model can be trained from start to finish and has complete differentiability.

2.2.2.11 Single Object Tracking with Two CNNs

The authors [32] presented an innovative single-object tracker based on two CNNs trained offline with data from extensive video libraries. The main idea is to alternate between tracking an object using motion information and changing its anticipated location based on how visually similar it is to other objects. Initially, they developed a deep regression network capable of learning broad relationships between object appearance models and their associated motion patterns. The position, size, and shape of the object's bounding box are then constantly changed to optimize a patch similarity function generated via CNN. These updates are driven by visual similarity limitations. Finally, a multi-resolution fusion of the two CNN outputs is conducted to achieve precise object localization.

2.2.2.12 Tracker Based on Appearance and Motion Features

Moving targets in satellite images, such as automobiles and planes, occupy only a small number of pixels, making them easily confused with the surrounding complex ground scenes. Due to resolution limitations, it is challenging to distinguish between objects with similar appearances that are located close to each other in satellite footage. Consequently, tracking drift caused by distractions remains a significant challenge. Traditional techniques, such as correlation filters with hand-crafted features, fail to produce satisfactory results when applied to satellite videos. However, deep learning technology can enhance object tracking in aerial videos [2], leading to more accurate outcomes. A simple regression network can be created by combining a regression model with convolutional layers and a gradient descent method [20]. To construct a robust tracker, the regression network makes the most of the abundant background context. Instead of handcrafted features, accurate object tracking employs both appearance and motion features derived from pre-trained deep neural networks. If ambiguous appearance information is supplied to the tracker [20], the motion characteristics can provide supplementary and discriminative information to improve tracking performance.

2.2.2.13 Visual Tracking of Generic Objects (Re3)

To monitor an object accurately, one must first understand its appearance, mobility, and evolution through time. An effective tracker should be capable of updating its model and incorporating new data. Re3 [14] introduces a real-time deep object tracker that can incorporate prior data into its current model. Rather than creating a model to monitor a specific instance at test time, a generic tracker is pre-trained on a diverse set of objects and efficiently updates on the fly. With a single forward pass, Re3 tracks and changes the appearance model. This lightweight model produces competitive benchmark scores while tracking objects at 150 frames per second.

2.2.2.14 Fusing Visual and Motional Descriptors

The goal of research [12] is to provide a system that can adaptively follow non-rigid objects by combining optical and motion feature descriptors. The proposed method is capable of automatically detecting an object from a range of angles of view as soon as soon as it begins to. In addition, an object model is built and then continuously updated to make use of both newly added and previously implemented capabilities. As a result, the approach may follow a non-rigid object even if it is spinning or deforming itself. The experimental data acquired from a grayscale camera is utilized to validate whether or not the proposed technique is effective.

2.2.2.15 Object Tracking Based on Adaptive Particle Filters

Occlusion identification and recovery is a difficult operation that must be completed successfully in real time for tracking non-rigid objects. Particle filtering [11] is shown to be particularly effective at tackling non-linear and non-Gaussian estimation problems using an adaptive particle filter approach for occlusion detection and recovery during object tracking. The normalization factor is employed in the first phase to identify obscured objects. An adaptive transition function is used in the second step of the occlusion recovery procedure. Lastly, the particle quantity varies based on the occlusion status. The results of this study show that the method can detect occlusion and quickly recover from it.

2.2.2.16 Natural Contour Tracking

The majority of systems for tracking by detection use bounding boxes, which lead to compounding tracking errors in subsequent frames. The study [49] aims to provide an accurate natural contour tracking method for tracking non-rigid objects. The proposed tracker [49] may follow natural contours. The suggested technique may successfully address tracking issues caused by interference, intricate backgrounds, and large changes in scale, shape, and illumination. As a result, the approach can follow the non-rigid target object properly while still delivering a precise natural contour. The experimental findings on a variety of datasets that are freely accessible demonstrate that this approach outperforms well-known non-rigid object tracking approaches in terms of the quality of its tracking results.

2.2.2.17 Supervised Level Set Model Tracking

The authors [40] offer a method for tracking non-rigid objects using supervised level set model (SLMSM) tracking. Unlike most existing trackers, which employ bounding boxes to characterize the monitored target, the approach obtains the correct contours as a tracking output. This allows for a more exact description of non-rigid objects and less contamination of the target model by the backdrop. The evolution of the SLSM's curve is overseen by object-oriented knowledge of the objectives to be pursued. Because of its excellent object-to-background discrimination, it first constructs the target's appearance model via online boosting. The model is then used to develop the contour probabilities of the level set in a Bayesian method, causing the curve to converge on the most likely candidate region. Lastly, the precise target region checks the samples utilized in the process and updates the target model for the next iteration. The two-phase SLSM mechanism is suggested for single-target and a multi-phase counterpart for multi-target scenarios. The learning rate slows down with time due to a positive decreasing rate, allowing tracking to continue even when there is an impediment on the way. The efficiency of the proposed technique is supported by simulation results on a range of sequences.

2.2.2.18 Tracker Based on Color Cluster Flow

The authors of the contribution [17] present a method for tracking moveable, non-rigid objects within a series of vivid photographs captured by a moving camera. The background is centered on assisting with vision-based driving in congested metropolitan environments. The first stage employs a divisive clustering algorithm to all of the pixels in the first image. This aids in determining which object sections will be used in later steps. A pixel's color and position both contribute to the definition of the feature space. For each succeeding image frame, the clusters discovered in the preceding image are updated iteratively via a concurrent k-means clustering technique. Individual points, edges, or areas are not followed; only the centroids of the clusters are traced through a series of images. The proposed technique not only significantly simplifies the problem of correspondence, but also ensures consistent monitoring behavior.

2.2.2.19 Tracking with Combined Techniques

A real-time multi-object tracking technique for both rigid and non-rigid objects is explored in [19]. The extraction of the backdrop, modification of the background, and identification of the object extracted from the image are the most significant parts of the system for tracking objects. The implemented techniques are improved inside each component without adding new layers of computational complexity. The fish tank experiment functioned as a test bed for the technique, which was designed to overcome problems with dynamic occlusions.

2.2.2.20 Tracker Based on Optical Flow Technique

The approach proposed in [21] employs a model based on knowledge about optical flow. This information is utilized to determine the objects' movement in the scene. Following the detection of moving regions in the first frame, the authors use the contour model to dynamically follow the objects in successive frames. These models are employed as a way of adding flow data into tracking to better comprehend the situation. The active contour model formulation can improve tracking speed by inserting an additional force-driven optical flow. This method works well for low-contrast videos, such as aerial footage.

2.2.2.21 Segmentation of Non-static Objects

The authors [24] propose a new method for segmenting moving objects and monitoring their motion in MPEG-4 movies that is based on an improved principal component analysis (PCA). Initially, the moving object contained within the first image sequence is segmented using an upgraded principal component analysis. At this level, stiff and non-rigid moving objects can be separated from the background in as few as three frames. The second stage of tracking is moving a window with three frames along the visual sequence and then repeating the first step multiple times within each window.

2.2.2.22 Object Tracking System for Blurry Frames

Blurry images, such as those produced by a rolling shutter camera, as well as occlusions, can readily disrupt an object tracking system. The work [26] aims to enhance the performance and robustness of trackers by employing both convolutional and recurrent neural networks. In this, it is proposed that a CNN be used to identify the target and then give the tracker with the discovered image. Additionally, this framework allows for the tracker to be updated after every "n" frame. An RNN is projected to learn the behavior of the object to assess and predict its position in unclear frames or when it is concealed by an obstruction. The feasibility of the proposed technique for improving tracker performance is validated through real-time use of the strategy.

2.2.2.23 Recurrent and Siamese Region Proposal Network

The work [51] presents an end-to-end trainable Siamese recurrent neural network and region proposal network (Siamese R-RPN). This is done to address the issues of imbalanced data and the neglect of temporal information in Siamese-based trackers. A Siamese R-RPN is made up of three components: a Siamese network, an RNN, and an RPN. The Siamese network extracts image features, which are then enhanced using channel and spatial attention methods before being sent to the RPN for classification and regression. The temporal information is processed by an RNN-based LSTM before being translated to RPN's anchor feature map for anchor selection. This aids in predicting the target's overall location. This method balances positive and negative samples more effectively during training. The proposed tracker achieves robust performance on three key benchmark datasets: VOT2016, VOT2018, and OTB 2015, due to its usage of both temporal and spatial information.

2.2.2.24 RNN for Direction Prediction

The authors [50] presented a tracking method based on RNN. Firstly, they use the temporal correlation offered by RNN to anticipate the movement of the object in the subsequent image. Secondly, they use RNN-predicted direction to determine the ROI. The next step is to locate the object within the ROI. The result of the object detection model is transferred to the direction prediction model in the final stage toward the realization of the object tracking framework. This model is used as the input for the next frame. The two benchmark datasets that researchers utilize to conduct exhaustive experiments are OTB and VOT2016. The approach achieves an accuracy of 0.826 on OTB100 while maintaining a speed of 41 frames per second, making it efficient.

2.2.2.25 Attentional RNN

Long short-term memory offers the benefit of being able to replicate long-term tasks. The study [45] proposes a state-of-the-art attentional recurrent neural network (ARNN) model for tracking. The core of this model is a two-layer bidirectional LSTM that runs along the x-y axes. By connecting multiple bidirectional LSTMs either in cascade or in parallel, the model can utilize multiscale target attributes, leading to more accurate object location tracking. Each bidirectional LSTM employs the convolutional features of a CNN contained within two bounding boxes from different frames to assess if the target in the current frame matches the target in previous frames. Furthermore, an attention mechanism has been included into the model to improve its ability to express the patch-level properties of the tracking targets. Both the attention mechanism and the bidirectional LSTM are trained concurrently. When the two of them collaborate, the accuracy of tracking improves noticeably. The trials have proven that the proposed online approach is successful and can generate results comparable to state-of-the-art tracking systems.

2.2.2.26 Anchor-Free Tracker

In article [15], the authors provide a unique Anchor-free Tracker based on Space-time Memory Network (ATSMN). This approach employs the space-time memory network, the memory feature fusion network, and the transformer feature cross fusion network in novel and imaginative ways. By leveraging these components synergistically, the tracker effectively utilizes temporal context information stored within memory frames associated with the object, enabling it to adapt better to changes in the object's appearance. This provides far more accurate categorization and regression findings. Extensive experiments on benchmark datasets demonstrate that ATSMN achieves tracking performance comparable to state-of-the-art (SOTA) Space-Time Memory Network.

2.2.2.27 RMNet for Object Segmentation

The authors [48] proposed the Regional Memory Network (RMNet) as a new local-to-local matching mechanism for semi-supervised Video Object Segmentation (VOS). RMNet constructs a precise regional memory by remembering local regions present in previous frames when searching for target objects. Using optical flow predicted from the preceding query frame, RMNet tracks and anticipates query regions for the current frame. This local-to-local matching approach effectively resolves ambiguity between similar objects in memory and query frames, facilitating efficient information transfer from regional memory to query regions. Experimental results demonstrate that RMNet outperforms previous state-of-the-art methods on YouTube-VOS and DAVIS datasets.

2.2.2.28 Enhanced Memory Network

The study [52] introduces an Enhanced Memory Network (EMN) for semi-supervised video object segmentation. Building on the effectiveness of Space-Time Memory Networks in leveraging guiding information, the authors enhance segmentation accuracy, particularly for smaller and unknown targets, using a finer-grained segmentation approach based on correlation attention maps. They employ a Siamese network to assess semantic similarity and relevance between tracked objects and the entire image. The feature map extracted from the Siamese network is applied to the cropped image and integrated with the full feature map as attention guidance. Additionally, an ASPP (Atrous Spatial Pyramid Pooling) module is employed to broaden the semantic receptive field, enhancing segmentation accuracy across different scales. The proposed algorithm achieves a j&F mean score of 81.8%, winning the YouTube-VOS 2019 Semi-supervised Video Object Segmentation Challenge. This success is attributed to multi-object integration and multi-scale ensemble strategies employed in the method.

2.2.2.29 Adaptive Detection Tracking

The authors [31] introduce a unique tracking framework centered on adaptive detection to enhance tracking algorithm performance in complex, unconstrained environments. The framework utilizes a RNN to predict the motion direction of the target, updating the RoI efficiently in subsequent frames. By focusing on a limited area of the next frame, the algorithm applies a correlation filter to initialize the predefined RoI based on a threshold. If the Intersection over Union (IOU) between the predicted and ground truth bounding boxes exceeds the threshold, the predicted bounding box is directly output as the result, adapting the detection within the defined RoI. The projected bounding box refines the motion model input for the next frame, completing the tracking process. Extensive testing across benchmark datasets such as OTB100, VOT2016, VOT2017, UAV123, and LaSOT consistently demonstrates state-of-the-art results in real-time, addressing significant challenges in tracking applications.

2.2.2.30 Object Detection and Tracking in Monocular Images

The technique [7] estimates the three-dimensional posture of a known object in real time under demanding conditions. Furthermore, because depth cameras are incapable of detecting metallic things, this method solely employs grayscale images. It can also handle badly textured objects as well as complex and dynamic settings, and the predicted pose declines gently when massive occlusions are present. The main purpose of the suggested methodology is to figure out how to anticipate the three-dimensional position of each component using just the two-dimensional projections from a limited number of control points. This methodology offers several advantages: firstly, it enables predicting the 3D pose of an object even with partial visibility; secondly, it facilitates combining multiple visible parts to enhance pose computation accuracy; and thirdly, it consistently delivers precise 3D pose estimations, even when only a few parts are visible.

2.2.2.31 Geometrical Tracking and Pose Estimation

The study described in reference [5] introduces demonstrations of geometric tracking and posture estimation using the homogeneous UVW inverse spherical coordinate system. It directly employs range data from a triangulation-based range sensor for calculations. In comparison to the conventional XYZ coordinate system, this approach exhibits superior performance in terms of accuracy, and processing speed. An illustrative example is provided to underscore these advantages. It contrasts the accuracy and resolution of a prototype 3D laser scanner that utilizes geometric monitoring to compute the relative posture of objects in three-dimensional space. The system integrates real-time geometric surface fitting with intensity processing to detect and track planar targets on objects. The demonstration employs a dual-axis laser scanner utilizing optical triangulation, Lissajous scanning patterns, geometric tracking, and photogrammetry (spatial resection) to estimate the relative position of objects in 3D space.

2.2.2.32 Transformer-Based Models

Transformer-based models have revolutionized various domains, particularly computer vision. These models have shown remarkable adaptability and efficacy in visual domains. Their application in object tracking represents an exciting frontier, but it comes with both significant strengths and notable challenges. The balance between leveraging their strengths and mitigating their weaknesses will be crucial for their successful implementation in real-world scenarios. The notable strengths and challenges are:

Strengths: Transformers leverage self-attention mechanisms that allow models to weigh the importance of different parts of the input data. This is particularly useful in object tracking, where the model needs to attend to relevant features of the target object and ignore irrelevant background information, improving tracking accuracy even in challenging conditions such as occlusions and rapid movements. The attention mechanism [42] captures the global context. This means they can better understand the overall scene context, leading to more robust tracking even when the object moves across different regions of the frame.

Unlike recurrent models, transformers allow for parallel processing of data, significantly speeding up training and inference, crucial in real-time object tracking applications. Transformers can be scaled up with more layers and parameters, potentially leading to better performance as more data and computational resources are available. Transformers can manage large datasets effectively, and their performance tends to improve with more data.

Transformer-based models can be adapted to various tracking tasks, including single-object tracking [6], multi-object tracking (MOT) [28], and even visual object tracking (VOT) [9]. This flexibility makes them versatile tools in the computer vision toolkit. Vision Transformers, specifically designed for image tasks, have shown that transformers can be directly applied to raw image patches. This integration simplifies the architecture and can improve performance by leveraging the strengths of transformers in modeling long-range dependencies. However, integrating transformers with traditional object tracking pipelines (e.g., feature extraction, motion modeling) involves complex engineering challenges.

Challenges: Transformers, particularly those with large numbers of parameters, require substantial computational resources for both training and inference. This can be a bottleneck, especially for real-time object tracking applications where speed is crucial. These models typically require large amounts of labeled data to achieve optimal performance. Thus, these models are prone to overfitting, particularly when the available training data is not sufficiently diverse. This can result in poor generalization to new or unseen tracking scenarios.

The extensive computations involved in self-attention mechanisms can lead to higher latency compared to more traditional approaches like CNNs. This is a critical concern in applications requiring real-time performance, such as autonomous driving and live video analytics. While transformers excel in capturing spatial relationships, maintaining temporal consistency over long sequences remains challenging. Ensuring smooth and consistent tracking across frames is critical in object tracking applications.

Recent Advances and Mitigations: Research is ongoing into more efficient transformer architectures, such as the use of sparse attention mechanisms or hybrid models combining CNNs or RNNs and transformers to reduce computational load while retaining performance benefits. To address data requirements, self-supervised learning methods are being explored. These approaches allow models to learn useful representations from unlabeled data, which can then be fine-tuned with smaller labeled datasets. The development of standardized benchmarks and datasets for object tracking using transformers helps in better evaluating and comparing different models. This drives improvements and innovations in the field by providing clear performance metrics.

2.3 Datasets and Approaches

Since a variety of tracker designs have been reported in the literature, a general form of tracker block diagram is presented in this section. The designs include online-trained, off-trained, and hybrid trackers. Following this, different datasets and performance measures that together function as performance benchmarks are discussed.

Online-trained Trackers: These are trained online: The predominant type of tracker often involves continual learning of features specific to the object of interest with each new frame. It encompasses key point-based and part-based trackers, correlation-based algorithms, and direct classification methods. These techniques typically expediently train a classifier to differentiate the object of interest from the background and potential occlusions. Due to the necessity for online trackers to continuously adapt to incoming frames, they often balance between speed and model complexity.

Offline-trained trackers: These methods excel in training data more efficiently than other machine learning approaches. Since these networks undergo complete offline training, they can quickly analyze data during testing, enabling both techniques to operate faster than real-time speeds. However, they lack the ability to adapt to new visual inputs. Offline trackers are inherently constrained because they cannot adjust to novel information.

Hybrid trackers: Hybrid trackers aim to address the challenges posed by both online and offline trackers by integrating the strengths of both approaches.

The general block diagram of the object tracker is displayed in Fig. 2.4.

The above block diagram shows various steps that need to be completed for building object trajectories. It starts with picking an image/video frame that is preprocessed before the object is detected. Most well-known object detectors are deep learning-based and involve training of data before tracking. This object, once recognized, is localized within the image frame for tracking purposes in subsequent frames. The success of object detection and tracking involves the use of various benchmark metrics that show performance scores. For online detectors and trackers, the objects are learned and tracked as frames arrive, whereas, in offline-trained, learning takes place entirely offline. Below, different image/video datasets and relevant performance metrics are discussed.

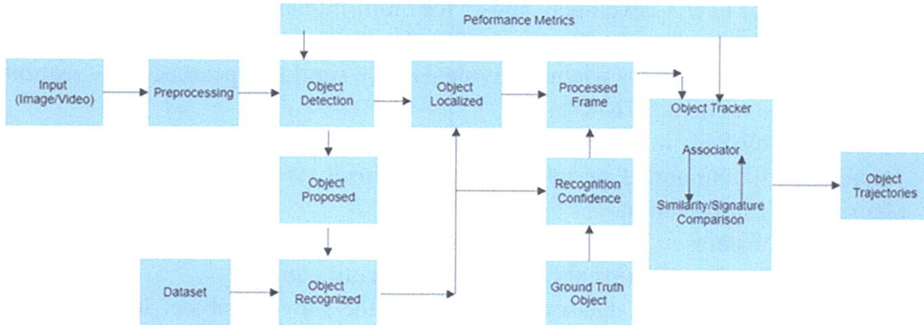

Fig. 2.4 Object detection and tracking functional diagram

2.3.1 Datasets

In this section, the well-known datasets that appear frequently in literature for object detection and tracking, are briefly introduced.

OTB (Object Tracking Benchmark): OTB is used to assess the performance of visual tracking algorithms. The dataset contains 100 annotated sequences frame-by-frame with bounding boxes and 11 challenge attributes. The OTB-2013 includes 51 sequences, while the OTB-2015 comprises all 100 sequences from the OTB dataset.

VOT2014: This dataset consists of 25 videos explicitly created for testing trackers. Many of the videos feature challenges such as significant appearance changes, camera motion, and heavy occlusions.

VOT2016 and 2017: These datasets each contain 60 challenging tracking videos, designed to assess the short-term tracking performance of algorithms under various attributes.

VOT2018: This version includes 60 videos with a total of 21,356 frames.

MOT15: The MOT2015 dataset is used for multiple object tracking. It features 11 different indoor and outdoor with pedestrians as the objects of interest. The dataset includes variations in camera motion and angle, and imaging conditions.

MOT17: This dataset includes video sequences captured by both moving and static cameras. It is widely used for multiple object tracking (MOT) and consists of 7 training sequences (5316 frames) and 7 testing sequences (5919 frames).

MOT20: Designed for highly crowded and challenging scenes, this version of the MOT dataset includes 4 training sequences (8931 frames) and 4 testing sequences (4479 frames).

KITTI: The KITTI dataset, developed by the Karlsruhe Institute of Technology and Toyota Technological Institute, is developed for autonomous driving tasks. It carries a low frame rate of 10 FPS and can be used for tracking pedestrians and cars and comprises 21 training sequences and 29 test sequences.

DanceTrack: This newly developed dataset for multi-human tracking supports MOT algorithms that focus on motion analysis rather than visual detection. It includes 100 group dancing videos where individuals have similar appearances but exhibit distinct motion characteristics.

UAV 123: Published in 2016, this dataset contains 123 low-altitude footage sequences of unmanned aerial vehicles, featuring variations in illumination, shape, scale, and rotation.

Okutama-Action dataset: This dataset contains fully annotated 43-minute sequences with 12 classes for concurrent human action identification.

MOR-UAV: A large-scale dataset designed for the moving object identification challenge, which involves the simultaneous localization and classification of moving objects in frames.

Semantic Drone dataset: This dataset is related to the semantic understanding of urban environments from an aerial perspective, comprising 400 training images and 200 testing images, all at a resolution of 6000x4000.

UAVid: A UAV video dataset for semantic segmentation, including 30 tilted episodes.

VisDrone: Collected in various metropolitan environments, this dataset addresses real-world challenges with obstacles, such as significant scale and viewpoint variations, as well as strong occlusions.

LaSOT: This dataset, which was published in 2019, is made up of 1400 high-quality densely annotated videos with 280 testing videos.

Deform-SOT: This dataset contains 50 unconstrained sequences.

MSCOCO: This has 80 real-world object categories and has become the industry standard for the detection of objects.

YouTube-Objects: A large-scale dataset sourced from YouTube in 2017, containing 924 annotated videos across 10 categories.

UA-DETRAC: This is a vehicle detection dataset produced from traffic scenarios.

Temple128 dataset: Published in 2019, this dataset consists of 128 sequences with ground truth, challenge factor annotations, and attribute annotations.

In Table 2.2, the attributes of well-known datasets mentioned above are listed to facilitate comparison for the benefit of the reader.

2.3.2 Strengths and Weaknesses of Trackers

As previously mentioned, various object-tracking approaches have been developed for tracking objects across video frames, and these approaches are often evaluated using benchmark datasets. Each method has unique strengths and weaknesses, making them suitable for different applications and scenarios. Selecting the appropriate dataset is crucial to ensure it aligns with the conditions in which the tracking algorithm will be used. Here is a breakdown of some common approaches in Table 2.3.

Table 2.2 Comparative view of datasets and corresponding attributes

Attribute	OTB2015	VOT18	MOT20	KITTI	Dance track	UAV 123	Temple 128
Year released	2015	2018	2020	2013	2021	2016	2015
Domain	Object tracking	Object tracking	Multi-object tracking	Autonomous driving	Object tracking	Object tracking	Object tracking
Number of Sequences	100	60	8	Various for different tasks)	100	123	128
Total frames	~59,000	~21,000	~13,410	Varies (about 40,000)	~40,000	~110,000	~60,000
Annotations	Bounding boxes	Bounding boxes	Bounding boxes	Bounding boxes, 3D bounding boxes	Bounding boxes	Bounding boxes	Bounding boxes
Objects per frame	Single object	Single object	Multiple objects	Multiple objects	Multiple objects	Single object	Single object
Categories	Various	Various	Pedestrians, vehicles	Cars, pedestrians,Cyclists	Pedestrians	Various	Various
Environment	Various	Various	Urban, Pedestrian areas	Urban, highway	Various	Aerial	Various

Table 2.3 Approaches, datasets used, and strengths and weaknesses

Approach	Strengths	Weaknesses	Suitable datasets
Correlation Filter-based	Efficient, simple, good for short-term tracking	Struggles with occlusion, scale variation, sensitivity to initialization	OTB, VOT
Deep learning based (Siamese Networks)	High accuracy, robust under occlusion, and appearance changes	Computationally intensive, data-dependent, complex to implement	GOT-10 k, LaSOT
Optical flow-based	Good for small motions, real-time performance	Struggles with large displacements, sensitive to illumination changes	MOT, KITTI
Feature-based	Robust to viewpoint changes, good for static environments	Computationally expensive, struggles with deformable objects	COCO, ImageNet VID
Kalman filter-based	Efficient, real-time, predictive capabilities	Limited to linear motion models, not robust to appearance changes	MOT, PETS
Reinforcement learning-based	Adaptable, capable of learning complex strategies	Training complexity requires many samples	OTB, LaSOT

Selecting an object-tracking algorithm hinges on the specific needs of the application. For example, real-time applications on devices with limited resources might prioritize speed and low computational complexity. In contrast, applications demanding high accuracy and robustness may utilize more complex and computationally intensive algorithms; and run it on powerful hardware for real-time performance. Balancing these trade-offs is crucial for choosing the right tracking method for a given use case. Below are trade-offs for some common approaches in Table 2.4.

2.4 Performance Metrics and Approaches

This section presents well-known metrics that are measured to investigate the performance of object trackers. Below, each of them is briefly stated.

MOTA: Multi-object tracking accuracy (MOTA), calculated using FP, FN, and IDs, focuses relatively more on performance. It quantifies the overall accuracy of the tracking and detection. Mathematically, it is computed as:

$$MOTA = 1 - \frac{|FN| + |FP| + |IDSW|}{|gtDet|} \tag{2.1}$$

Table 2.4 Comparison based on accuracy, speed, and computational complexity

Algorithm	Accuracy	Speed	Computational Complexity	Notes
Kalman filter (KF)	Medium	High	Low	Ideal for linear, Gaussian motion models; real-time capable.
Particle filter (PF)	High	Medium to low	High	Effective for non-linear, non-Gaussian models; resource-intensive
Mean-shift (CamShift)	Medium	High	Medium	Works well with distinct color features; struggles with occlusions
Kernelized correlation filter (KCF)	High	High	Medium to high	Efficient with FFT operations; robust to appearance changes
Discriminative correlation filter (DCF)	High	Medium to high	Medium	Robust with contextual information; slightly slower than KCF
Siamese network-based trackers (SiamFC, SiamRPN)	Very high	Medium to high	High	Highly robust; real-time with optimized models and GPUs
Deep learning-based trackers (e.g., DeepSORT)	Very high	Medium	Very high	Excellent for complex scenarios; the detection phase is costly

Here FP, FN, IDSW, and gtDet stand for false positive, false negative, ID switch, and ground truth detection, respectively.

MOTP (Multi-object tracking precision): MOTP measures the localization accuracy of detection by averaging the overlap across correctly matched predictions and their ground truth. It is similar to mAP metrics.

$$MOTP = \frac{1}{|TP|} \sum_{TP} S \tag{2.2}$$

where TP and S stand for true positive and similarity scores respectively.

IDF1: This metric focuses on association accuracy instead of detection accuracy, and combines ID Precision and ID Recall. Mathematically, it is stated as:

$$IDF1 = \frac{|IDTP|}{|IDTP| + 0.5 * |IDFN| + 0.5 * |IDFP|} \tag{2.3}$$

HOTA (High Order Tracking Accuracy): HOTA combines the detection score (DetA) and the association score (AssA), balancing the impacts of accurate detection and association into one unified metric. Mathematically,

$$HOTA = \frac{1}{19} \sum_{\substack{\alpha = 0.05 \\ \alpha += 0.05}}^{0.95} HOTA_{\alpha},\ where\ HOTA_{\alpha} = \sqrt{DetA_{\alpha}.AssA_{\alpha}} \tag{2.4}$$

$$\boldsymbol{DetA_{\alpha} = Det - IOU = \frac{|TP|}{|TP| + |FN| + |FP|},\ and}$$

$$\boldsymbol{AssA_{\alpha} = \frac{1}{|TP|} \sum_{c \in TP} \frac{|TPA(c)|}{|TPA(c)| + |FNA(c)| + |FPA(c)|}}$$

FAF: Number of false alarms per frame.

MT: This refers to the number of primarily tracked trajectories where the target maintains the same label for at least 80% of its lifespan.

ML: The number of mostly lost trajectories, meaning the target is not tracked for at least 20% of its lifespan.

ID: The number of times an ID switches to a different previously tracked object.

Frag: The number of fragmentations where a track is interrupted by a missed detection.

FM: These are the times that trajectories are disconnected.

EFO: A normalized speed used to evaluate operating efficiency.

Accuracy (A): This metric is computed as an overlap between predicted and ground truth bounding boxes during tracking periods, where accuracy at time step t is given by overlap at time t:

$$Acc_t = \frac{\left(A_t^p \cap A_t^g\right)}{\left(A_t^p \cup A_t^g\right)} \tag{2.5}$$

Robustness (R): Robustness quantifies tracking failures in a dataset. A lower value indicates greater reliability, with failures reported when IoU overlap between prediction and ground truth is zero, prompting tracker re-initialization after 5 frames. Mathematically, robustness is represented as:

$$R = \frac{\{Acc_t \leq \tau\}_{k=1}^{N}}{\mathrm{N}} \tag{2.6}$$

where N and τ stand for the run time of the tracker in frames and overlap threshold (zero in this case) respectively.

EAO (Expected average overlap): EAO is used to assess the performance of the tracking algorithms. This metric combines both Accuracy and Robustness. Mathematically, it is measured by computing the average of overlaps ($\mathrm{EAO_{Ns}}$) over typical sequence lengths, from $\mathrm{N_l}$ to $\mathrm{N_h}$ as:

$$EAO = \frac{1}{N_h - N_l} \sum_{N_s=N_l}^{N_h} EAO_{Ns} \tag{2.7}$$

CLE (Central location error): CLE is measured as the Euclidean distance computed between the tracker and the target ground truth. Mathematically, CLE is represented as:

$$CLE = \sqrt{(x_i - x)^2 + (y_i - y)^2} \tag{2.8}$$

where $(x_{\mathrm{i}}, y_{\mathrm{i}})$ are positions computed using a tracking algorithm, and (x, y) are values of ground truth.

Overlap success (OS): This metric is defined as the area between the ground truth and the estimated position, calculated using a threshold of 0.5. The overlap success rate is determined by dividing the number of frames where the overlap area exceeds the 0.5 threshold by the total number of frames.

$$AUC = \frac{area\left(A_e \cap A_g\right)}{area\left(A_e \cup A_g\right)} \tag{2.9}$$

Distance precision (DP): This metric is defined as the pixel distance between the ground truth and estimated position, typically calculated using a 20-pixel threshold as a standard practice.

Table 2.5 Results on the VOT2018 dataset

	LADCF	DaSiamRPN	MFT	RCO	SPM	ASRCF	ECO	Siam R-RPN
A	0.510	0.586	0.276	0.507	0.580	0.490	0.480	0.594
R	0.243	0.159	0.280	0.140	0.155	0.300	0.234	0.280
EAO	0.389	0.384	0.383	0.376	0.338	0.328	0.276	0.398

Table 2.6 Results of MOT20 benchmark

Trackers	HOTA	IDF1	MOTA	AssA	DetA	IDs
SORT	36.1	45.1	42.7	35.9	36.7	4470
CrowdTrack	55.0	68.2	70.7	52.6	57.7	3198
RelationTrack	56.5	70.5	67.2	56.4	56.8	4243
MAATrack	57.3	71.2	73.9	55.1	59..7	1331
ReMOT	61.2	73.1	77.4	58.7	63.9	1789
ByteTrack	61.3	75.2	77.8	59.6	63.4	1223
DeepSORT	57.1	69.6	71.8	55.5	59.0	1418
StrongSORT++	62.6	77.0	73.8	64.0	61.3	770

Table 2.7 Results of KITTI benchmark

Trackers	HOTA	IDF1	MOTA	AssA	DetA
CenterTrack	41.8	35.7	86.8	22.6	78.1
FairMOT	39.7	40.8	82.2	23.8	66.7
QDTrack	45.7	44.8	83.0	29.2	72.1
TransTrack	45.5	45.2	88.4	27.5	75.9
TraDes	43.3	41.2	86.2	25.4	74.5
ByteTrack	47.7	53.9	89.6	32.1	71.0
StrongSORT++	55.6	55.2	91.1	38.6	80.7

2.4.1 Comparative Benchmark Results

The results of well-known state-of-the-art trackers using previously mentioned metrics measured on databases are presented in this section to compare the performance. Table 2.5 shows the results of some state-of-art trackers assessed on the VOT2018 dataset ([52]; & [26]). The performance measures used are EAO, A, and R. The results suggest the superior performance of Siam R-RPN in terms of accuracy and expected area overlap.

The results reported in (Bowley et al. 2016; & [10]) compare the performance of various detectors using different sets of metrics on the MOT20 benchmark sequence. The results are shown in Tables 2.6, which suggest the better performance of ByteTrack based on the MOTA benchmark metric.

The authors [10] have also reported results of MOT-based methods on KITTI and DanceTrack datasets. The resulting metric measurements are shown in Tables 2.7 and 2.8. Based on Tables 2.7 and 2.8 results, StrongSORT++ and PermaTrack perform better than other trackers based on the MOTA benchmark metric.

Table 2.8 Results on DanceTrack benchmark on car tracking

Trackers	HOTA	MOTA	AssA	IDs
TrackMPNN	72.3	87.3	70.6	481
CenterTrack	73.0	88.8	71.2	254
QD-3DT	72.7	85.9	72.2	206
QDTrack	68.4	84.9	65.5	313
LGMTracker	73.1	87.6	72.3	448
Eager	74.4	87.8	74.2	239
PermaTrack	77.4	90.8	77.7	275
StrongSORT++	77.7	90.3	78.2	440

The authors [35] have also reported results of state-of-art trackers on OTB2015, Temple128, and UAV123 datasets, and showed CLE, DP, and OS metric values. These are displayed in Tables 2.9, 2.10, and 2.11. Based on the results of overlap success, CCOT performs better on both OTB2015 and UAV123 datasets, whereas DSLT performs better than others on the Temple128 dataset.

The authors [54] report the results of different algorithms on the VisDrone2018 benchmark using CLEAR-MOT evaluation protocol, and metric results are displayed in Table 2.12, which shows V-IOU performing better than other trackers based on MOTA and MOTP benchmark values.

Lastly, to conclude the comparative view of this research that lists datasets, key findings of approaches with methodological advantages, and challenges encountered, the following tabular view provides a useful summary of the information discussed in this section and Sect. 2.3 (Table 2.13).

2.5 Conclusions and Future Directions

Object tracking is a continuously evolving field. The researchers have created a wide range of ways to handle diverse issues in object detection and tracking, ranging from traditional feature-based methods to cutting-edge deep learning approaches in applications such as healthcare, military, civil defense, etc. [1, 29, 30]. Both traditional and freshly proposed object detectors and trackers were discussed in this chapter. Various benchmark datasets and performance criteria for assessing the performance of various detection and tracking systems were also presented. Object detection is often regarded as the initial step in several approaches presented in this chapter to generate objects, and then tracking algorithms are established to link the object instances to build trajectories. Thus, tracking systems benefit from object detector accuracy to create more accurate tracking results by utilizing temporal information. Some multiple object trackers structure the task as a data association challenge, to generate object trajectories by associating object detections in sequential frames. As a result, the object detection accuracy has a considerable impact on performance. Some academics have also attempted to create end-to-end

Table 2.9 Results on OTB2015 benchmark

	CCOT	MCPF	TRACA	MemTrack	ACT	CREST	Siam RPN	Siam Tri	ADNet	Baseline
CLE	13.99	20.86	27.63	27.83	15.78	21.19	19.21	33.13	14.65	15.41
$OS_{0.5}$	0.82	0.78	0.74	0.78	0.76	0.78	0.82	0.74	0.80	0.79

Table 2.10 Results on Temple128 benchmark

	CCOT	DSR	CREST	DSLT	MEEM	Struck	KCF	Frag	MIL
CLE	33.33	41.07	32.26	25.62	42.60	50.70	66.26	59.71	62.81
$OS_{0.5}$	0.702	0.652	0.689	0.729	0.615	0.545	0.480	0.469	0.428

Table 2.11 Results on UAV123 benchmark

	CCOT	DSLT	SRDCF	MEEM	SAMF	MUST	DSST	Struck	ASLA
DP_{20}		0.746	0.676	0.627	0.592	0.591	0.586	0.578	0.571
OS_{0AUC}	0.517	0.530	0.464	0.392	0.396	0.391	0.356	0.381	0.407

Table 2.12 Results of the VisDrone 2018 Challenge

Trackers	MOTA	MOTP	IDF1	FAF	MT	ML	IDs	FM
V-IOU	40.2	74.9	56.1	0.76	297	514	265	1380
TrackCG	42.6	74.1	58.0	0.86	323	395	779	3717
SCtrack	35.8	75.6	45.1	0.39	211	550	798	2042
GOG_EOC	36.9	75.8	46.5	0.29	205	589	354	1090
Ctrack	30.8	73.5	51.9	1.95	369	375	1376	2190
FRMOT	33.1	73.0	50.8	1.15	254	463	1043	2534

systems to handle detection and tracking problems concurrently. Object detection and tracking approaches can thus complement each other to improve performance.

The obstacles for aerial imaging are varied, such as motion blur, small objects, changing viewpoints, and so on. The existing well-known tracking approaches in this arena claim promising outcomes but fall short of eliminating related difficulties.

Table 2.13 Summary of works with a focus on datasets, findings, and challenges

Research work	Dataset	Research focus	Key findings	Methodological advantages	Challenges encountered
[23]	VOT 2018	Visual object tracking	Novel algorithms improving tracking accuracy	Benchmark for online tracking performance	Handling object appearance changes and occlusions
[53]	MOT20	Multiple object tracking	Advancements in multi-object tracking	In real-world scenarios, benchmarking multiple trackers	Dealing with crowded scenes and complex motions
[3]	KITTI	Object tracking	Evaluation of tracking in driving scenarios	High-quality dataset, real-world driving scenarios	Variability in weather conditions and lighting
[16]	Dance track	Human tracking	Techniques for robust human pose estimation	Dance-specific motions, pose estimation algorithms	Complex and diverse human movements
[41]	OTB 2015	Object tracking	Comparative evaluation of tracking methods	Large-scale dataset, standardized evaluation metrics	Handling various object scales and motions
[27]	Temple 128	Object tracking	Improved tracking in challenging environments	Ground truth annotations, challenge-specific metrics	Complex object interactions and occlusions
[41]	UAV 123	Aerial object tracking	Tracking algorithms for UAV applications	Aerial perspective, benchmarking UAV tracking	Handling fast-moving and small objects
[43]	VisDrone 2018	Visual object tracking	Tracking performance under diverse conditions	Diverse scenarios, benchmarking visual tracking	Dealing with scale variations and occlusions

It was discovered in the literature that performance measures are not the same for different methods. This is because, in some applications, different metrics have varying degrees of value for detection and tracking. Because trajectory accuracy is critical in surveillance applications, more emphasis is placed on trajectory fragmentations, ID switches, and false positives, whereas false negatives are more important than other factors in autonomous driving situations.

With the current availability of large-scale public datasets and more powerful computing resources, more advancements in this field are expected in the coming years.

The directions for future research in this field can be thought of as follows:

- Integrating detection and tracking into a unified architecture by leveraging spatiotemporal information is a natural way to increase performance.
- Creating an assessment process that fits the needs of various scenarios of object detection and tracking.
- Creating a comprehensive motion model that makes use of the motion information
- Gathering large-scale datasets and benchmarks for small objects to improve accuracy.

References

1. Ali, Z., & Memon, Q. (2013). Time delay tracking for multiuser synchronization in CDMA networks. *Journal of Networks, 8*(9), 1929.
2. Bachir, N., & Memon, Q. (2024). Benchmarking YOLOv5 models for improved human detection in search and rescue missions. *Journal of Electronic Science and Technology, 22*(1), 100243.
3. Bernad, J., Ramajo-Ballester, A., & Moreno, J. (2024). Three-dimensional vehicle detection and pose estimation in monocular images for smart infrastructures. *Mathematics, 12*(13), 2027.
4. Bewley, A., Ge, Z., Ott, L., Ramos, F. T., & Upcroft, B. (2016). Simple online and real-time tracking'. In *IEEE International Conference on Image Processing (ICIP)* (pp. 3464–3468).
5. Blais, F., Beraldin, J., El-Hakim, S., & Cournoyer, L. (2001). Real-time geometrical tracking and pose estimation using laser triangulation and photogrammetry. In *3rd international conference on 3-D digital imaging and modeling*, Quebec City (pp. 205–212).
6. Carion, N., Massa, F., Synnaeve, G., Usunier, N., Kirillov, A., & Zagoruyko, S. (2020). End-to-end object detection with transformers. In *European conference on computer vision* (pp. 213–229).
7. Crivellaro, A., Rad, M., Verdie, Y., Yi, K., Fua, P., & Lepetit, V. (2015). A novel representation of parts for accurate 3D object detection and tracking in monocular images. In *IEEE international conference on computer vision* (pp. 4391–4399).
8. Deng, Y., & Zheng, H. (2018). Memory network for tracking with deep regression'. In *IEEE International Conference on Image Processing, Applications and Systems, Sophia Antipolis* (pp. 273–278).
9. Dosovitskiy, A., et al. (2020). An image is worth 16x16 words: Transformers for image recognition at scale. In *International conference on learning representations* (p. 11929).
10. Du, Y., Song, Y., Yang, B., & Zhao, Y. (2023). StrongSORT: Make DeepSORT great again. *IEEE Transactions on Multimedia, 25*, 8725–8737.
11. Duan, Z., Cai, Z., & Yu, J. (2009). Occlusion detection and recovery in video object tracking based on adaptive particle filters. In *Chinese control and decision conference* (pp. 466–469).
12. Firouzi, H., & Najjaran, H. (2010). Adaptive non-rigid object tracking by fusing visual and motional descriptors. In *International conference on digital image computing: Techniques and applications* (pp. 58–62).
13. Gao, J., Zhang, T., Yang, X., & Xu, C. (2018). P2T: Part-to-target tracking via deep regression learning. *IEEE Transactions on Image Processing, 27*(6), 3074–3086.
14. Gordon, D., Farhadi, A., & Fox, D. (2018). Re3:Re al-time recurrent regression networks for visual tracking of generic objects. *IEEE Robotics and Automation Letters, 3*(2), 788–795.
15. Han, G., Cao, C., Liu, J., & Kwong, S. (2023). Anchor-free tracker based on space-time memory network. *IEEE Multimedia, 30*(1), 73–83.
16. He, Z., Zhao, K., & Zeng, D. (2024). TLtrack: Combining transformers and a linear model for robust multi-object tracking. *AI, 5*, 938–947.
17. Heisele, B., Kressel, U., & Ritter, W. (1997). Tracking non-rigid, moving objects based on color cluster flow. In *IEEE conference on computer vision and pattern recognition* (pp. 257–260).
18. Held, D., Thrun, S., & Savarese, S. (2016). Learning to track at 100 FPS with deep regression networks. In *European conference on computer vision, lecture notes in computer science* (pp. 749–765, 9905).
19. Hsu, H., Shih, T., Tang, C., & Liao, Y. (2005). Real-time multiple tracking using a combined technique. In *19th international conference on advanced information networking and applications* (pp. 111–116).
20. Hu, Z., Yang, D., Zhang, K., & Chen, Z. (2020). Object tracking in satellite videos based on convolutional regression network with appearance and motion features. *IEEE Journal of Selected Topics in Applied Earth Observations and Remote Sensing., 13*, 783–793.
21. Jayabalan, E., Krishnan, A., & Pugazendi, R. (2007). Non-rigid object tracking in aerial videos by combined Snake and optical flow technique. In *Computer graphics, imaging and visualisation* (pp. 388–396).

22. Kalman, R. E. (1960). A new approach to linear filtering and prediction problems. *ASME Journal of Basic Engineering., 82*(1), 35–45.
23. Kristan, M., et al. (2019). The sixth visual object tracking VOT2018 challenge results. In L. Leal-Taixé & S. Roth (Eds.), *Computer Vision—ECCV 2018 Workshops. ECCV 2018, lecture notes in computer science* (p. 11129).
24. Li, C., Li, Y., Zhuang, Q., Li, Q., Wu, R., & Li, Y. (2005). Moving object segmentation and tracking in video. *International Conference on Machine Learning and Cybernetics, Guangzhou, 8*, 4957–4960.
25. Liu, X., Tao, D., Song, M., Zhang, L., Bu, J., & Chen, C. (2015). Learning to track multiple targets. *IEEE Transactions on Neural Networks and Learning Systems., 26*(5), 1060–1073.
26. Lotfi, F., Ajallooeian, V., & Taghirad, H. (2018). Robust object tracking based on recurrent neural networks. In *6thRSI international conference on robotics and mechatronics* (pp. 507–511).
27. Lu, X., Ma, C., Ni, B., Yang, X., Reid, I., & Yang, M. H. (2018). Deep regression tracking with shrinkage loss. In V. Ferrari, M. Hebert, C. Sminchisescu, & Y. Weiss (Eds.), *Computer Vision—ECCV 2018. ECCV 2018, lecture notes in computer science* (p. 11218).
28. Meinhardt, T., Kirillov, A., Leal-Taixé, L., & Feichtenhofer, C. (2022). TrackFormer: Multi-object tracking with transformers. In *IEEE/CVF conference on computer vision and pattern recognition* (pp. 8834–8844).
29. Memon, Q., & Khoja, S. (2012). RFID–based patient tracking for regional collaborative healthcare. *International Journal of Computer Applications in Technology, 45*(4), 231–244.
30. Memon, Q., & Valappil, N. (2021). On multi-class aerial image classification using learning machines. In *Computer vision and recognition systems using machine and deep learning approaches: Fundamentals, technologies, and applications* (Vol. 15, pp. 351–384).
31. Ming, Y., & Zhang, Y. (2020). ADT: Object tracking algorithm based on adaptive detection. *IEEE Access, 8*, 56666–56679.
32. Mocanu, B., Tapu, R., & Zaharia, T. (2017). Single object tracking using offline trained deep regression networks. In *7thinternational conference on image processing theory, tools and applications* (pp. 1–6).
33. Ning, G., et al. (2017). Spatially supervised recurrent convolutional neural networks for visual object tracking. In *IEEE international symposium on circuits and systems* (pp. 1–4).
34. NVIDIA Developer. (2022). *Autonomous machines*. https://www.nvidia.com/en-us/autonomous-machines/embedded-systems/. Accessed 6 Nov 2022.
35. Pu, S., Song, Y., Ma, C., Zhang, H., & Yang, M. (2021). Learning recurrent memory activation networks for visual tracking. *IEEE Transactions on Image Processing, 30*, 725–738.
36. Runze, W., Yuxing, W., & Jianlin, Z. (2017). Improved object tracking algorithm based on tracking-leaning-detection framework. In *7thIEEE international conference on electronics information and emergency communication* (pp. 74–77).
37. Shi, B., Fan, T., & Liu, Q. (2015). Online object tracking and learning with sparse deformable template models. In *8thinternational symposium on computational intelligence and design (ISCID)* (pp. 67–70).
38. Soleimanitaleb, Z., Keyvanrad, M., & Jafari, A. (2019). Object tracking methods: A review. In *9thinternational conference on computer and knowledge engineering* (pp. 282–288).
39. Sommer, L. W. (2022). *Deep learning based vehicle detection in aerial imagery*. Scientific Publishing.
40. Sun, X., Yao, H., Zhang, S., & Li, D. (2015). Non-rigid object contour tracking via a novel supervised level set model. *IEEE Transactions on Image Processing, 24*(11), 3386–3399.
41. Taufique, A., Minnehan, B., & Savakis, A. (2020). Benchmarking deep trackers on aerial videos. *Sensors, 20*(2), 547.
42. Vaswani, A., Shazeer, N., Parmar, N., Uszkoreit, J., Jones, L., Gomez, A. N., Kaiser, Ł., & Polosukhin, I. (2017). Attention is all you need. *Advances in Neural Information Processing Systems*, 5998–6008.
43. Walambe, R., Marathe, A., & Kotecha, K. (2021). Multiscale object detection from drone imagery using ensemble transfer learning. *Drones, 5*(66).

44. Wang, B.-y., Chen, F., & Deng, P. (2014). Online object tracking based on sparse subspace representation. In *26th Chinese control and decision conference* (pp. 3975–3980).
45. Wang, Q., Yuan, C., & Lin, Z. (2017). Learning attentional recurrent neural network for visual tracking. *IEEE International Conference on Multimedia and Expo*, 1237–1242.
46. Wojke, N., Bewley, A., & Paulus, D. (2017). Simple online and real-time tracking with a deep association metric. In *IEEE international conference on image processing (ICIP)* (pp. 645–3649).
47. Wong, S. C., et al. (2017). Track everything: Limiting prior knowledge in online multi-object recognition. *IEEE Transactions on Image Processing, 26*(10), 4669–4683.
48. Xie, H., Yao, H., Zhou, Z., & S., & Sun, W. (2021). *Efficient regional memory network for video object segmentation* (pp. 1286–1295). IEEE/CVF Conference on Computer Vision and Pattern Recognition.
49. Ying, G., Liu, S., Liu, Z., & Jin, Y. (2015). Accurate natural contour tracking for non-rigid object. In *IEEE international conference on information and automation* (pp. 1382–1387).
50. Zhang, Y., Ming, Y., & Zhang, R. (2018). Object detection and tracking based on recurrent neural networks. In *14th IEEE international conference on signal processing* (pp. 338–343).
51. Zhao, X., Liu, Y., & Han, G. (2021). Cooperative use of recurrent neural network and Siamese region proposal network for robust visual tracking. *IEEE Access, 9*, 57704–57715.
52. Zhou, Z., et al. (2019). Enhanced memory network for video segmentation. In *IEEE/CVF international conference on computer vision workshop* (pp. 689–692).
53. Zhou, X., Chan, S., Qiu, C., Jiang, X., & Tang, T. (2023). Multi-target tracking based on a combined attention mechanism and occlusion sensing in a behavior-analysis system. *Sensors, 23*(6), 2956.
54. Zhu, P., et al. (2022). Detection and tracking meet drones challenge. *IEEE Transactions on Pattern Analysis and Machine Intelligence, 44*(11), 7380–7399.

Chapter 3
Safeguarding Smart Infrastructure: A Review of Deep Learning Techniques for Automatic Pipeline Defect Detection

Ata Jahangir Moshayedi, Amir Sohail Khan, Zeashan Hameed Khan, and Xiaohong Zhang

Abstract Pipelines serve as a backbone for a wide on-ground and underground industrial infrastructure, such as oil, gas, water, and sewage. They protect the environment by localizing and transporting their contents in safe housing. However, a significant challenge is faced in case of leakage due to pipeline defects, which may arise due to multiple factors, ranging from manufacturing processes in the factory to on-site operations. The presence of these defects not only carries environmental risks and associated maintenance costs but can also result in substantial disruptions and financial loss within pipeline transportation operations. Thus, detecting defects at every stage of production and usage is crucial. Currently, various methods are employed to identify these defects. However, the integration of visual machine learning techniques, particularly in conjunction with deep learning methodologies, has opened up new avenues for pipeline monitoring and troubleshooting. This chapter details a comprehensive comparison of deep learning-based methods, provides a succinct overview of conventional techniques, and evaluates the performance of these methods in terms of accuracy, applicability, and their ability to detect the sizes and types of defects in pipelines. Furthermore, it explores the challenges and potential prospects of implementing these algorithms, providing valuable insights for researchers in the field.

Keywords Deep learning (DL) · Pipelines defects · Artificial intelligence (AI) · Machine learning · Defects detection

A. J. Moshayedi (✉) · A. S. Khan · X. Zhang
Jiangxi University of Science and Technology, Ganzhou, China
e-mail: ajm@jxust.edu.cn; xiaohongzh@jxust.edu.cn

Z. H. Khan
IRC-IMR, King Fahd University of Petroleum & Minerals, Dhahran, Saudi Arabia
e-mail: zeashan.khan@kfupm.edu.sa

N. E. M. Khalifa, M. H. N. Taha (eds.), *Empowering AI Applications in Smart Life and Environment*, https://doi.org/10.1007/978-3-031-78038-7_3

List of Abbreviations

AI	Artificial Intelligence
ANFIS	Adaptive network-based fuzzy inference system
ANN	Artificial Neural Network
CASAE	Cascade autoencoder
CCTV	Closed Circuit Television
CNN	Convolutional Neural Network
CPM	Cathodic Protection Monitoring
DCNN	Dilated Convolutional Neural Network
DL	Deep Learning
GANs	Generative adversarial nets
GPR	Ground Penetrating Radar
HOG	Histogram of Oriented Gradients
ILI	In-Line Inspection
k-NN	k-Nearest Neighbors
LBP	Local Binary Patterns
LS	Laser Scanning
MFL	Magnetic Flux Leakage
ML	Machine Learning
NLP	Natural language processing
PG	Pipeline Pigging
PPM	Pipeline Potential Measurement
RT	Radiographic Testing
SGDM	Stochastic gradient descent with momentum
SMOTE	Synthetic minority over-sampling technique
SPP	Spatial pyramid pooling
SVM	Support Vector Machines
UT	Ultrasonic Testing
VECT	Visual and Eddy Current Testing
VI	Visual Inspection
YOLO	You only look once

3.1 Introduction

Pipelines constitute a vital component of industries and serve as a means to transport resources from one point to another. They ensure smooth flow, optimize processes, and enhance productivity.Pipelines carry gas, oil and water from one place to another [1]. As pipelines are used for transportation of chemicals and waste water, it is important to use the best quality, and any deterioration in pipelines, like leakage or defect, can cause a huge disaster for industries and the environment [2]. Pipe defect detection is vital for safety, preventing accidents, and safeguarding the environment from leaks and pollution. It extends infrastructure life, maintains operational efficiency, and reduces long-term costs. Compliance with regulations builds public trust, while data-driven methods enhance decision-making and resource management. In essence, it ensures reliable, efficient, and responsible pipeline systems [3]. On the other hand, with respect to pipe production quality control, detecting defects in pipes has significant importance. By identifying flaws early in the manufacturing process, the manufacturer can ensure that pipes meet safety standards, have optimal structural integrity and durability. This proactive approach minimizes costly rework, reduces waste, and maintains customer satisfaction [4]. It's important to highlight that this issue plays a crucial role in both environmental preservation and the efficient transmission of flows. Ensuring the high quality of pipeline production is vital for the industry, necessitating the use of top-notch materials. This holds particular significance during pipeline manufacturing and welding processes [5]. A pipeline can face many different challenges at different stages. In [6], the main defect in pipelines is referred to as "Corrosion". It occurs when the material of the pipeline deteriorates due to chemical reactions with its surroundings, leading to thinning of the pipe walls and potential leaks or failures. Corrosion is a significant concern in many industries, especially those involving the transport of liquids or gases, as it can compromise the integrity of the pipeline and pose safety and environmental risks. Other common pipeline defects include cracks, erosion, mechanical damage, and weld defects [7]. The defects a pipeline faces can be internal or external. These can be structural, construction, or defects that occur in the maintenance stage of the life cycle [8]. Welding plays an important role because; any improper welding can lead a pipeline to different flaws which can greatly affect the strength and longevity of the pipe.

Most recent studies focus on various defects that can occur during welding which occupies the greatest percentage of faults in pipelines [9]. Detecting and addressing these defects is essential to ensure the safe and efficient operation of pipelines [10]. A global picture of most common pipeline defects is shown in Fig. 3.1 with respect to three categories. These are structural, construction and maintenance defects along with defect detection methods [11]. The main contribution of our book chapter are listed as follows:

- Introduction to deep learning as a novel approach for pipeline defect detection.
- Addressing different DL methods used in detection of pipeline defects and their potential consequences.
- Analyzing recent research, comparing strengths and limitations of deep learning methods.
- Evaluating the accuracy of deep learning models for diverse defect types.

The authors believe that this review will be beneficial not only for the researchers but also for engineers and scientists working in pipelines defect detection area. It will assist them in exploring the potential of innovative DL methods, encouraging the creation and utilization of new models to get rid of the existing limitations of current approaches [12]. This chapter is organized as follows: Sect. 3.2 describes the various defect types in pipeline networks followed by sensing techniques in

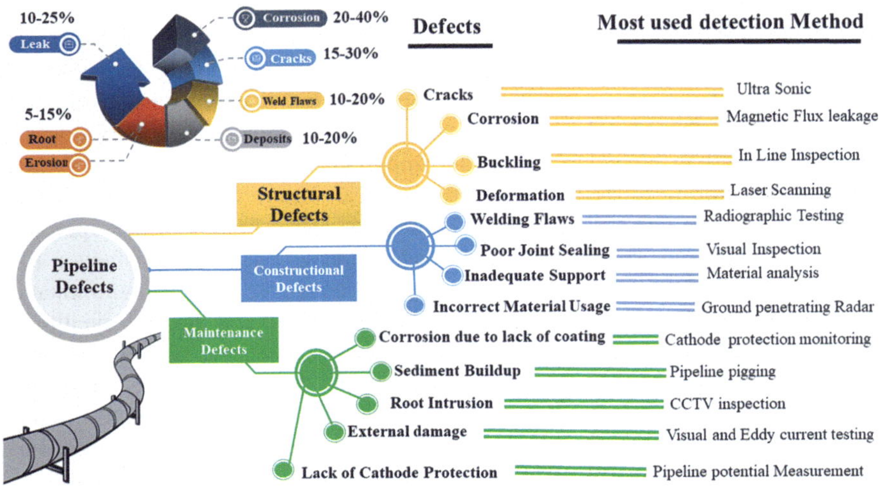

Fig. 3.1 Pipeline defects and preferred detection method

remote monitoring of these systems in Sect. 3.3. Next, typical applications of deep learning in defect detection is highlighted in Sect. 3.4. Finally, the discussion is highlighted in Sect. 3.5. In the end, the chapter is concluded with some insights into future endeavors.

3.2 Types of Defects

The pipeline defects can be broadly grouped into the following three categories:

3.2.1 Structural Defects

It is the most common type of defect a pipeline can face. These structural defects occur because of the poor quality of materials used, which greatly affects the life and longevity of a pipe. Mainly, this defect involves physical weakness, potentially leading to ruptures. Other consequences include cracks, joint deformation, holes, and even structural collapse, compromising their stability [14]. Table 3.1 shows some structural defects in pipelines which manifest themselves as cracks, which are fissures in the pipeline material that weaken its strength, while corrosion results from chemical reactions with fluids or the environment, leading to material

Table 3.1 The Pipeline defect category and detection methods, Ultrasonic Testing (UT), Magnetic Flux Leakage (MFL), In-Line Inspection (ILI), Laser Scanning (LS), Radiographic Testing (RT), Visual Inspection (VI), Material Analysis (MA), Ground Penetrating Radar (GPR), Cathodic Protection Monitoring (CPM), Pipeline Pigging (PP), Closed Circuit Television (CCTV) Inspection, Visual and Eddy Current Testing (VECT), Pipeline Potential Measurement (PPM) [13]

Category	Defects	Description	Common detection (%)
Structural defects	Cracks	Fissures or fractures in the pipeline material that can weaken its structural integrity.	UT: 30%
	Corrosion	Deterioration of the pipeline material due to chemical reactions with the environment or fluids.	MFL: 25%
	Buckling	The formation of wrinkles or bends in the pipeline due to compressive forces or uneven soil settling.	INI: 20%
	Deformation	Changes in the shape of the pipeline caused by external forces, impacting its flow and strength.	LS: 15%
Construction defects	Welding Flaws	Inadequate or faulty welding during construction, leading to weak points in the pipeline.	RT: 40%
	Poor Joint Sealing	Improperly sealed joints that can result in leaks and water infiltration.	VI: 35%
	Incorrect Material Usage	Using materials that are not suitable for the pipeline's intended purpose, leading to premature failure.	MA: 15%
	Inadequate Support	Lack of proper support or anchoring, leading to stress concentrations and potential failure.	GPR: 10%
Operation and maintenance defects	Corrosion Due to Lack of Coating	Absence or degradation of protective coatings, making the pipeline vulnerable to corrosion.	CPM: 30%
	Sediment Buildup	Accumulation of sediments and deposits that can reduce flow capacity and cause blockages.	PP: 25%
	Root Intrusion	Tree roots infiltrating the pipeline, causing blockages, cracks, and leaks.	CCTV: 20%
	External Damage	Physical damage to the pipeline from construction activities, excavation, or accidents.	VECT: 15%
	Lack of Cathodic Protection	Failure to provide cathodic protection, resulting in accelerated corrosion.	PPM: 10%

deterioration. Buckling involves the formation of wrinkles or bends due to external pressure, while deformation refers to changes in the pipeline's shape caused by forces, affecting both its flow and structural integrity.

3.2.2 *Construction Defects*

Construction defects result from installation errors or welding, impacting flow efficiency and causing leaks. This second group of defects involve improper welding during pipeline construction due to which some weak points are left leading to leaks and water infiltration. Low quality material usage involves choosing materials not suitable for the pipeline's construction, risking early failure, where inadequate support can stress pipeline segments, leading to potential failures.

3.2.3 *Operational Defects*

Operation and maintenance issues introduce root intrusion, deposits, infiltration, and obstructions, stemming from negligence or wear. These defects collectively jeopardize pipeline integrity, triggering leaks, ruptures, and environmental risks. Addressing these issues ensures pipeline safety, reliability, and longevity. Inspection and maintenance are thus crucial to detect and address defects, preventing accidents, leaks, and environmental damage. Early intervention reduces downtime, costly repairs, extends pipeline lifespan, and ensures regulatory compliance. Proactive measures are preferred to uphold operational reliability, data accuracy, and product quality across industries.

The major defects are produced by corrosion are due to the lack of protective coatings, making pipelines susceptible to degradation, while sediment buildup accumulates and hampers flow capacity, causing obstructions. Root intrusion involves tree roots infiltrating pipelines, leading to blockages and leaks. External damage can result from construction, excavation, or accidents, impacting pipeline integrity. Lack of cathodic protection accelerates corrosion, compromising the pipeline's durability.

It should be mentioned that Pipeline defects vary, but a general composition of faults include corrosion 20–40%, cracks 15–30%, imperfect weld 10–20%, and deposits 10–20%. Root intrusion and erosion might contribute 5–15% each, while leaks encompass 10–25%, contingent on factors such as materials, environment, and maintenance. Figure 3.2 shows different types of welding faults. Regular monitoring and maintenance are essential to mitigate these risks [16]. The Table 3.1 provides a comprehensive comparison and detailed description of each category, highlighting the most prevalent detection methods along with their corresponding usage in percentage.

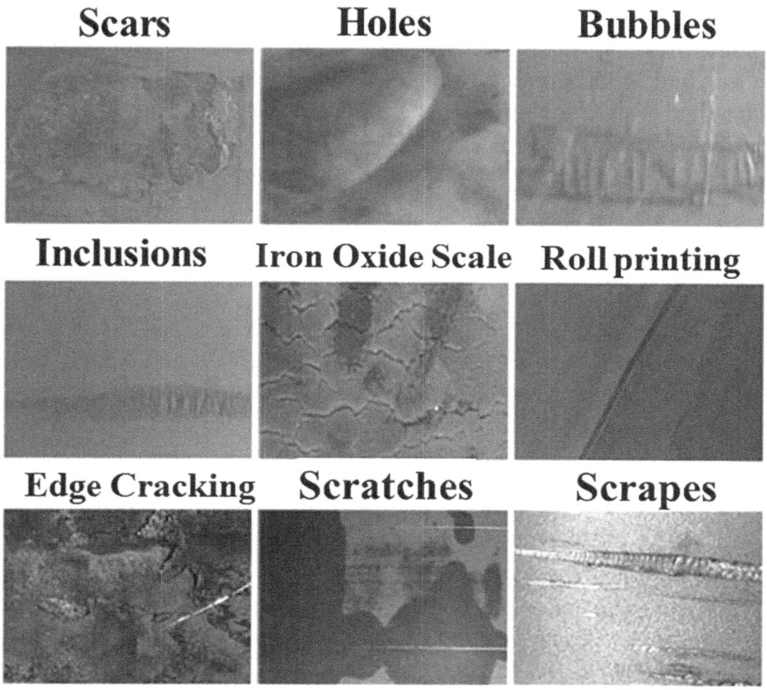

Fig. 3.2 Images showing laser welding anomalies [15]

3.3 Sensing and Post-processing for Defects Detection

A series of steps are required to sense and detect defects after processing of the raw data. These are explained below:

3.3.1 Non-contact and Contact Based Sensing

In non-contact pipe defects sensing, a sensing device or technology is used which never comes in contact with the pipes such as ultrasonic inspection using hand-held devices or Drones; while contact based sensing involves in-pipe inspection using robots or eddy current testing etc.

3.3.1.1 Ultrasonic and Radio-Graphic Sensing

As shown in Table 3.1, corrosion is commonly identified through Ultrasonic Testing, while Erosion often requires Visual Inspection. Magnetic Particle Testing detects

Cracks, and Leaks are pinpointed via Pressure Testing. Weld Defects call for Radio-graphic testing, Blockages necessitate CCTV Inspection, and Material Flaws are spotted using Eddy Current Testing. Misalignment is measured through Laser techniques, and Wall Thinning is gauged using Guided Wave Ultrasonic. Pitting, in turn, can be detected by Eddy current testing [17]. These approaches collectively safeguard industrial systems by addressing diverse pipe integrity challenges.

3.3.1.2 Visual Sensing

Within the above mentioned methods, Visual defect detection [18] provides a straightforward and immediate view of the pipeline's external surface, making it a cost-effective initial screening method [19]. However, it is restricted to surface defects, and is limited by the access, environmental factors, and human error.

3.3.1.3 CCTV and Machine Vision Sensing

CCTV is mainly used to acquire data in machine vision for inspecting objects [20]. The CCTV inside the pipe captures everything and gives a complete video film of the pipe from inside. Mainly CCTV is applicable for inspecting pipelines that are not easily accessible to check if the pipeline is defective [21, 22]. Even recently, in-pipe robots have been preferably used and the video is mapped with the robot's position to detect the precise location of the fault within pipe [23]. But the main problem for defect detection based on vision system and image features remains related to the feature extraction and fault detection/identification system. For the intelligent detection, ML algorithms are equipped with the AI tools [24] for pipeline defect detection [25]. Images of various defects of pipelines are used for training the ML model that can be used in many mobile applications specially made for pipeline defect detection [26]. The purpose of defect detection within manufacturing processes is to ensure the high quality of end products.

The retrospective analysis of prior techniques, including the traditional feature extraction and ML approach, comprises of methods such as Histogram of Oriented Gradients (HOG), Local Binary Patterns (LBP), and color histograms. These distinctive attributes were subsequently input into ML classifiers like Support Vector Machines (SVM), Random Forests, and k-Nearest Neighbors (k-NN) to effectively discriminate between defective and non-defective images [27].

3.3.2 Feature Extraction and Classification for Defect Analysis

Some key researchers such as Wang and Liao [28] designed a system to detect the weld defects of a pipeline. Using radiography images, 12 non-identical attributes

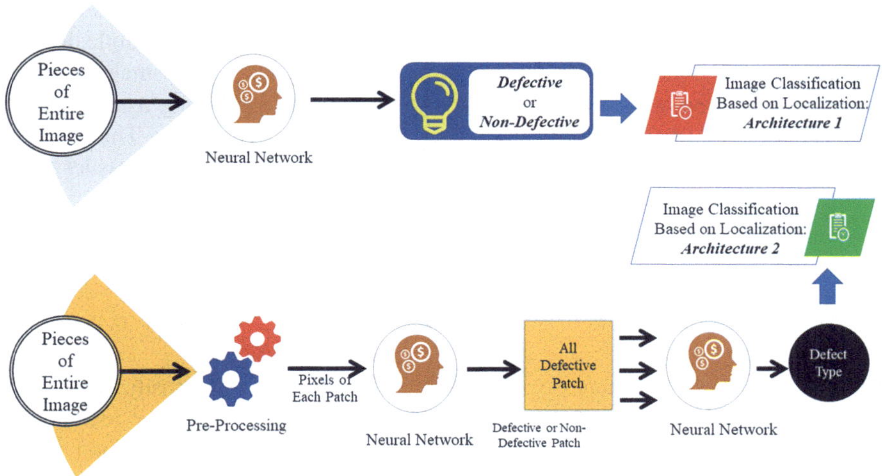

Fig. 3.3 Defect detection utilizing image classification-based defect localization

were used as input. For the detection of welding defects, two well-known networks were applied: one is known as a fuzzy *k*-nearest neighbour (fuzzy KNN), and the other network used was multi-layer perception (MLP) neural networks; the accuracy of fuzzy KNN and MLP obtained as 91.57% and 92.39% respectively. In another work, Zapata et al. employed a two-fold approach involving convolutional neural classifiers: an adaptive network-based fuzzy inference system (ANFIS) and an artificial neural network (ANN) [29]. Following comprehensive experimentation of both classifiers, it became evident that the ANN achieved an accuracy of 78.9%, which was comparatively less than the ANFIS counterpart. Input for the ANFIS model is designed utilizing twelve distinct geometrical attributes extracted from X-ray images which resulted in achieving an accuracy of 82.6% for the ANFIS detection. Figure 3.3 shows the defect detection architectures using the image classification method.

In Fig. 3.3, the image classification process for defect localization begins with an input image, followed by a neural network training model. The trained system then generates an output for evaluating defect detection. This process not only identifies defects but also classifies them by type and name [30]. In another research, Kumar et al. undertook a divergent trajectory by leveraging the grey-level co-occurrence (GLCM) texture features [31]. This distinctive methodology achieved an accuracy of 86.1% for defect classification. Also, Kumar et al. [32] applied a different method known as geometrical features and gained an accuracy of 87.34%, higher than the previous method he used to classify defects detection.

Notably, the above methods relied upon domain expertise and feature extraction proficiency. The modality of texture analysis used Gabor filters and co-occurrence matrices, which found prevalent application in capturing peculiar patterns embedded within images. These techniques were especially good at spotting subtle defects that were dependent on variations in texture spread across the image canvas. Template matching was a similar process that involved comparing a template of a defect with the target image, trying to identify areas of similarity. This method was good at spotting defects that had consistent patterns, but it had issues with accommodating variations within the patterns of defects.

3.3.3 Image Segmentation for Defect Analysis

Another approach is image segmentation and region-based classification, that involved segmenting images to identify areas which were likely to be recognized as defects. Then, extracting specific attributes from these segments and using them for classification resulted in increased accuracy, especially when defects were distributed randomly across the image. However, these methods had some limitations in terms of adaptability, accuracy and scalability. These drawbacks led to a demand for more complex and automated systems, which eventually resulted in the widespread adoption of systems that rely on deep learning for defect detection. This shift to deep learning solves the limitations mentioned above, creating solutions that are accurate and effective.

In [33], used a sequential backward selection (SBS) technique to combine texture and geometrical features to select functional features. This method can cause a lower risk of analytical complexity, and the designed classifier of the ANN for classification resulted in 85.4% accuracy. Soomro et al. [34] resulted in detection of corrosion that pose a threat to the integrity and longevity of oil and gas pipelines within the energy infrastructure.

The corrosion types addressed encompass CO_2 corrosion, also identified as Sweet Corrosion, Pitting corrosion, Stress corrosion cracking (SCC), Hydrogen Induced Cracking (HIC), and sulfide stress cracking (SSC). Through this comprehensive exploration, the authors discern and underscore the multifaceted challenges posed by these corrosive processes. Furthermore, the scholars delve into the realm of integrity assessment for corroded pipelines through the innovative lens of machine learning (ML) techniques. Such methods encompass the application of pivotal frameworks such as Artificial Neural Networks (ANN), Support Vector Machines (SVM), and Hybrid Machine Learning Models (HML). This advanced suite of methodologies is strategically harnessed with the ultimate ambition of facilitating defect detection mechanisms intrinsic to the intricate landscape of pipelines. By embracing deep learning paradigms, the authors endeavor to enhance the efficacy and precision of defect identification within the pipeline domain [35, 36].

3.4 Deep Learning for Anomaly Detection

3.4.1 *Traditional Approaches in Pipelines Fault Detection*

The traditional methods employed for pipe defect detection encompass a range of techniques: For example, Edge Detection, Thresholding, Blob Analysis, Texture Analysis, Template Matching, Hough Transform, Morphological Operations, and Region-Based Segmentation to name few. Also, other traditional machine learning techniques like Support Vector Machines (SVM), Random Forests, k-Nearest Neighbors, and classical neural networks were also employed for pipe defect detection prior to the rise of deep learning [37]. Since, these methods are not robust, the accuracy of these methods can significantly fluctuate as they are vulnerable to the type of defect, lighting conditions, image quality, and the complex and time varying characteristics of the surrounding environment. Thus, no universal solution was available that can guarantees maximum accuracy across all defect types [38].

3.4.2 *Deep Learning for Diagnosis and Prognosis of Pipeline Faults*

The utilization of deep learning in pipe defect detection represents a relatively modern advancement in the last decade that has rapidly gained popularity due to its potential to transform inspection processes across diverse industries [39]. The evolution cycle is shown in Fig. 3.4 where the inception of deep learning into the spotlight commenced in 2012 with the unveiling of AlexNet. This pioneering deep convolutional neural network (CNN) made a groundbreaking impact by achieving exceptional performance in the ImageNet Large Scale Visual Recognition (LSVR)

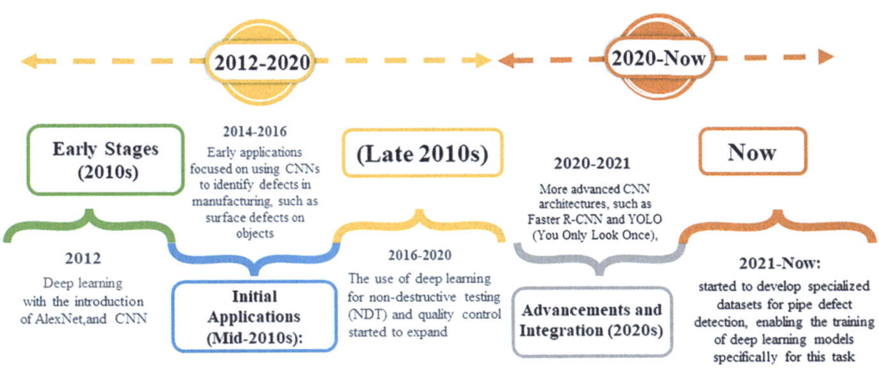

Fig. 3.4 History of deep learning in pipeline defect detection, Convolutional neural network (CNN), Non-destructive testing (NDT), Recurrent Neural Network (RNN)

challenge. This marked the beginning of the application of deep learning in image classification tasks. Between 2014 and 2016, a new phase began as researchers and engineers explored the implementation of deep learning for anomaly detection across various industrial sectors [40]. CNNs became the predominant technique for identifying defects in manufacturing environments, such as the detection of surface cracks in structural materials. From 2017 to 2019, the use of deep learning seamlessly expanded into the domain of NDT and quality control. During this period, deep learning began to expand due to its applications in pipe defect detection. As a result, they focused on the use of CNNs to detect irregularities by examining offline images obtained from visual inspections of pipelines. During 2020s, the development of DL for pipe defect detection witnessed remarkable growth [41].

Continued work in 2020 and 2021 led to more advanced but intricate CNN learning architectures, like R-CNN or YOLO, which were given a lot of attention for complex tasks like object detection. These architectures were useful for finding defects in pipes because they showed high accurate in real-time. Thus, during 2021–2023, specialised datasets were created to train deep learning models to detect pipe defects. These datasets cover a lot of different things, like pipe materials, wide range of faults in different environments, thus incorporating the complexity of real-world situations. In short, the application of using deep learning to detect pipe defects is rapidly progressing with new learning architecture, and a commitment to innovation.

3.4.2.1 Real Time Condition Monitoring Architectures

In pursuit of DL architectures for real time condition monitoring and preventive maintenance, Tao et al. [42] presented a seminal contribution where the authors obtained a high percentage accuracy of 89.60% for correct detection by using CNN in the analysis of segmented outputs, thereby facilitating the classification of defective regions. This architecture is composed of ten convolutional layers, wherein each stratum was composed of 3×3 convolutional operations. However, a down side of the proposed model is its dependency on manual data labeling which requires sufficient time and resources. Hou et al. [43] utilized the GDXray platform as their foundation for investigating weld defect detection, a domain of paramount significance. In their quest, the authors recognized three distinct weld defect categories by using deep convolutional neural networks (DCNNs) as analytical instrument. The architecture of the proposed DCNN method incorporated a combination of four connected Convolutional layer blocks, seamlessly interlinked with four pooling layers, combined into a singular, fully connected layer resulting in an accuracy of 97.2%, showing its efficacy when trained over a dataset rich in various weld defects.

Remarkably, this dataset was complemented through the integration of synthetic minority over-sampling technique (SMOTE), ensuring the equitable representation of diverse defect categories. Moreover, the researchers ventured to extrapolate the effectiveness of their approach across datasets using divergent defect profiles.

Herein, two distinctive techniques, namely random over-sampling (ROS) and random under-sampling (RUS), were deftly employed to re-calibrate the datasets. Following the systematic application of these techniques, the DCNN method upheld its prowess, rendering a sustained accuracy of 96.3% for the ROS-adapted dataset. Conversely, the application of the RUS technique yielded a comparatively modest accuracy, settling at 79.9%, thereby showing better performance.

3.4.2.2 CNN Architecture for Diverse Weld Defects

Another CNN classification model was harnessed to diagnose a diverse spectrum of weld defects was proposed by [44], with an optimized design. The aim is to detect anomalies embedded within the aluminum alloy when used for robotic arc welding by utilizing a 11-layer CNN structure resulting in 99.38% precision rate for a single category of weld material. It is worth noting that the dataset for this research, were different from conventional radiographic imagery, as they were obtained from a Charge-Coupled Device (CCD) camera. However, an obvious constraint of this methodology poses limitations due to restricted navigation illustrated by scenarios where obtaining images of concealed cavities and holes within a pipeline is not trivial [45].

In another study, Zhang et al. [46] employed the innovative Generative Adversarial Nets (GANs) technique for weld defect detection. The authors adeptly categorized defects into distinct categories; such as cracks, porosity, and burn-through. Following a triad of comprehensive experimental investigations, they noted that assemblages of isolated dots may be classified as porosity, while elongated shadows, vertically oriented or parallel to the weld's perimeter, correspond to cracks. Furthermore, anomalous configurations depicted on X-ray images were coined as "burn-through". Nevertheless, a problem faced with this approach is due to its bounded and circumscribed definition of anomaly, thereby leading to an inadvertent oversight of a considerable portion of the defect spectrum. However, the proposed algorithm is able to exhibit a commendable accuracy of identifying 94% defects. Yang et al. [47] examined different deep learning methodologies for the identification of pipeline defects during the manufacturing phase. They considered welding defects, which predominantly manifest within the manufacturing context. Among the diverse array of deep learning techniques included in their study, the authors highlighted the convolutional neural network (CNN), auto-encoder neural network, depth residual neural network, full convolution neural network, and recurrent neural network. Significantly, the authors affirmed that the CNN classifier exhibited a remarkable proficiency in discerning pipeline defects with an accuracy of 99%. This outstanding success is achieved through a large datasets i.e. by training the model over 12,000 images involving more than 200 distinct pipelines.

In another research, Naddaf-Sh et al. [48] successfully performed detection and categorization of welding defects within pipelines during the maintenance phase. They also used DL to address this exigent challenge using digital radiography to capture high-resolution images encapsulating the diverse spectrum of pipeline defects. Using CNN model for training through the stochastic gradient descent with momentum (SGDM) methodology, a ubiquitous optimization algorithm combined with deep learning, constituting a novel classifier. In this research, an expansive dataset comprising 5000 images of welded pipelines, each replete with an array of weld defects, was used for training. Remarkably, the resultant outcomes exhibited an exceptional accuracy of 96% for defect detection. Based on these results, the authors concluded the applicability of CNN as a robust instrument for detecting and localizing defects within pipelines.

Another deep learning method for classifying the pipelines defects with image signals were proposed by [49]. The authors achieved classification based on an analysis of rough set concept and AI network. Using the Back Propagation (BP) AI network model, the upgraded BP-AI network model, and the improved PSO-SVM model to identify and categorise the obtained feature signals and compare their results. All three models achieved 85% accuracy. For recognition and classification, PCA and SVM are integrated and used to the MNIST handwriting digit collection. This considerably enhances the algorithm's performance, with identification accuracy of 98% and processing times reduced by 90% approximately.

3.4.2.3 CNN Architecture for Surface Cracks in Pipes

Surface lesions and deep cracks in pipes provide an important clue for anomaly. Bhatt et al. [50] embarked on a pioneering endeavor, delineated in their scholarly contribution under the title "Image-based Surface Defect Detection". Their proposed algorithm comprised of a distinctive methodology tailored for the discrimination of faults. At its core, this methodology harnessed the profound efficacy of CNN in image-based surface defect detection within pipeline systems.

A major breakthrough in the deployment of deep learning framework for the defect detection application is dependent on the dataset available. The researchers meticulously conducted a multifaceted exploration of the trends, augmenting the robustness of their approach through the integration of three discrete methodological avenues [51]. The first strategy is based on defining a wide range of features to detect complex faults. The second strategic dimension emerged as a thorough examination of the academic tapestry through the lens of machine learning. The third methodological trajectory is relevant to the system architecture for targeting both the aspects of defect location and classification. Thus, based on this approach an average error rate of 90% is achieved. This empirical success demonstrated the robustness of their methodology, and demonstrated the usefulness of their contributions in the domain of image based surface defect detection.

3.4.2.4 CNN for Composite Faults in Sewer Pipes

In relation to safe environment, different other types of pipes are also important for surveillance outside the oil and gas industry, for example a commonly used sewage pipes network also need attention. Siu et al. [52] presented a compendium of techniques aimed at enhancing the efficacy of automatic sewer pipe detection, as documented in their work. Central to their approach was the deployment of a closed-circuit television (CCTV) robot, meticulously dispatched into the interior of the pipe to discern latent defects. This novel methodology hinged upon the assimilation of deep learning principles, specifically the Convolutional Neural Network (CNN) facial technique, to train these robotic agents. The objective was to imbue them with the acumen required for defect identification within the intricate recesses of the pipelines.

A dataset comprising 578 images for cracks, 3240 images capturing deposits, and 1650 images depicting the influence of tree roots on pipeline integrity were used for the purposes of empirical validation. Remarkably, the peak accuracy attained by the proposed methodology culminated at 23.92%. Notably, these images were captured by an autonomous robot, which was strategically navigated within the confinements of the sewer pipelines. The authors also discussed about the faster R-CNN, that can predict the class of the defects and also the coordinates of predicted defect class. This can be done by applying regional proposal network (RPN) combined with the faster R-CNN. However, even with this approach, the trained model of a robot gives inaccurate results for some cases. In their recent works, style-transferred synthetic images were found to upgrade the faster-RCNN model's precision. As an experiment, when a data augmentation technique was used, it increased the accuracy of the sewer pipes model by 2.7%. Zhou et al. [53] introduced an innovative paradigm in the domain of defect detection, encompassing the utilization of a transformer-based deep learning framework, aptly named TransPCNet. This pioneering approach enhanced the feature extraction, as an outcome of incorporating long-range contextual insights and using advanced learning mechanisms. From this study, authors highlighted the convincing performance of TransPCNet, particularly in classifying diverse anomalies that affect the sewer pipelines. The empirical results corroborate the notion that TransPCNet depicts a superior performance vis-à-vis other contemporary benchmarks.

In their recent investigation, Zhang et al. [54] have presented an enhanced methodology for the detection of sewer faults utilizing YOLOv4. In the quest of performance, they incorporated the spatial pyramid pooling (SPP) module which augmented the model's receptive field, thereby amplifying its capability to assimilate contextual information across disparate receptive domains. The construction of a dataset comprising 2700 photographs, encompassing four distinct categories of faults, increased the efficacy of computer vision algorithms. The empirical insights garnered from this study demonstrate that this model yields a mean average precision (mAP) of 92.3% and a recall of 89.0% for the identification of sewage defects resulting in better performance than the baseline YOLOv4 model. The improved accuracy of the refined model augments its potential to significantly improve the precision and classification of sewer-related anomalies.

In a recent investigation, Saberironaghi et al. [55] conducted an incisive review that encapsulates the advances and challenges within the domain of pipeline defect detection. The experiment used deep learning technology with a dataset of X-ray welding images combined with the efficacy of CNN fortified by the application of the Rectified Linear Unit (ReLU) activation function. This method found success in the detection of anomalies within industrial pipelines, particularly for the case of cracks and porosities. The outcome of their work empirically substantiated that the CNN methodology yielded an unprecedented accuracy quotient of 98.8%, thereby witnessing an outstanding efficacy of this approach.

3.4.2.5 CNN for Magnetic Flux Leakage Detection

In a distinct work where deep learning is utilized for pipeline defect detection, Xu et al. [56] introduced a notable advancement in the form of an image recognition model designed specifically for pipeline magnetic flux leakage (MFL) detection. This approach is composed of an integration of YOLOv5 and CNN models which followed a two-fold process: First, it initiates with object identification to systematically classify targets discernible within MFL images. Subsequently, the classification output is used for feature extraction of defects using a CNN-driven regression model. Thus, a dual objective of classification within MFL pseudo-color maps as well as simultaneous recognition of metal loss depth is achieved using this approach. The synergy between object detection and image regression forms the main idea of this comprehensive framework which ensures the robustness of the model's capability in target identification, with a precision of 96%. Moreover, the model's capacity for metal loss depth detection is underscored by a mean absolute error of 1.14. This framework not only enhances the precision of identification but also imparts flexibility to the pipeline defect detection domain.

3.5 Discussion

Defect detection in pipelines is challenging as it is not trivial to detect faults in large datasets under varying conditions. However, with the advent of deep learning in image processing and computer vision, these can help recognize and detect the faults in time to avoid any loss and prolong a pipeline age. Different deep learning methods are utilized for pipeline defect detection, each offering unique advantages and considerations. CNNs excel in automatic feature learning from visual data, yielding high accuracy. However, they demand large labeled datasets and substantial computational resources. Recurrent Neural Networks (RNNs) capture temporal patterns in sensor data, though they may struggle with lengthy sequences offering moderate accuracy. Generative Adversarial Networks (GANs) generate synthetic data for potential high accuracy, but face challenges in training dynamics and mode collapse.

The choice of deep learning method depends on factors such as the available data, the nature of defects, computational resources, and the desired speed of detection. While CNNs are widely used for real-time visual defect detection, other methods

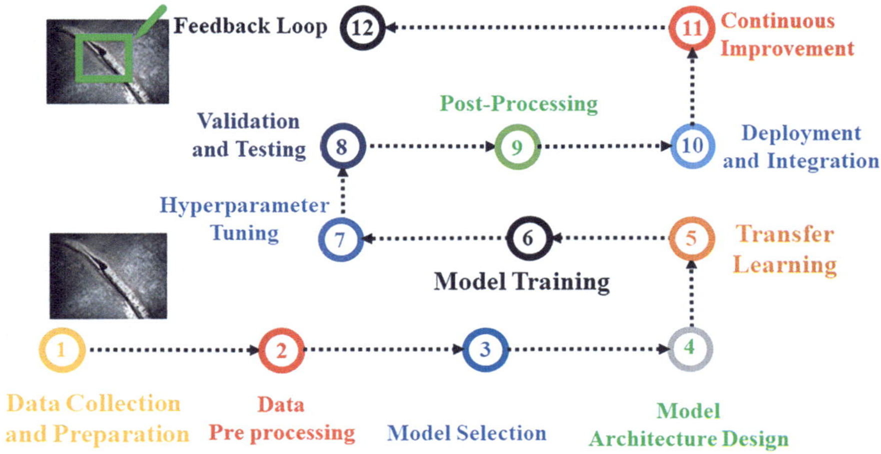

Fig. 3.5 Process for pipe defect detection utilizing deep learning

like RNNs and LSTM can be effective for time-series data from sensor readings. GANs and transfer learning provide unique advantages in data generation and leveraging pre-trained models, respectively. The percentage of use varies based on industry and application requirements [57]. Based on the reported research, weld defects are mostly covered in fault studies. To establish an effective process for pipe defect detection utilizing deep learning as it shown in Fig. 3.5, the following steps are recommended:

1. As depicted in Fig. 3.5, the first step is Data collection and preparation where we collect a diverse dataset of pipe images, encompassing a comprehensive set of both defective and non-defective cases under a variety of lighting conditions, angles, and pipe materials.
2. Then, we proceed to Data Pre-processing in which the images are resized to a consistent size and scale. After that, they are organized within the dataset as training, validation, and testing groups. The dataset robustness is augmented through image rotation, flipping, and subtle color adjustments, which contribute to the model's ability to generalize.
3. Model Selection is the next crucial step in which a deep learning architecture is selected (such as CNN) that best-suits for image analysis.
4. For tasks involving more intricate object detection, consider advanced architectures like Faster R-CNN or YOLO, which provide enhanced capabilities. In the process of Model Architecture Design, tailor the selected architecture as per the requirements of defect detection task.
5. Transfer Learning offers a valuable strategy in which pre-trained models trained on extensive image datasets such as ImageNet are used. This approach enables the model to harness learned features from these datasets, expediting the training process for the specific defect detection task at hand.

6. The Model Training phase involves training the chosen model using the designated training dataset. Implement appropriate loss functions (e.g., categorical cross-entropy for classification, mean squared error for regression) and optimization algorithms (e.g., Adam, RMSprop) to effectively minimize loss and enhance model performance.
7. Hyper-parameter tuning is used to optimize the model's performance by varying a range of hyper-parameters, including learning rates, batch sizes, and regularization techniques, to discover the configuration that yields the best results.
8. Validation and Testing are pivotal stages where we assess the model's performance on the validation set during training to guard against over-fitting.
9. In the subsequent step of Post-Processing, refine the model's predictions. Employ techniques such as non-maximum suppression, thresholding, and clustering to eliminate redundant or false-positive detection's, thereby enhancing the accuracy of defect identification.
10. Upon achieving satisfactory results, proceed to Deployment and Integration of the model into the pipeline, whether through real-time monitoring of pipe sections or batch processing of collected images.
11. Embrace the principle of Continuous Improvement by monitoring the model's performance in real-world scenarios, actively seeking feedback and insights. Periodically retrain the model with fresh data to accommodate changes in lighting conditions, pipe materials, and defect variations, ensuring its relevance over time.
12. Finally, establish a Feedback Loop. Incorporate user feedback and manual inspections to further fine-tune the model's accuracy. This iterative process enables ongoing enhancements, gradually refining the model's performance and its utility in real-world fault detection applications.

In Table 3.2, a summary of the reported deep learning technologies that can be used to detect pipeline defects is provided, along with their advantages and the accuracy for each method.

Table 3.2 shows the details of technologies that can be used for the pipeline's defects detection. Deep learning technology has a very higher accuracy compared to any other technology. Also, the speed of detection in deep learning is comparatively higher. As we can see from Table 3.2, the DL technology mostly used CCTV and different Neural Networks like CNN, Mask R-CNN and ANN. In comparison, the most successful deep learning method was CNN with 99.38% accuracy. Transformer Networks process sequences and complex patterns, requiring significant computational resources and training. Auto encoders learn compact data representations but necessitate careful tuning and provide moderate accuracy. YOLO enables real-time object detection in images, with moderate accuracy, yet it may encounter difficulties with small or crowded objects. These methods find application in above-ground and underground pipelines, with varying percentages of use. Detection scenarios range from real-time to offline, depending on the method. While they each contribute to defect detection, the selection relies on factors like

Table 3.2 Comparative Analysis of Diverse Deep Learning Defect Detection Approaches Across Multiple Pipelines. Convolutional Neural Network (CNN), Cascade autoencoder (CASAE), Synthetic minority over-sampling technique (SMOTE), Generative adversarial nets (GANs), Deep Learning (DL), Stochastic gradient descent with momentum (SGDM), Closed Circuit Television (CCTV), spatial pyramid pooling (SPP), You Only Look Once (YOLO)

Method	Advantages	Accuracy	Highlights	Ref
A. Defect Type: Weld Defects				
CNN	High Accuracy of recognition.	89.60%	2720×2040×3 pixels images were used, based on 10 layer convolution, each layer containing 3×3 convolutional operations.	[43]
DCNNs	Using SMOTE lies in its ability to balance the data-set by generating synthetic samples of the weld defective pipelines.	97.2%	Three different re-sampling methods were applied to three balanced datasets. Subsequently, we utilized a deep learning approach to extract the classification capabilities of five distinct types of features.	[44]
GANs	GANs method can be used in weld defect detection. GANs can help in identify defects such as, porosity, cracks and burn through.	94%	The training dataset for weld defects comprises 7606 X-ray images labeled with RGB information. Among these, 2038 images were normal welds, 1907 images were burn-through defects, 2097 images showcasing cracks, and 1564 images were porosity issues.	[46]
CNN	Utilizing a CNN classification model proves effective in identifying defects, particularly in the context of robotic arc welding involving aluminum alloys. Employing an 11-layer CNN architecture enhances the precision of defect detection within the welding process.	99.38%	Welding defects detection based on deep learning with multiple optical sensors during disk laser welding of thick plates.	[47]
SGDM	SGD with Momentum (SGDM) serves as a valuable tool for training CNNs in classification. By iteratively adjusting the CNN's weights and biases, this method efficiently minimizes the loss function.	96%	Over 100,000 X-ray images of diverse welds were meticulously categorized.	[48]
CNN	CNNs in pipeline defect detection can automatically learn and extract relevant features from raw images without the need for manual feature engineering.	99%	DL methods were used and compared to detect the welding defects that occurs at manufacturing stage of pipeline. 12000 images were trained with more than 200 different pipelines for testing this method.	[50]

(continued)

Table 3.2 (continued)

Method	Advantages	Accuracy	Highlights	Ref
CNN	The use of the CNN method with Rectified Linear Unit (ReLU) activation function on X-ray welding images achieved a remarkable accuracy and effectiveness in detecting cracks and porosity in industrial pipelines.	98.8%	The CNN method, applied to X-ray welding images, achieved an impressive accuracy of 98.8% for detecting pipeline defects, showcasing its effectiveness.	[55]
YOLOv5 and CNN	The model combines object detection and image regression for strong target identification and precise metal loss depth detection.	96%	Novel YOLOv5 and CNN-based system achieves precise metal loss depth detection (mean absolute error 1.14) by integrating object identification and image regression.	[56]
CNN	Can recognize and classify image signal accurately.	98%	The fusion of rough set theory and artificial intelligence for image recognition, achieving 85% accuracy with three models. Combining PCA and SVM for MNIST digit recognition boosts accuracy to 98% and reduces running times by 90%.	[49]
CNN	High accuracy of detection	90%	CNN-based method for pipeline surface defect detection with high accuracy. Three review strategies were applied, achieving over 90% average accuracy.	[51]
C. Pipeline Type Sewer Pipelines				
CNN	A CCTV robot trained through deep learning can be sent inside a pipeline to detect the defects.	23.92%	A total of 1296 synthetic images were experimented with.	[52]
Transformer based deep learning model	Can extract features and long range contextual information	–	Enhances the potential for detecting defects within pipelines. This approach empowers the model to excel in feature extraction, capturing long-range contextual insights, and optimizing the learning process.	[53]
YOLOv4 and SPP	The use of the SPP module enhances the model's capacity to merge context data in separate receptive fields, improving sewer flaw identification.	92.3%	Improved YOLOv4-based model achieves 92.3% mAP and 89.0% recall for sewer flaw identification, promising significantly enhanced accuracy.	[54]

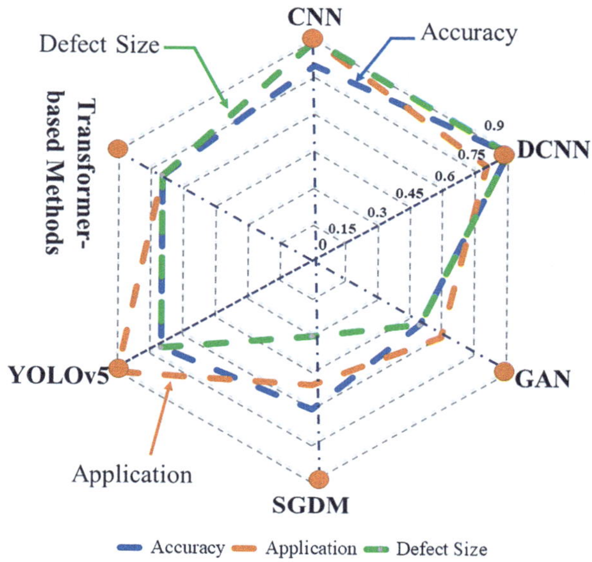

Fig. 3.6 Exploring Advanced Deep Learning Models: From Convolutional Neural Networks (CNNs) to You Only Look Once (YOLO), Enhanced Optimization with Stochastic Gradient Descent and Momentum (SGDM), Creative Power of Generative Adversarial Networks (GANs), to the Versatility of Dilated Convolutional Neural Networks (DCNNs)

defect types, data availability, computational resources, and desired detection speed and accuracy.

A more extensive comparative analysis comprising of the methodologies in terms of Accuracy, Application, and Defect Size is graphically shown within Fig. 3.6. As shown, the Convolutional Neural Network (CNN) has occupied the top position due to its adept performance in image based defect detection. CNNs hold a pervasive utility in the fields of image classification, segmentation, and object recognition, covering all three dimensions. Their pertinence extends seamlessly to the identification of anomalies within pipeline images, provided a sufficiently diverse dataset is available which cover a spectrum of defect dimensions.

The Dilated Convolutional Neural Network (DCNN), is a refinement of the conventional CNN paradigm, which introduces the concept of dilated convolutions, a stratagem conducive to multivariate feature capture across multiple scales. This augmentation serves as a mean for enhancing precision through the assimilation of complex but contextual insights. The DCNN architecture is uniquely suited to such defects which necessitate an analysis of both proximate and comprehensive contextual elements. Noteworthy, among these are fractures or irregularities transpiring across varying dimensions. The DCNN's proclivity for discerning anomalies of heterogeneous dimensions stems from its capacity to accommodate differential dilation rates, thereby constituting an inherent advantage.

The GAN, though primarily associated with the generation of data, proffers ramifications for direct defect detection that are not without merit. While inclined toward data augmentation and the synthesis of synthetic samples emblematic of pipeline defects, GANs furnish a salient resource for the creation of lifelike defect templates, thereby augmenting the reservoir of training data available to models such as CNNs or DCNNs. Though proficient in engendering defects spanning diverse magnitudes, GANs' primarily work well in generating data that bears a multifarious character.

The Stochastic Gradient Descent with Momentum (SGDM), is an optimization algorithm that exists in contradistinction to a deep learning method, bespeaks the potential for amplifying the speed of model convergence during neural network training, thereby exerting an indirect influence upon precision. In addition to its utility in the training phase, the SGDM's benefit extends across various deep learning methodologies, encompassing CNNs, DCNNs, and Transformers. Its purview, however, lies not in the direct calibration of defect dimensions, but rather in expediting the training process itself.

You Only Look Once version 5 (YOLOv5), is a preeminent instantiation within the object detection domain tailored for real-time applicability, embarks upon a quest for a balance between speed and exactitude. Its calibration inaccuracy is contingent upon factors inclusive of model scale and training datasets. Favourable for deployment in scenarios necessitating prompt and meticulous object detection within pipeline contexts, YOLOv5's ability in effectuating such tasks is eminently perceptible. In addition, it is equipped to accommodate an array of defect dimensions, with its predilection for anchor-based detection constituting a foundational asset, though potential reservations exist when confronted with micro anomalies.

Transformation-based methodologies, are effective to tasks entailing sequence-to-sequence bridging, notably in domains such as natural language processing (NLP). These methodologies, when applied to image-based domains such as Vision Transformers, inscribe their relevance into the history of image analysis. In consequence, they show their supremacy when tasked with detecting pipeline defects characterized by subtle interplay and protracted dependencies that bear pivotal implications for defect detection. Nevertheless, it is not without caveat that the preeminence of Transformers within image domains necessitates a stipulation such as the exigencies of ample data availability and considerable computational resources. As a whole, the selection of the most fitting methodology is dependent upon the user requirements within the pipeline defect detection ecosystem, encapsulating dimensions such as data availability, computational endowment, and the idiosyncrasies intrinsic to defect manifestations. A judicious amalgamation of methodologies—predicated on the pairing of CNNs or DCNNs for meticulous defect localization and Transformers for contextual embedment—renders a prognosis that guarantees optimal outcomes.

3.6 Conclusion

The domain of pipeline defect detection holds paramount importance across a spectrum of scientific domains, encompassing metallurgy, material science, and computer science, among others. It captivates researchers due to the pervasive utilization of pipelines across diverse industries. The breadth of this sphere spans from pipeline manufacturing to defect detection methods, each bearing a crucial responsibility in ensuring product safety and quality preservation. In the contemporary landscape, a multitude of techniques exists for pipeline defect detection. Among these, machine vision-based approaches have gained popularity, primarily driven by the challenge of accessing the pipeline's internal environment and propelled by advancements in photographic tools. These innovative methodologies find application on pipe-rolling robots or within mobile applications, well praised as the next generation of defect detection tools. Operating on the principles of machine vision, they meticulously analyze images via specialized algorithms to identify anomalies concealed within the pipeline. This chapter rigorously explores a diverse array of deep learning techniques proposed by distinct authors within recent publications. The focus is on characterizing pipeline defects to uphold the safety of these conduits. The study culminates in a comparative analysis of the presented methodologies. Impressively, all the deep learning algorithms discussed above exhibit an average accuracy surpassing 90%. This noteworthy accuracy substantiates the proficiency of technologies and algorithms in real-time defect detection. Notably, the Circular Conventional Neural Network (CCNN) structure, a prominent deep learning method, holds potential for diagnosing pipeline defects, offering enhanced diagnostic precision and speed. While certain sources may lack precision data, traditional methods still display an average accuracy exceeding 85%. Despite this lower figure compared to deep learning, their established reliability in numerous industries warrants recognition. As a future consideration, the review and adoption of proposed deep learning models, embedded in a shared database and processor, seemed as a promising avenue for future advancements in this dynamic field. Further innovations in this field can be categorized as Transfer Learning, Generative Adversarial Networks, Self-Supervised Learning, Attention Mechanisms, Meta-Learning, and Automated Machine Learning (AutoML) to name few. In a nutshell, the domain of deep learning remains in a perpetual state of dynamic evolution. Pioneering researchers and innovators tirelessly tackle challenges while concurrently pushing the boundaries of deep learning's capacities. This collective endeavor promises continued advancements that will undoubtedly reshape the future of technology and discovery.

References

1. Yang, D., Yan, S., Zhou, D., Shao, T., Zhang, L., & Xing, T. (2020). Reinforcement learning methods on optimization problems of natural gas pipeline networks. In *2020 4th International Conference on Smart Grid and Smart Cities (ICSGSC)*, August (pp. 29–34).
2. Li, J., Zhan, X., & Jin, S. (2009). Research on ultrasonic phased array system for automatic defect detection of pipeline girth welds. In *2009 9th International Conference on Electronic Measurement & Instruments*, August (pp. 1–903).
3. Jiang, J., Men, Y., Pang, T., Tang, S., Hou, Z., Luo, M., & Zheng, Y. (2023). An integrated supervision framework to safeguard the urban river water quality supported by ICT and models. *Journal of Environmental Management, 331*, 117245.

4. Kholil, M. (2023). Implementation of lean manufacturing for improvement of gas pipe product quality with six sigma approach and value stream mapping in oil and gas. *International Journal of Scientific and Academic Research, 3*(6), 29–37.
5. Yan, Y., Liu, D., Gao, B., Tian, G.Y., & Cai, Z.C. (2020). A deep learning-based ultrasonic pattern recognition method for inspecting girth weld cracking of gas pipeline. *IEEE Sensors Journal, 20*(14), 7997–8006.
6. Laleh, M., Xu, Y., & Tan, M.Y. (2023). A three-dimensional electrode array probe designed for visualising complex and dynamically changing internal pipeline corrosion. *Corrosion Science, 211*, 110924.
7. Say, D., Zidi, S., Qaisar, S.M., & Krichen, M. (2023). Automated categorization of multiclass welding defects using the X-ray image augmentation and convolutional neural network. *Sensors, 23*(14), 6422.
8. Singh, S. (2018). Analysis of various defects involved in welding metallurgy. *International Journal of Pure and Applied Mathematics, 120*(6), 6267–6280.
9. Long, Y., Huang, S., Peng, L., Wang, W., Wang, S., & Zhao, W. (2021). Internal and external defects discrimination of pipelines using composite magnetic flux leakage detection. In *2021 IEEE International Instrumentation and Measurement Technology Conference (I2MTC)*, May (pp. 1–6).
10. Waqar, M., Louati, M., & Ghidaoui, M.S. (2023). Time-reversal technique for pipeline defect detection. *Water Research, 243*, 120375.
11. Moradi, S., Zayed, T., & Golkhoo, F. (2019). Review on computer aided sewer pipeline defect detection and condition assessment. *Infrastructures, 4*(1), 10.
12. Ribalta, M., Bejar, R., Mateu, C., and Rubión, E. (2023). Machine learning solutions in sewer systems: a bibliometric analysis. *Urban Water Journal, 20*(1), 1–14.
13. Altabey, W.A., Kouritem, S.A., Abouheaf, M.I., & Nahas, N. (2022). A deep learning-based approach for pipeline cracks monitoring. In *2022 International Conference on Electrical, Computer, Communications and Mechatronics Engineering (ICECCME)*, November (pp. 1–6).
14. Xie, M., Zhao, J., & Pei, X. (2023). Maintenance strategy optimization of pipeline system with multi-stage corrosion defects based on heuristically genetic algorithm. *Process Safety and Environmental Protection, 170*, 553–572.
15. Honggui, D., Yu, C., Feng, Y., & Xiang, J. (2021). Industrial laser welding defect detection and image defect recognition based on deep learning model developed. *Symmetry, 13*(9), 2073–8994.
16. Lu, S., Yue, Y., Liu, X., Wu, J., & Wang, Y. (2022). A novel unbalanced weighted KNN based on SVM method for pipeline defect detection using eddy current measurements. *Measurement Science and Technology, 34*(1), 014001.
17. Khawaja, A.H., Huang, Q., & Khan, Z.H. (2017). Monitoring of overhead transmission lines: a review from the perspective of contactless technologies. *Sensing and Imaging, 18*, 1–18.
18. Tang, R., Liu, Z., Song, Y., Duan, G., & Tan, J. (2023). Hierarchical multi-scale network for cross-scale visual defect detection. *Journal of Intelligent Manufacturing, 35*, 1–17.
19. Oh, C., Dang, L.M., Han, D., & Moon, H. (2022). Robust sewer defect detection with text analysis based on deep learning. *IEEE Access, 10*, 46224–46237.
20. Xu, G., Khan, A.S., Moshayedi, A.J., Zhang, X., & Shuxin, Y. (2022). The object detection, perspective and obstacles in robotic: a review. *EAI Endorsed Transactions on AI and Robotics, 1*(1).
21. Duran, O., Althoefer, K., & Seneviratne, L.D. (2007). Automated pipe defect detection and categorization using camera/laser-based profiler and artificial neural network. *IEEE Transactions on Automation Science and Engineering, 4*(1), 118–126.
22. Moshayedi, A.J., Fard, S.S., Liao, L., & Eftekhari, S.A. (2019). Design and development of pipe inspection robot meant for resizable pipelines. *International Journal of Robotic Control, 2*(1), 25.
23. Sun, L., Zhu, J., Tan, J., Li, X., Li, R., Deng, H., & Zhu, X. (2023). Deep learning-assisted automated sewage pipe defect detection for urban water environment management. *Science of the Total Environment, 882*, 163562.

24. Fries, D., Phillips, J., McInnis, M., & Tate, C. (2021). Rapid multi-sensor fusion and integration using ai-enabled machine vision for real-time operator physiological status. In *2021 IEEE Research and Applications of Photonics in Defense Conference (RAPID)*, August (pp. 1–2).
25. Situ, Z., Teng, S., Liao, X., Chen, G., & Zhou, Q. (2023). Real-time sewer defect detection based on YOLO network, transfer learning, and channel pruning algorithm. *Journal of Civil Structural Health Monitoring, 14*, 1–17.
26. Ji, C., Wang, H., & Li, H. (2023). Defects detection in weld joints based on visual attention and deep learning. *NDT & E International, 133*, 102764.
27. Mohamed, A., Hamdi, M.S., & Tahar, S. (2019). Decision tree-based approach for defect detection and classification in oil and gas pipelines. In *Proceedings of the Future Technologies Conference (FTC) 2018* (Vol. 1, pp. 490–504).
28. Wang, G., & Liao, T.W. (2002). Automatic identification of different types of welding defects in radiographic images. *NDT & E International, 35*(8), 519–528.
29. Zapata, J., Vilar, R., & Ruiz, R. (2011). Performance evaluation of an automatic inspection system of weld defects in radiographic images based on neuro-classifiers. *Expert Systems with Applications, 38*(7), 8812–8824.
30. Ren, Z., Fang, F., Yan, N., & Wu, Y. (2022). State of the art in defect detection based on machine vision. *International Journal of Precision Engineering and Manufacturing-Green Technology, 9*(2), 661–691.
31. Kumar, J., Anand, R.S., & Srivastava, S.P. (2014). Multi-class welding flaws classification using texture feature for radiographic images. In *2014 International Conference on Advances in Electrical Engineering (ICAEE)*, January (pp. 1–4).
32. Kumar, J., Anand, R.S., & Srivastava, S.P. (2014). Flaws classification using ANN for radiographic weld images. In *2014 International Conference on Signal Processing and Integrated Networks (SPIN)*, February (pp. 145–150).
33. Valavanis, I., & Kosmopoulos, D. (2010). Multiclass defect detection and classification in weld radiographic images using geometric and texture features. *Expert Systems with Applications, 37*(12), 7606–7614.
34. Soomro, A.A., Mokhtar, A.A., Kurnia, J.C., Lashari, N., Lu, H., & Sambo, C. (2022). Integrity assessment of corroded oil and gas pipelines using machine learning: a systematic review. *Engineering Failure Analysis, 131*, 105810.
35. Dai, L.S., Feng, Q.S., Sutherland, J., Wang, T., Sha, S.Y., Wang, F.X., & Wang, D.P. (2020). Application of MFL on girth-weld defect detection of oil and gas pipelines. *Journal of Pipeline Systems Engineering and Practice, 11*(4), 04020047.
36. Yuan, J., Mao, W., Hu, C., Zheng, J., Zheng, D., & Yang, Y. (2023). Leak detection and localization techniques in oil and gas pipeline: a bibliometric and systematic review. *Engineering Failure Analysis, 146*, 107060.
37. Shen, D., Liu, X., Shang, Y., & Tang, X. (2023). Deep learning-based automatic defect detection method for sewer pipelines. *Sustainability, 15*(12), 9164.
38. Sircar, A., Yadav, K., Rayavarapu, K., Bist, N., & Oza, H. (2021). Application of machine learning and artificial intelligence in oil and gas industry. *Petroleum Research, 6*(4), 379–391.
39. Moshayedi, A.J., Khan, A.S., Yang, S., & Zanjani, S.M. (2022). Personal image classifier based handy pipe defect recognizer (HPD): design and test. In *2022 7th International Conference on Intelligent Computing and Signal Processing (ICSP)*, April (pp. 1721–1728).
40. Fu, G., Zhang, Q., Zhu, L., Lin, Q., Wang, Y., Fan, S., & Xiao, C. (2024). Towards high-resolution specular highlight detection. *International Journal of Computer Vision, 132*(1), 95–117.
41. Mao, J., Shi, S., Wang, X., & Li, H. (2023). 3D object detection for autonomous driving: A comprehensive survey. *International Journal of Computer Vision, 131*(8), 1909–1963.
42. Tao, X., Zhang, D., Ma, W., Liu, X., & Xu, D. (2018). Automatic metallic surface defect detection and recognition with convolutional neural networks. *Applied Sciences, 8*(9), 1575.
43. Hou, W., Wei, Y., Jin, Y., & Zhu, C. (2019). Deep features based on a DCNN model for classifying imbalanced weld flaw types. *Measurement, 131*, 482–489.
44. Zhang, Y., You, D., Gao, X., Zhang, N., & Gao, P.P. (2019). Welding defects detection based on deep learning with multiple optical sensors during disk laser welding of thick plates. *Journal of Manufacturing Systems, 51*, 87–94.

45. Zang, Y., Zhou, K., Huang, C., & Loy, C.C. (2023). Semi-supervised and long-tailed object detection with CascadeMatch. *International Journal of Computer Vision, 131*(4), 987–1001.
46. Zhang, H., Chen, Z., Zhang, C., Xi, J., & Le, X. (2019). Weld defect detection based on deep learning method. In *2019 IEEE 15th International Conference on Automation Science and Engineering (CASE)*, August (pp. 1574–1579).
47. Yang, J., Li, S., Wang, Z., Dong, H., Wang, J., & Tang, S. (2020). Using deep learning to detect defects in manufacturing: a comprehensive survey and current challenges. *Materials, 13*(24), 5755.
48. Naddaf-Sh, M.M., Naddaf-Sh, S., Zargarzadeh, H., Zahiri, S.M., Dalton, M., Elpers, G., & Kashani, A.R. (2021). Defect detection and classification in welding using deep learning and digital radiography. In *Fault diagnosis and prognosis techniques for complex engineering systems* (pp. 327–352). Academic Press.
49. Zhao, Y., & Wei, G. (2021). Using an improved PSO-SVM model to recognize and classify the image signals. *Complexity, 2021*, 1–12.
50. Bhatt, P.M., Malhan, R.K., Rajendran, P., Shah, B.C., Thakar, S., Yoon, Y.J., & Gupta, S.K. (2021). Image-based surface defect detection using deep learning: a review. *Journal of Computing and Information Science in Engineering, 21*(4), 040801.
51. Wang, M., Kumar, S.S., & Cheng, J.C. (2021). Automated sewer pipe defect tracking in CCTV videos based on defect detection and metric learning. *Automation in Construction, 121*, 103438.
52. Siu, C., Wang, M., & Cheng, J.C. (2022). A framework for synthetic image generation and augmentation for improving automatic sewer pipe defect detection. *Automation in Construction, 137*, 104213.
53. Zhou, Y., Ji, A., & Zhang, L. (2022). Sewer defect detection from 3D point clouds using a transformer-based deep learning model. *Automation in Construction, 136*, 104163.
54. Zhang, J., Liu, X., Zhang, X., Xi, Z., & Wang, S. (2023). Automatic detection method of sewer pipe defects using deep learning techniques. *Applied Sciences, 13*(7), 4589.
55. Saberironaghi, A., Ren, J., & El-Gindy, M. (2023). Defect detection methods for industrial products using deep learning techniques: a review. *Algorithms, 16*(2), 95.
56. Xu, Z., Liu, K., Gu, B., Yan, L., Pang, X., & Gao, K. (2023). Image recognition model of pipeline magnetic flux leakage detection based on deep learning. *Corrosion Reviews, 41*, 689–701.
57. Ma, D., Liu, J., Fang, H., Wang, N., Zhang, C., Li, Z., & Dong, J. (2021). A multi-defect detection system for sewer pipelines based on StyleGAN-SDM and fusion CNN. *Construction and Building Materials, 312*, 125385.

Chapter 4
AI Enabled Smart IoT Data Platform

Mohamed Sohail and Said Tabet

Abstract Over the last decade, advances in AI and Machine learning accelerated, and the adoption of IoT and Big Data created a perfect environment for this next generation of IT-OT systems. Data centers are now pressured and needed to process challenging AI-intensive workloads while becoming more sophisticated and agile to address other important concerns such as power consumption and personalization of customer requirements including cost management. This brings up the necessity to optimize the current infrastructure handling techniques of the IoT platforms to adapt to the new nature of the IoT data including "computing, storage, and networking". In this book chapter, we propose a novel technique to enhance IoT data platforms to optimize the whole ecosystem performance for read and write intensive applications. This approach uses AI techniques including small and large models to adapt to this new era of consuming digital transformation generated data and get the most out of it in near real-time.

Keywords IoT · AI · Data analytics · Data center · Multi-layered platforms

4.1 Introduction

Many IoT use-cases and some cloud-based applications are shown distinct patterns such as Intensive Data generation. As part of the modern workloads massive amounts of data are generated in non-stopping 24*7 fashion from huge number of devices & sensor nodes. For instance, a Smart Field could have multiple sensors installed every ten meters, then we can have approximately one million sensors for a ten square KM field space. If we can assume the size of 1 (one) KB data (for instance temperature or humidity) can be generated per sensor every minute. With a simple calculation we could have around ~1 TB of data ingested per day. Another

M. Sohail · S. Tabet (✉)
Dell Technologies, Cairo, Egypt
e-mail: Mohamed.Sohail@dell.com; Said.Tabet@dell.com

N. E. M. Khalifa, M. H. N. Taha (eds.), *Empowering AI Applications in Smart Life and Environment*, https://doi.org/10.1007/978-3-031-78038-7_4

clear example of the huge amount of data is the video surveillance generated data which brings even more massive data.

One of patterns is Global accessibility. Once we have that huge data ingested, they'll be looped to be accessed in a global level by different type of consumers (Apps) from different locations (cross cities, cross sites, or even countries) for a wide array of use cases. This will be more important and common. Such data, once created & shared, can be much easier to access or analyze by different organizations. Another pattern is Intensive read / write. Once the Data is generated by the edge sensors nodes/devices, they could be distributed or replicated to a few or more Data Centers or geolocations. Many applications / users globally can access or analyze that data in a read intensive mode (Eventually analyzing the data is the most important stage in the IoT data life cycle).

In Fig. 4.1 below a holistic view of the increasing IoT Market by 2030. We can notice a huge number of sensors and data that will be generated out of these sensors. This will need a new way to process and store such a huge amount of data.

Artificial Intelligence (AI) is revolutionizing various fields by enabling advanced data processing, pattern recognition, and decision-making capabilities. It can be used to enhance crop management and quality control [1]. In healthcare, innovative models can be used to optimize COVID-19 diagnosis leading to more accurate and efficient electrocardiography analysis [2]. Additionally, AI plays a critical role in improving the robustness of diagnostic tools against adversarial attacks which fortify cancer diagnosis systems in deep learning against malicious interference [3]. These examples highlight the transformative impact of AI across diverse sectors, driving advancements that are reshaping industry standards and improving outcomes.

The integration of Artificial Intelligence (AI) into IoT ecosystems [4] is essential for managing the vast amounts of data generated by millions of sensors and devices in smart environments. AI algorithms, particularly those designed for real-time data processing and analysis, play a crucial role in handling this data deluge. They enable

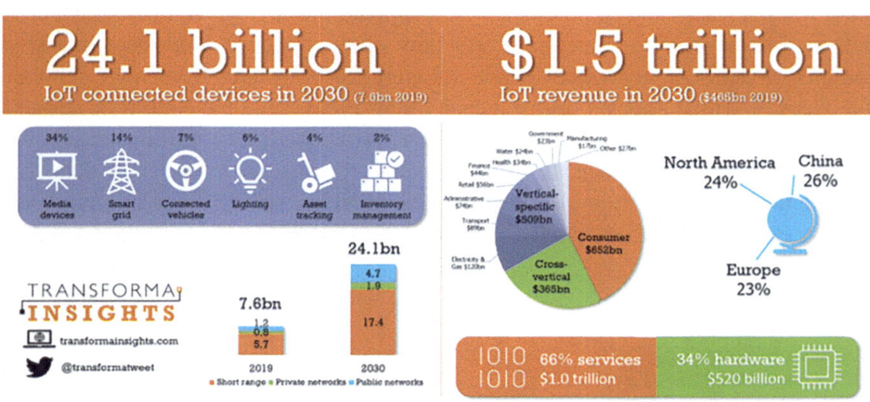

Fig. 4.1 IoT market from 2019–2030

the extraction of actionable insights from the continuous streams of information generated by these sensors.

Furthermore, AI enhances global accessibility and the intensive read/write operations characteristic of IoT data management [5] . As data is distributed across multiple data centers and geolocations, AI-driven algorithms optimize the retrieval and processing of information, ensuring that applications worldwide can access and analyze data efficiently. This capability is particularly important for applications that require real-time data analysis, such as predictive maintenance, where AI can rapidly analyze sensor data to forecast equipment failures before they occur. As the IoT market continues to expand, with an increasing number of sensors and devices generating unprecedented volumes of data, the role of AI in processing, analyzing, and managing this data will become even more critical.

4.2 Challenges

IoT data is usually generated in a rapid way, in large volumes and the types of data may vary a lot with potentially incomplete information and even often erroneous data. We are tackling a series of challenges here. The ubiquitous sensors, RFID readers, and other devices involved in the IoT systems can generate data massively. So the data has to be processed with in a high throughput fashion [6]. Furthermore, and due to the fact that the data volume is huge as we illustrated before, and is increasing rapidly, a data storage solution oriented for IoT usage should not only be capable of storing massive data efficiently, but also have an elastic support and horizontal scaling using new AI techniques to address such new challenges in the IoT data landscape. Moreover, the IoT data can be gathered from many different sources and consists of various structured and unstructured data. So, Data Storage systems are expected to have the ability to deal with such heterogeneous data resources.

4.2.1 Storage Backend Reliability

In a generic Cloud computing environment, Storage back-end is not IoT aware and doesn't optimize data handling to enhance IoT data cloud performance. This is even more pronounced with AI Data Workloads.

4.2.2 Data Center Operations for Heterogenous Devices

The enormous number of heterogeneous devices, coupled with the sheer volume, velocity, and structure of IoT data, will create challenges for data center operators, manifesting in areas such as data storage management and servers. Those challenges can't be ignored, as real-time business processes are at stake [7].

4.2.3 Data Movement and Latency

There could be many kinds of Apps running on top of IoT data, clearly, we don't want to modify them. Instead, it's desired to provide transparent ways to access the data at proper location in fast way. The concept of accessing data with suitable latency and location, eliminating unnecessary data movement [8].

4.2.4 Propagational Delay and QoS

Performance (Bandwidth, Delay, or Latency) requirements in a typical cloud computing environment are a challenge for QoS (Quality of Service) satisfaction [9]. The propagation delay is based on the distance between cloud users and the hosting Data Centers to access the data. It has a dominant impact on the overall delay in cloud computing. Bandwidth is crucial for the data analytics to load massive data sets. Thus, it's highly demand to minimize the IoT data access latency, especially when it comes to IoT read-intensive applications for data analytics with no matter they may come from which location [10].

4.3 Steps to Address the Challenges

4.3.1 Step 1: Establishing AI Enabled Smart DB Allocation Service

Choose the suitable DB type Dynamically based on a pre-defined criterion. This may include data type, sensors functions, and application types (for instance column stores Vs. row stores or in-memory databases for real time analysis (field system sensors) Vs Hadoop for batch analysis (surveillance videos).

Pre-data preparation: Depending on the type of application, perform early data preparation in storage for batch processing.

As an illustration:

(a) **Camera Data**: Prepare the data by pre-structuring it so that it is ready for batch processing when needed.
(b) **Traffic data**: Prepare it for batch processing at any time by cleaning, summarizing, and storing it.

The **AI enabled IoT-Smart platform** resides between the 'Sensor Network' and the backend infrastructure (such as Cloud platform) with the following logic:

4.3.1.1 Storage Path Optimization Engine

The AI engine will send large data chunks on the storage layer instead of sending it on the devices layer. This puts the focus on optimization. For example, if I send data from one "Sensor" to the other over the internet, then insert the data on the assigned storage layer (into the same Data Store) and only send the relevant metadata, and pointers over the network to save time and battery [11]. This means that if all the storage is cloud based, why send the data (if I do not want to process/read it now) if we can just modify the "Data ownership" metadata from one owner device to the other and move/copy the data from the internal Data Store within the same Data Center.

Why is the above approach best suited for M2M communication especially sensors in smart city environments?

This is due to the following:

(a) sensors tend to act as data generators, they do not consume or process data instantly. Instead, they just need to store it for further processing by central servers.
(b) sensors are very critically constrained devices in energy (battery) and bandwidth and require minimum traffic possible over the network/internet.

Figure 4.2 illustrates the proposed framework architecture for IoT Oriented data storage. Multiple sources and streams of data from various IoT devices (including sensors, cameras, radars, and other devices and potentially wearables) are part of the overall IoT data ecosystem. Ingest of data is managed taking into consideration the semantic of each data input and the characteristics of the devices as well as their context (some data is transient and other data is required for long term storage for various reasons including reporting and regulatory compliance).

In Fig. 4.3, we propose the algorithm that will control the upload process of the data in scope. With the Storage Path Optimization algorithm, as illustrated in Fig. 4.4, the data will be received by the IoT server, then we will check the frames from the sender to the receiver, then we will map the device address with the device ID. The data will be stored in the respective LUN, then the data can be copied from the sender LUN to the destination LUN, then the IoT server will send a trigger to the receiver device that the data has been written in its respective LUN [12].

In Fig. 4.5, we show the theory of the operation without applying the SPO from the initial writing of the data until it reaches the destination data store of the other devices. This will help in saving the time and effort for the large and big files that shouldn't be reprocessed multiple times.

In Figs. 4.6 and 4.7, it shows the modification that we have using the SPO algorithm.

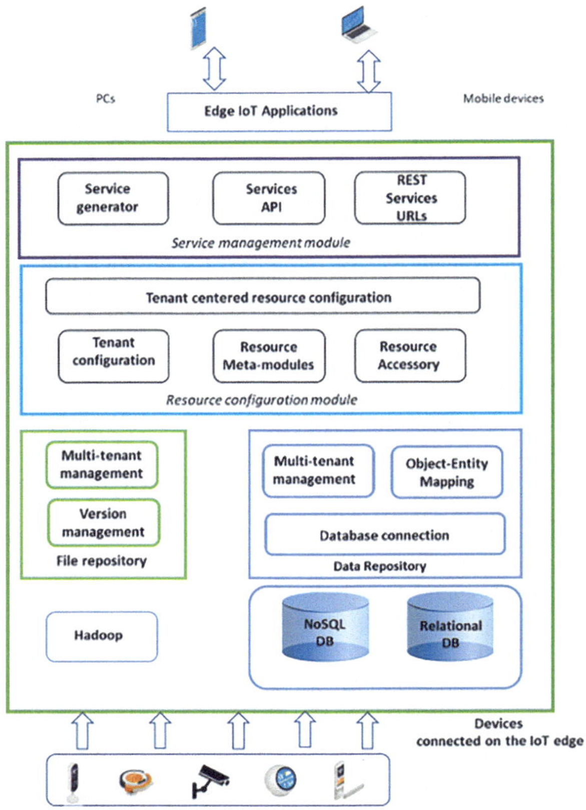

Fig. 4.2 IoT oriented data storage framework

Here we have Implemented the SPO algorithm using environment simulation (**MATLAB**) and tested its performance over the current storage and networking approaches (for TCP and UDP) [13]. Results showed up to 25% improvement for the average delay per user.

4.3.1.2 Data Profiling

IO Profiling It's important to understand the behavior of deployed IoT devices. Some IoT devices tend to send more than receive data while other devices tend to receive data more than send. For example: health monitor sensors or production line sensors in Oil and gas industry connected to the internet are more likely to send data (reports and notifications) to other devices such as mobile phones as illustrated in Fig. 4.8.

To manage the massive IoT data requirements in the cloud, the Data Storage framework should be able to deal with the relevant challenges of database.

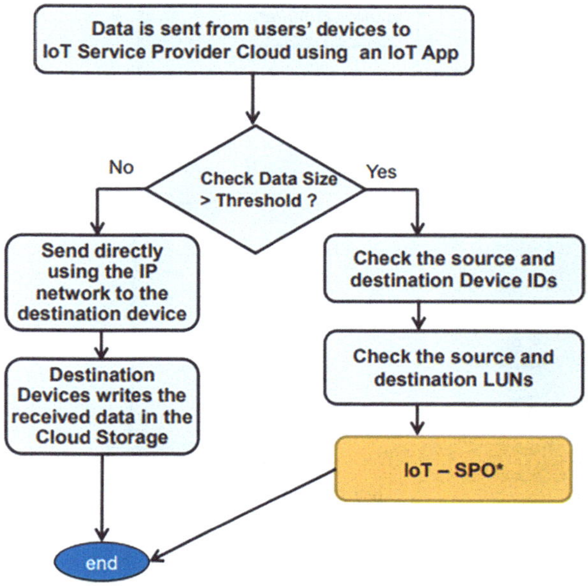

Fig. 4.3 Storage path optimization algorithm

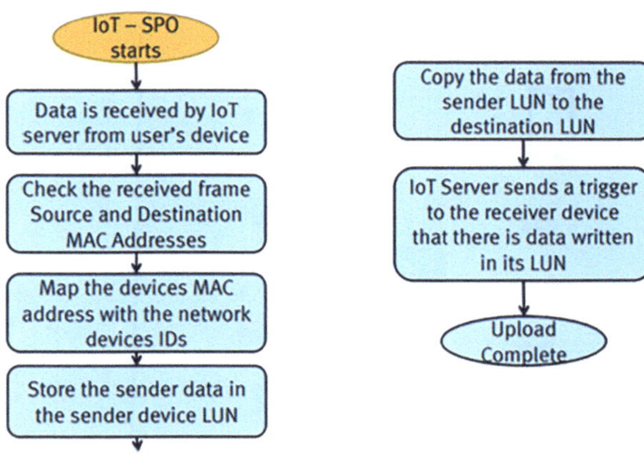

Fig. 4.4 Data upload flowchar

(a) Locate data for the "Send intensive Devices" in a storage/RAID type that is suitable for high read performance such as RAID 5.
(b) Locate data for the "Receive-intensive Devices" in a storage/RAID type that is suitable for high Write performance such as RAID10

In this section, we have used a scenario that focuses on a "Logistics Delivery" scenario. For instance, to proof how this framework can perform. In this logistics scenario, a considerable amount of logistics orders is tracked and processed by an IoT-based technologies such as RFID readers, multiple types of sensors, and also cameras. The generated data by the devices are firstly collected and preprocessed by some of the terminals, and then they are also sent to a logistics management

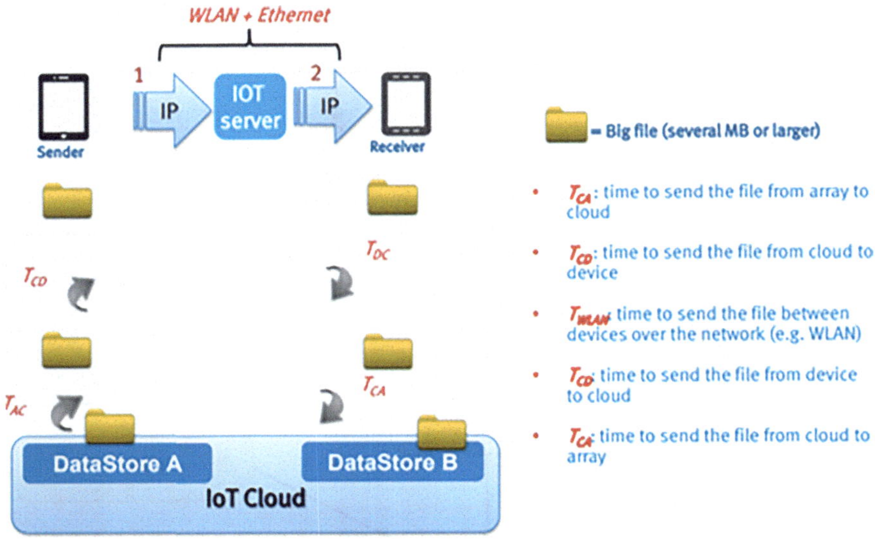

Fig. 4.5 Theory of operations—without SPO

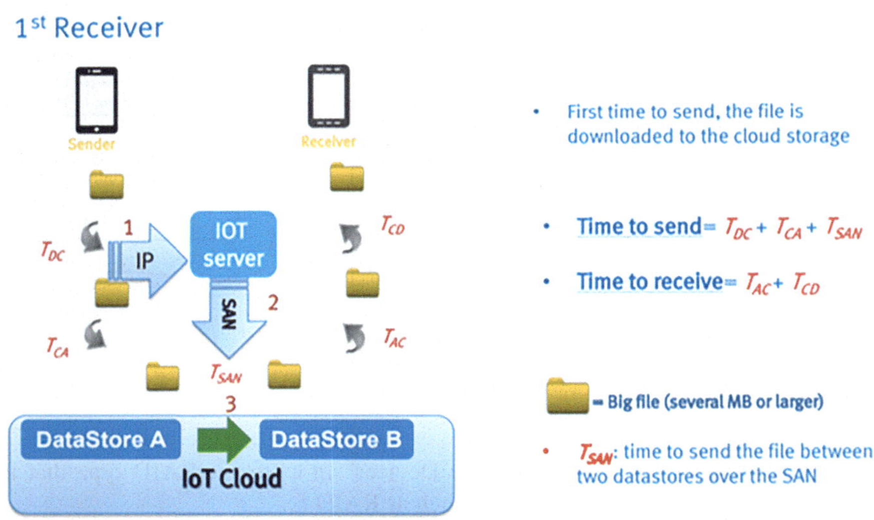

Fig. 4.6 Theory of operation with SPO

dedicated application, which is developed based on the framework of the data storage we proposed earlier. To deploy an improved performance of the data storage and accessibility, all the data types are stored in different types of Data bases such as (MySQL database, file repository, and MongoDB), as shown in Fig. 4.9 below.

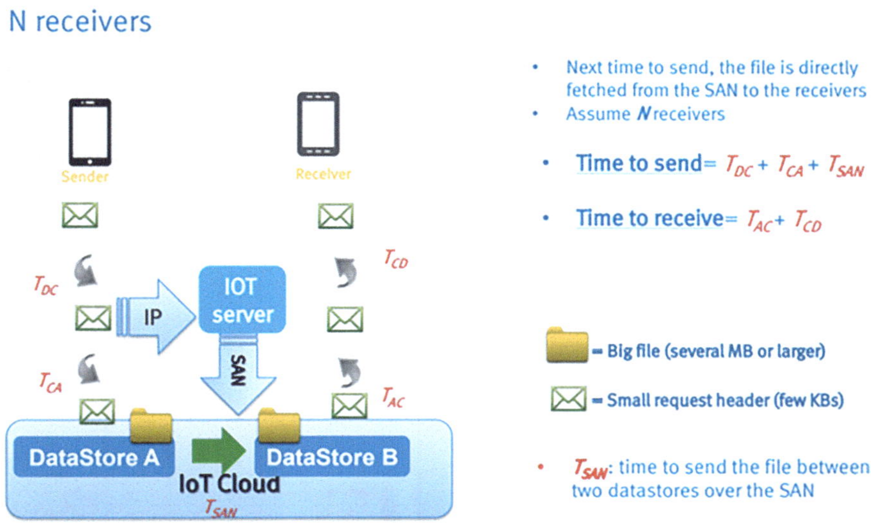

Fig. 4.7 Theory of operation with SPO Continued

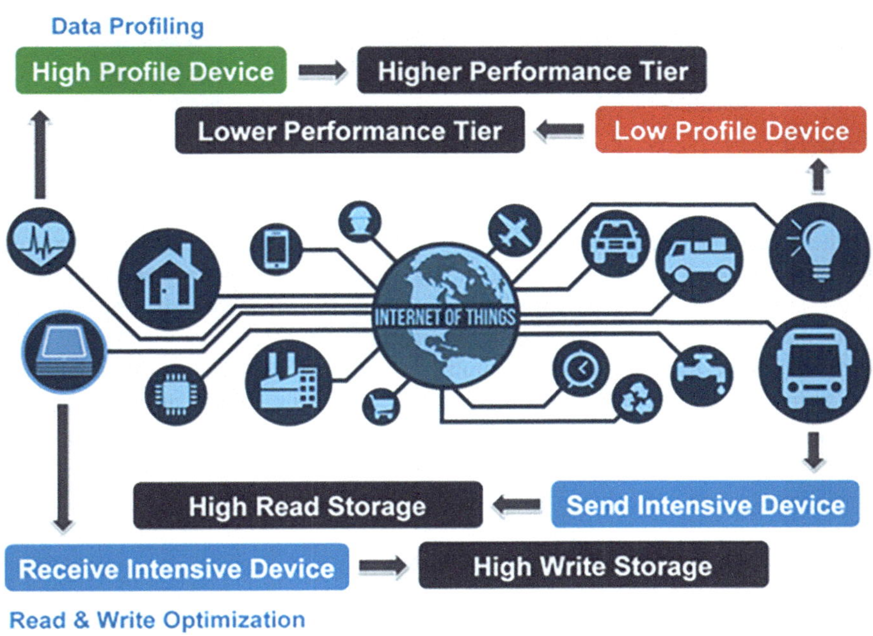

Fig. 4.8 Data profiling chart

Logistics Data storage: In a typical logistics system, package delivery can be traced by a series of devices and generates data frequently. In Fig. 4.9 below, we can

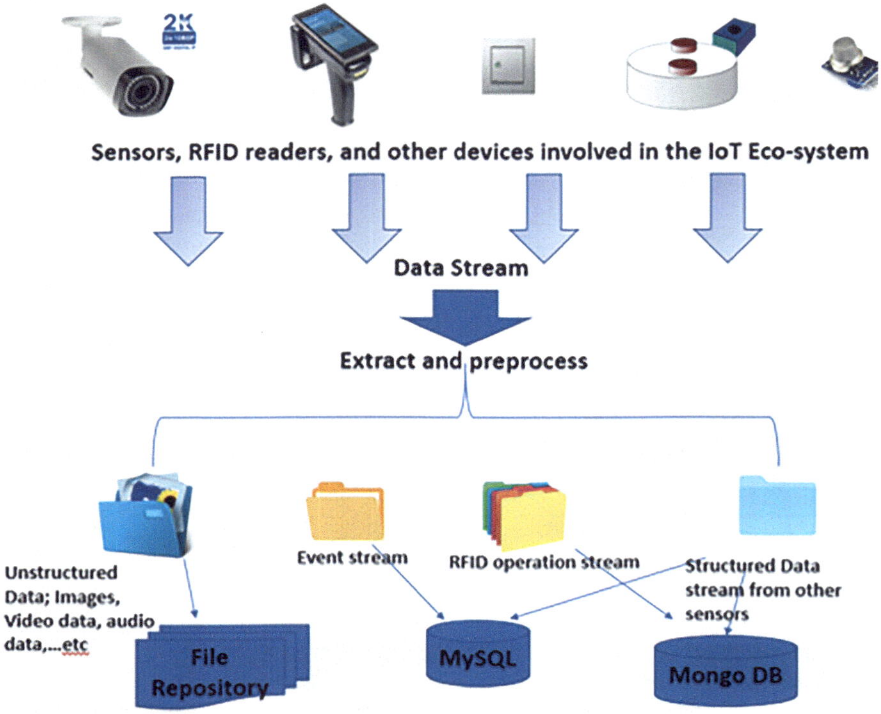

Fig. 4.9 Process of storing logistics data as example

see the procedure of the data generated by each device and persisted in the proposed storage framework. The generated data by each device is preprocessed in some of the terminals before reaching the logistics management system. The logistics management system can then process the tracing data in the proposed storage [14]. The data can be firstly divided into multiple types of data such as structured data, which are stored in the databases, and unstructured data, which can be stored in a file repository model. Furthermore, the structured data is stored into a separate mode in different databases based on the metadata captured into the configuration.

4.3.1.3 Cluster-Aware Resource Allocation

The data generated by the devices are firstly captured and preprocessed by some terminals and then sent to the application of the "logistics management" application, which is built as per the data storage framework [15]. To enhance the performance of data storage and data access, all types of data are stored in relevant storage platforms (MySQL database, MongoDB, and file repository).

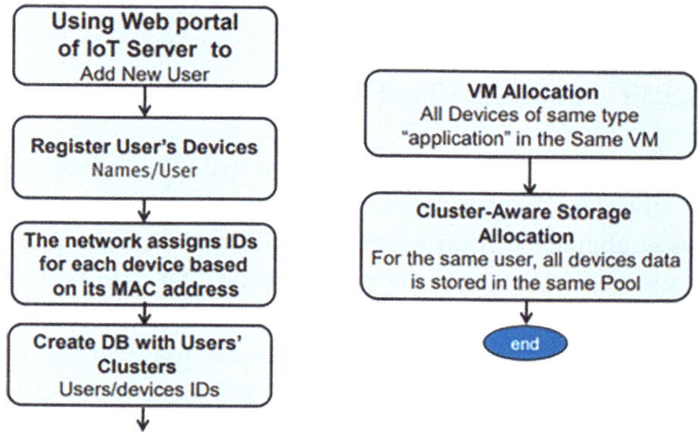

Fig. 4.10 Data classification using the cluster aware method

User	Device	MAC	IoT Net ID	VM	Pool	LUN
User 1	Mobile	x....1	M1	VM1	Pool 1	100
	Cooker	z....2	C1	VM2		101
	E-Curtains	y....3	C2	VM3		102
	Door	a....4	D1			103
User 2	Mobile	b....5	M2	VM1	Pool 2	104
	Laptop	f....6	L1			105
	Cooker	i....7	C3	VM2		106
	Car	e....8	C4	VM4		107

Same Application/platform devices are in same VM
Same User devices are in same pool

Fig. 4.11 Resource management DB

Cluster-Aware Resource allocation: Data in IoT tends to move between a set of devices "Cluster" that belong to certain profile such as same user or between sensors in the same area reporting data to an aggregator point. Hence, the engine will locate data for the same "Cluster" in the same datastore to get maximum performance as data mobility inside the cluster is high. Copying data inside the same datastore or same array is much faster than copying data between sites or different arrays as illustrated in Fig. 4.10.

In the below Fig. 4.11, we have provided a demo for Resource Management Database doing this allocation on the compute level (VMs) and storage level (Pool).

4.3.2 Step 2

4.3.2.1 Creating Cloud Enabler Service

To handle these challenges, we need to deploy a data storage platform that is enabled to store and manage efficiently massive structured and unstructured IoT data. In this book chapter we have proposed a Smart Storage platform for IoT data. We have leveraged some previous work around "Storage path optimization for IoT" with a granted patent 'US9882985B1'. In addition, we have proposed an enhancement to use an AI based method to handle the IoT Data to manage both the structured / unstructured data using the smart IoT layer (Cloud Enabler Service) based on a combined set of algorithms to implement a novel version of IoT data management.

In Fig. 4.12, we illustrate how multiple Data Centers relate to different routes, along with Cloud Enabler Service orchestrating the data movement between them. Since multi-cloud computing might be considered as a global network with multi-continent connectivity, signal propagation delay plays an important role in the cloud read/write access performance and is considered a serious challenge. The main goal behind our approach is to optimize the read/write and latency/bandwidth using the layer of the Cloud Enabler Service (CES).

We achieved this by deploying a replica-aware and performance-aware layer that can coordinate with any replication system. This will help in choosing the fastest route to write the data & allows a dynamic way to define the best path to achieve the most efficient performance way to read or write the generated data. The Cloud Enabler Service can intelligently choose the right action to seek the higher performance, thus replica site could be fully utilized to minimize any read/write penalty to the minimum possible.

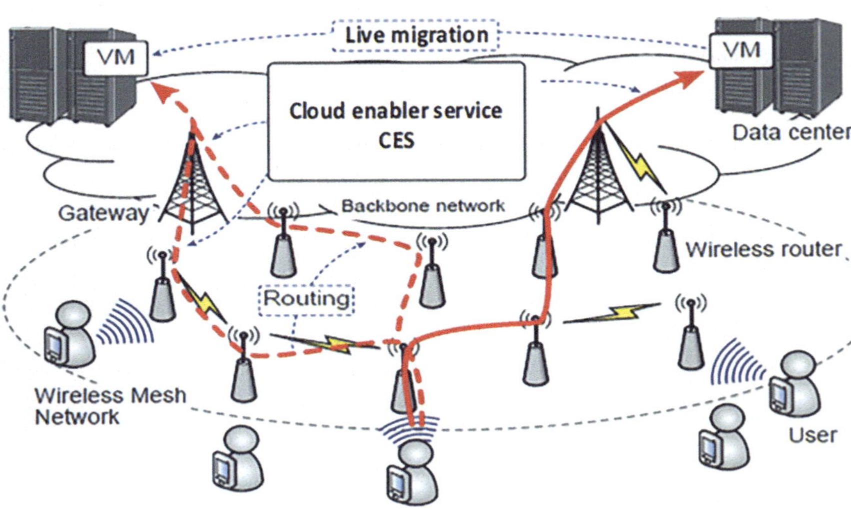

Fig. 4.12 Multi-cloud data centers with cloud enabler service

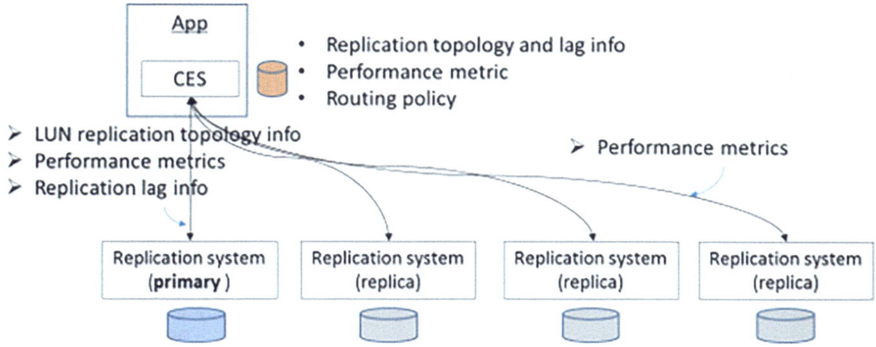

Fig. 4.13 Advanced routing policy & replication/routing coordination

4.3.2.2 Advanced Control Policy

The Cloud Enabler Server (CES) or the routing layer can efficiently coordinate with any storage replication system. The replication load and the replication lag status, with such info is supposed to be exported to or collected at close-to-App routing layer. The Cloud Enabler Server CES engine also supports control over scenarios like replica-aware, performance-aware, lag-aware, affinity etc., so that IoT application read/write requests can be automatically and intelligently routed to the proper site for better performance, load-balance etc. See Fig. 4.13 for detailed policy below:

Algorithm Illustration Example:

In the below diagrams, we show Storage Path Optimization algorithm in action. This has already been presented in our previous USPTO US9882985B1. A sender device is supposed to send a large file to another device. For each use case, we created a formula for the time calculation before and after applying the SPO algorithm.

Before CES:

The below flowchart describes the current treatment for a request in case of RecoverPoint replication technique existence as illustrated in Fig. 4.14.

After CES:

After using the CES, the hosts IOs should be handled as shown in the below flow chart in RecoverPoint system as presented in Fig. 4.15.

The idea is to add a Cloud Enabler service layer as an additional coordination module talking to a replication system like RecoverPoint for VMs. This module function is to detect the write performance of a request and compare the previously discussed parameters to achieve the best route to handle such write request.

Fig. 4.14 Flowchart describes the current treatment for a request in case of RecoverPoint replication technique existence

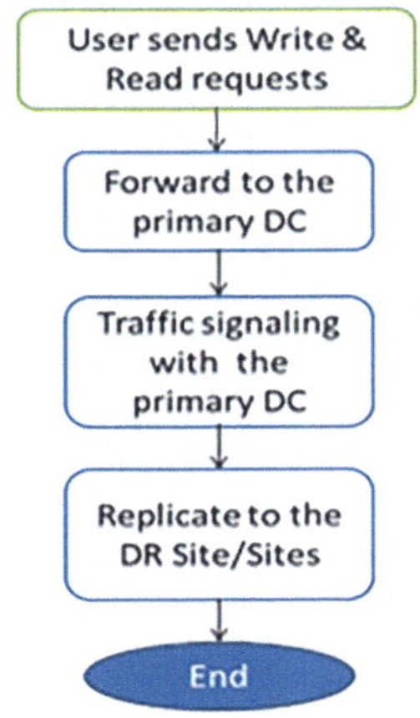

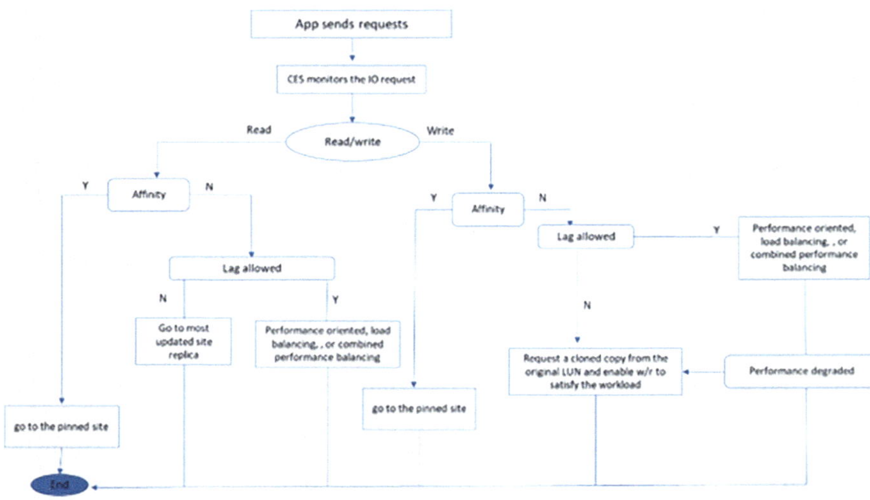

Fig. 4.15 RecoverPoint system

(a) **Write Optimization**: The engine will be able to determine the large data chunks requests and evaluates each request to check if it is a candidate for optimization. For instance, in a typical Machine to Machine M2M communication it is easier if sensor "A" needs to send data to sensor "B" over a specific network, the engine will make sure to send the request data on the underlying storage layer (inside the same datastore) or the storage and send just the metadata and pointers over the network to save time and energy consumption. This means that if all the storage is cloud based, why send the data (if I do not want to process/read it now) if we can just edit the "Data ownership" from one device to the other and copy data internally inside Data Center!

Why is the above approach best suited to Machine to Machine M2M communication especially sensors in smart city environments?

This is due to the following reasons:

1. Sensors are often treated as data generators and in some scenarios as aggregators, they do not consume or process data instantly. Instead, they just need to store it for further processing by central servers or advanced edge computing nodes.
2. Sensors are very critical and constrained devices in energy (battery) and bandwidth, and they require minimum traffic over the network/internet.

(b) **Replica-aware**: As replication system like Dell Recover Point "RP" can configure or change its primary & target points, the routing layer may also regularly pull or push such information, then update its local datastore (as metadata). Any given application from a given location would have more flexibility in the choices to write its data either in primary or replica site. If a site is lost or unavailable, RecoverPoint RP system (primary site) may also push urgent messages to the routing layer and clone the volume / LUN and make it writable.

(c) **Performance-aware**: The routing layer running on a specific host together with a given application periodically monitors the access performance to all available sites, including primary replica, latency, and bandwidth. For example:

(d) Let's consider the following scenarios:

   (i). In the background, it may ping the primary/replica site to collect networking latency then rank the latency
   (ii). or in background, it may measure both latency and bandwidth from reading test data from the primary or replica sites., processing
   (iii). or for real IO to specific site, it can also measure latency and bandwidth. Such performance datasets can later be leveraged for read traffic routing or combined with other policies including balancing, affinity and locality.

(e) **Load-aware**: The routing layer may also balance its issued IO to multiple sites, for example, it may implement a round-robin solution to all site or consider a more sophisticated approach using the above performance measurement as weight in addition the IO amount to specific site, then use a weighted balance.

(f) **Lag-aware**, Locality and affinity: The routing layer can also support advanced settings, such as

   – Lag-aware: If replication or Continuous Data Protection CDP system configured multiple replica sites which could be common for enterprise users, even all replica sites running in (Continuous Data Protection) CDP mode, data replication performance from primary to each replica site may be different due to unpredictable interconnection, which leads to different replication lag. Replication system (the primary) could monitor such lag (RecoverPoint already did this), then report it to the data routing layer (it is also possible the routing layer could push the info), based on that, the routing layer may apply weights to the policy, based on the needs of applications and services

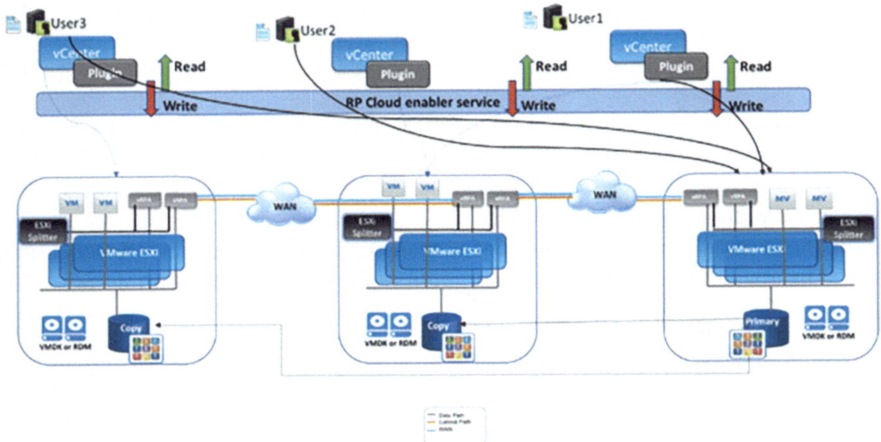

Fig. 4.16 Cloud enabled for VMs system

needing more real-time data, they could choose primary or the most updated replica site as presented in Fig. 4.16.

- **Locality and consistency**: By default, all written requests should always be directed to the primary site. An example is data generation from deployed sensors and other edge nodes.

4.3.3 Performance Analysis and Testing Results

Performance analysis and testing is illustrated here using a simulation model and a dataset. The implementation exercise was based on the Matlab framework. However, the reader may choose to replicate simulation testing using any other simulation platform. The platform was also used to generate synthetic data for testing purposes as stated in Fig. 4.17.

4.3.3.1 Testing Results

MATLAB Simulation Model:

1 sender, M receivers, N frames (UDP)

- Total_Delay_4_without = Twlan+T_AP_to_Server+(N1)*T_AP_to_Server +T_IOT_server+N*T_LUN_write+N*T_AP_to_Server+N*Twla
- Total_Delay_4_with = Twlan+T_AP_to_Server+(N1)*T_AP_to_Server +T_IOT_server+N*T_LUN_write+N*T_Copy+T_notification

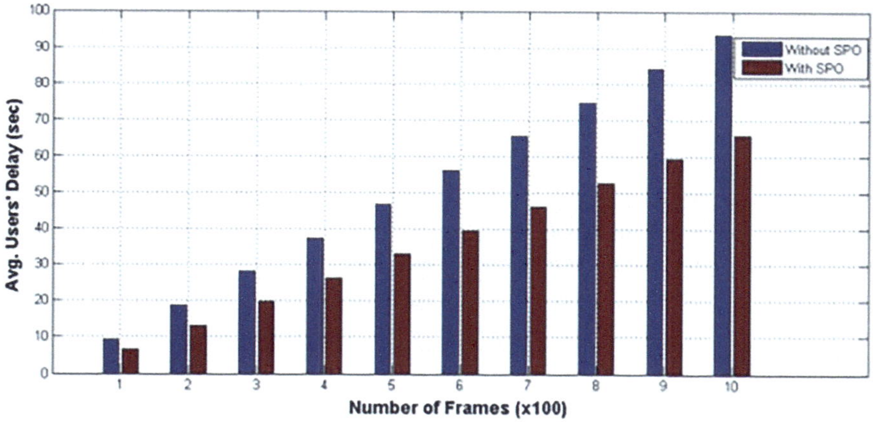

Fig. 4.17 With SPO & without SPO example

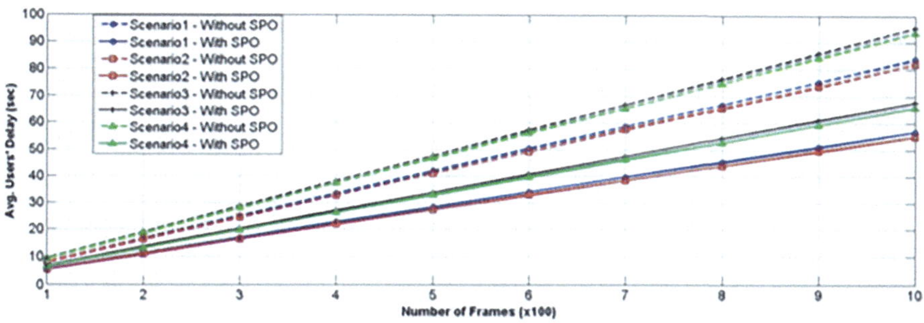

Fig. 4.18 Scenario comparison

We used four scenarios with and without SPOs as shown above in Fig. 4.18.

4.4 Conclusion

In a complex cross continent cloud deployment system, we often experience important delays in both read / write functions, leading to poor user experience. The problem is even more pronounced in IoT read intensive applications. In this book chapter we proposed a solution using AI to optimize the IOT platform. We use a Cloud Enabler Server (CES) that directs the write requests to the primary site as its default policy but directs the read requests to the proper site intelligently with an AI-based declarative policy engine. By optimizing the propagation delay in the cloud and datacenter, the suggested solution seeks to decrease the read latency. In a multi-continent cloud computing environment, propagation latency has a dominant value and a linear relationship with distance. The patented technique is expected to deliver considerable improvement in user access latency.

The use of AI techniques enables the systems to be continuously trained to reduce its performance degradation and improve the decision-making precision. We hope that this chapter provides the reader with an approach highlighting the challenges and the solution to address them. The use of AI techniques is just a starting point. Ultimately, we look to see more advanced autonomous systems (agent-based) dynamically orchestrated that will enable more precise training and inferencing to optimize this framework in real-time.

References

1. Khalifa, N. E. M., Wang, J., Hamed, M., Taha, N., & Zhang, Y. (2024). DeepDate: A deep fusion model based on whale optimization and artificial neural network for Arabian date classification. *PLoS One, 19*(7), e0305292.
2. Khalifa, N. E., Wang, W., Mawgoud, A. A., & Zhang, Y.-D. (2024). COECG-resnet-GWO-SVM: An optimized COVID-19 electrocardiography classification model based on resnet50, grey wolf optimization and support vector machine. *Multimedia Tools and Applications*, 1–21.
3. Abd El-Aziz, A. A., El-Khoribi, R. A., & Eldeen Khalifa, N. (2024). RDMAA: Robust defense model against adversarial attacks in deep learning for cancer diagnosis. *International Journal of Computing and Digital Systems, 15*(1), 1273–1287.
4. Katare, G., Padihar, G., & Qureshi, Z. (2018). Challenges in the integration of artificial intelligence and internet of things. *International Journal of System and Software Engineering, 6*(2), 10–15.
5. Do, J., et al. (2020). Cost-effective, energy-efficient, and scalable storage computing for large-scale AI applications. *ACM Transactions on Storage (TOS), 16*(4), 1–37.
6. Allioui, H., & Mourdi, Y. (2023, Jan). Exploring the full potentials of IoT for better financial growth and stability: A comprehensive survey. *Sensors, 23*(19), 19. https://doi.org/10.3390/s23198015
7. Godavari, A., & Sudhakar, C. (2024, Jan). A survey on deduplication systems. *International Journal of Grid and Utility Computing, 15*(2), 143–159. https://doi.org/10.1504/IJGUC.2024.137902
8. Lei, Z., Ren, S., Hu, Y., Zhang, W., & Chen, S. (2022). Latency-aware collaborative perception. In S. Avidan, G. Brostow, M. Cissé, G. M. Farinella, & T. Hassner (Eds.), *Computer vision—ECCV 2022* (pp. 316–332). Springer. https://doi.org/10.1007/978-3-031-19824-3_19
9. A review on quality of experience (QoE) in cloud computing | Journal of Reliable Intelligent Environments. Accessed: 11 Aug 2024. [Online]. Available: https://link.springer.com/article/10.1007/s40860-023-00210-y
10. Palumbo, F., Aceto, G., Botta, A., Ciuonzo, D., Persico, V., & Pescapé, A. (2021, Jan). Characterization and analysis of cloud-to-user latency: The case of azure and AWS. *Computer Networks, 184*, 107693. https://doi.org/10.1016/j.comnet.2020.107693
11. Sethi, P., & Sarangi, S. R. (2017). Internet of things: Architectures, protocols, and applications. *Journal of Electrical and Computer Engineering, 2017*(1), 9324035. https://doi.org/10.1155/2017/9324035
12. Dongjie, Z., Haiwen, D., Yundong, S., Zhaoshuo, T., & Ning, C. (2022). A data grouping model based on cache transaction for unstructured data storage systems. *International Journal of Intelligent Systems, 37*(8), 4488–4514. https://doi.org/10.1002/int.22728

13. Hutter, F., Hoos, H. H., Leyton-Brown, K., & Murphy, K. P. (2009, Jul). An experimental investigation of model-based parameter optimisation: SPO and beyond. In *Proceedings of the 11th annual conference on genetic and evolutionary computation, in GECCO '09* (pp. 271–278). Association for Computing Machinery. https://doi.org/10.1145/1569901.1569940
14. Ding, Y., Jin, M., Li, S., & Feng, D. (2021, Jul). Smart logistics based on the internet of things technology: An overview. *International Journal of Logistics Research and Applications, 24*(4), 323–345. https://doi.org/10.1080/13675567.2020.1757053
15. Zhao, X., Huang, A., Wang, D., & Zhang, G. (2024). Cluster-aware scheduling in multitasking GPUs. *Real-Time Systems, 60*(1), 1–23.

Chapter 5
Automated Mango Quality Assessment in Smart Environments: A Custom YOLO Model for Surface Characteristic Analysis

Akshatha Prabhu, N. Shobha Rani, Arun Sri Krishna, Zhenglin Wang, and N. Manohar

Abstract This chapter proposes a computer vision-based technique for defect detection in Mango fruits by utilizing the efficiency of deep learning-based object detection models. A dataset consisting of 1600+ samples with defects at various stages of ripening is considered for experimentation. The dataset is collected with the help of a specialized controlled environment adopted in industries during the production process for grading and sorting. Additionally, two publicly accessible datasets, which comprise images of fruits with defects captured in real-world scenarios, are also considered for experimentation so as to demonstrate the robustness of the proposed object detection model. A customized deep learning-based object detection model is devised to perform defect detection. The model's initial layers perform the data preprocessing and augmentation followed by object detection and, finally, classification of detected regions into classes—defects, bruises, rotten ripe, ripe, partially ripe, and ripe stages. The experimentations on the proposed and publicly available datasets achieve a mean Average Precision (mAP) of 64.8%, precision of 76.3%, and recall of 65.01%, respectively. An object loss of less than 2.5% is observed with a class loss of less than1.5% and box loss of 1.7% for 300 epochs at a learning rate of 0.01. The visual results of experiments are prone to be consistent with the subjective assessment results.

A. Prabhu · N. Manohar
Department of Computer Science, School of Computing, Amrita Vishwa, Vidyapeetham, Tamil Nadu, India

N. S. Rani (✉)
Department of Artificial Intelligence and Data Science, GITAM School of Technology, GITAM (Deemed to be University), Bengaluru, India

A. S. Krishna
The Math Company, AI and Analytics, Bengaluru, India

Z. Wang
School of Engineering and Technology | Tertiary Education Division, Institute for Future Farming Systems, CQ University Australia, Sydney, Australia

N. E. M. Khalifa, M. H. N. Taha (eds.), *Empowering AI Applications in Smart Life and Environment*, https://doi.org/10.1007/978-3-031-78038-7_5

Keywords Defect detection · Sustainable agriculture · Automation · Supply chain efficiency · Postharvest loss reduction · Food security

5.1 Introduction

Defect detection in fruits plays a vital role in many agricultural postharvest and preharvest-related applications [1]. Enabling automated detection of defects in Mango fruits using computerized grading and quality assessment systems enhances the quality of packaging productivity and economic growth of the country [2, 3]. Defect detection using computer vision techniques is the key to developing computerized grading and quality assessment systems. These technologies explore the mango surface characteristics of texture, color, and stiffness to determine the quality [4, 5].

Defect detection using computerized grading of quality assessment systems provides valuable insights during the production process in industries and postharvest agricultural procedures for preventing the spread of infections [6]. Rapid identification of diseases/infections at various stages of mango ripening is crucial for preventing the spread of pathogens to other fruit samples, allowing timely interventions [7]. Defect detection in mango fruits during postharvest procedures helps adapt pest agricultural practices, while fruit grading leads to effective disease management.

Carrying out defect detection at various ripening stages is crucial in industrial processing and agricultural applications [8]. The reason for defect detection to be conducted at various stages of ripening includes early identification of defects, enabling the interventions to reduce risks of disease infestations [9, 10]. Next, defect detection in the unripe stage ensures diligent control of infestation of other fruit samples, ensuring quality control throughout the supply chain. The early form of infestation in mangoes will appear in the form of bruises, a crucial aspect of quality control in the Agricultural and Food industry, as bruises on mangoes can critically affect the appearance, taste, and shelf life [11]. It is essential to detect the bruises early to maintain the overall product quality. The other mango defects include sooty mold, anthracnose, bacterial black spots, internal browning, fruit flies, spongy tissues, sunburns, spoiled fruits, irregular ripening, and pest damage [12]. Among these, the mango skin's bacterial black spots and dark lesions are considered vital and rapidly spreading infestation in the postharvest stage. As a result, BBS leads to detrimental effects during storage and transportation [13].

Bacterial black spots are caused by the bacterium Xanthomonas campestris pv. Mangiferae indcae is a famous infestation in the postharvest stage of mangoes [14]. Lack of timely detection of this defect can lead to internal damage, resulting in rotting. Bacterial black spots appear in the form of dark lesions and are developed from bruises, and spread rapidly in warm and humid environments. The bacterial black spots affected fruit samples when kept close to other mango fruit samples;

there is a high chance of contamination, leading to the whole batch of fruits having reduced shelf life and making it unsuitable for the supply chain process.

Furthermore, bacterial black spots reduce the marketability of fruit due to export restrictions and stringent quality standards. Trade regulations often prohibit the entry of fruits with bacterial diseases; therefore, infecting mangoes are discarded, resulting in increased waste and economic losses for producers. Thus, it is crucial to develop preventive harvesting techniques with the help of computerized disease control systems.

In this investigation, the defect detection method is devised to automatically detect the bacterial black spots, bruises, rotting, and maturity stages—unripe, partially ripe, and ripe. Integrating the ripening stage detection and defect detection is beneficial to provide a comprehensive understanding of fruit quality by assisting optimized postharvest procedures and timely decision-making throughout the supply chain. The maturity stage detection and defect detection help to enhance quality control by reducing the fruit drop to the rotten stage. Detecting bruises at the early ripening stage helps us control the spread of infestations and ensure quality packaging standards, improving customer satisfaction.

This research focuses on developing a comprehensive deep learning-based defect detection model for detecting bruises, bacterial black spots, and rotting along with the maturity stage of mango. The research objectives formulated as part of the study are resented subsequently.

1. A comprehensive dataset of 1600 samples of defect detection at various maturity stages is contributed for investigation. The dataset is accessible via Mendeley (Prabhu, Akshatha; Rani, N Shobha (2024), "MangoFruitDefect," Mendeley. Data, V2, doi: 10.17632/jnp9tmyrt6.2).
2. The study proposes a customized deep-learning model for defect detection for mangoes.
3. A comprehensive performance evaluation is conducted to test the efficacy of the proposed model with a self-built dataset and two publicly available datasets.
4. The proposed model is evaluated against YOLOV7 model to demonstrate its robustness.

5.2 Literature Review

Numerous works are reported to perform defect detection in fruits; some of the significant works are summarized as follows.

Sahu and Potdar [15] investigated an image processing-based method for defect detection in mango fruit images. The samples used are captured in controlled environment with classes being labelled as immature and matured. The work does not focus towards the identification of specific type of defects based on fruit surface. The techniques used follows a sequel of preprocessing, combination of contour approach, and thresholding for segmenting the defects. The sample collection does not comprise the early stage of defects and specific maturity stage at which it occurred. In a work by Mim et al. [16], a decision tree-based classifier is applied for the classification of the maturity stage of mango into six classes via using a thresholding method and color features analysis. The image dataset consider only 25 samples, resulting in poor precision and recall rate. Later, Nithya et al. [17] investigates the technique for defect detection in mangoes using deep learning networks with single convolution layers. The classes into which the fruits are classified include fully ripe with minor defects and ripe with no texture variations. The robustness is not evaluated towards the datasets with early-stage defects that include bruises. In a work by Raghavendra et al. [18], defect detection is interpreted in mango fruits using NIR spectroscopy by combining Fourier transformation and filter-based feature selection techniques. Subsequently, Patel et al. [19] employed a computer vision technique for defect detection in Chausa and Dashehari varieties. After experimental analysis it is noticed that accuracy is reported as 88.6% and 93.3%, respectively.

Subsequent investigations by Tiemtud et al. [20] performs mango surface analysis for detection of defects using non-extensive entropy with Gaussian modelling. Multiple defect type such as cracks, dark spots, and bruises are detected as part of investigation. Later Abbas [21], in his work used an image analysis method for defect detection in samples captured in controlled environments. Later, Huang et al. [22] introduced a method which adapts a flow of preprocessing, thresholding, and morphological operations for computing defective areas in mangoes. Gururaj et al. [23] devised a multi-level grading using deep learning, computer vision, and image processing techniques using the convolutional neural networks for feature extraction and classification using Random Forest classifier. The mango varieties such as Banganapalli, Neelam, and Rumani are considered for experimentations and achieved an accuracy of 93.23% and 95.11%. Next, Vishwanath et al. [24] introduced a technique for mango defect detection using image analysis techniques for improving the efficiency of the sorting process. A work by Li et al. [25], a mango fruit defect detection method using hyperspectral imaging and thresholding is used. Dimensionality reduction is applied on features extracted based on NIR spectroscopic methods for determining defective areas and achieved an accuracy of 96.67%. Subsequent investigation by Ashok et al. [26], a quality evaluation method for determining external and internal defects in mango fruits based on color and X-ray imaging is investigated.

In a work by Velásquez et al. [27], hyperspectral image analysis is carried out for detection of infected fruit at early stage of anthracnose is applied on mango cultivars such as Keitt and Osteen. Next, Rungpichayapichet et al. [28] developed calibration models for firmness, total soluble solids, titratable acidity, and ripening index assessment using regression analysis to classify the mango ripeness stage. In another work, fruit images are inspected for exploration of infected and intact areas of mangoes that are captured with 650–1100 nm hyperspectral images for distinguishing defective from non-defective mangoes by Rivera et al. [29]. Then, in a work by Ardila et al. [30], a spectro-radiometer based method is followed for classifying ripening stages of mango into healthy, asymptomatic, and diseased.

Consequently, Gabriëls et al. [31] employed VNIRS to predict the internal browning in mango cultivar Keitt.

The survey shows that most of the research on defect detection in mango fruits is based on the following aspects. The majority of works are carried out for defect detection in mangoes in the ripened stage. In contrast, few works focus on defect detection using infrared spectrum, X-rays, and hyper-spectral data related to fruit samples. Furthermore, some works also focus on fruit detection directly from tree image samples, which only covers some ripening stages with defects ranging from early to rotten. On the other hand, works that are based on image analysis using preprocessing and thresholding techniques are sensitive to the method of image modality along with variations in texture, etc. Thus, there exists a need to develop a robust method for defect detection in various stages of mango suiting for industrial processing needs.

5.3 Materials and Methods

5.3.1 Dataset Collection and Preparation

Based on the observations from the state-of-the-art datasets related to fruit maturity and quality assessment, the proposed study inclines to collect the mango fruit dataset with defects in various forms at various stages of fruit maturity. The samples of mango fruits are collected by adapting to naturally progressive ripening methods as that leads to obtaining a highly comprehensive feature representation with characteristics implying the severity of defect from the raw stage to the rotten stage of the fruit. The methodology followed after the fruit harvest of the samples collected proceeded with decapping, washing, drying, layering in the haystack, and storage in containers. The samples are chosen carefully after the harvest by ensuring no external visual defects exist in the harvest stage. The fruit samples are collected from multiple mango tree orchards from different trees to ensure the diversity of fruit sample collection. The locations include the University of Horticulture, Mysuru, Madanahalli, Hullahalli, Maritikyatanahalli, and Nanjungudu, Mysuru, Karnataka, India. The dataset is acquired in three years in four to six batches each year. Table 5.1 presents the batch-wise sample collection details. Figure 5.1 shows the samples collected from harvest to the post-desapping stage.

5.3.2 Image Acquisition Model

In the proposed study, an Image Acquisition setup is in close proximity to the industry-oriented fruit quality monitoring unit. The overall setup involves one ring light, two fill lights, a camera, and an object placement base. The objective of the

Table 5.1 Overall dataset collection details

Year	# of samples	Batches	Samples per batch	Total images captured	Locations
2020	52	6	7 to 8	278	Mysuru, Nanjungudu
2021	56	4	10 to 13	325	Hullahalli, Madanahalli
2022	177	5	34 to 36	1062	University of Horticulture, Madanahalli

Fig. 5.1 Visual illustration of samples collected in the harvest stage (**a**–**d**) Samples in harvest stage (**e**–**h**) Samples before decapping (**i**–**l**) Samples in various stages of maturity

proposed setup is to capture high-contrast images of mango fruit with an optimal lighting effect that ensures the visibility of texture variations of various ripening stages and any defects/infestations, enabling efficient feature analysis. Fruit samples are captured in six orientations to ensure the prominent variations in terms of defects along with the texture. The image acquisition setup employs a 6-inch diameter ring light for shadow-free, uniformly illuminated image acquisition, two fill lights for

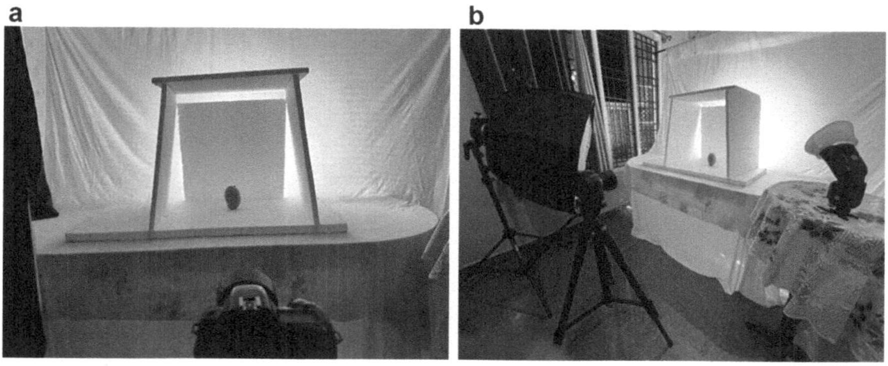

Fig. 5.2 Image acquisition setup (**a**) front view (**b**) side view

contrast adjustment, a NikonD3300 camera for high-quality image capturing, and a stable placement base. The ring lights facilitate capturing high-quality images with minimum light variations, which is crucial for feature analysis. Additionally, two fill lights are placed in two diagonal cameras, resulting in improved brightness and contrast throughout the fruit.

Furthermore, the camera settings of Nikon D3300 include ISO800 image sensors with a shutter speed of 1/60 per second. Finally, a secured object placement base for accommodating the fruit in its position is crafted using polystyrene foam with rectangular base dimensions of 60 cm length and 30 cm width. The foam is covered with one layer of salt, above which the clean, hygienic white cloth is affixed using ball pins, creating a neutral background for the fruit's visual appearance. Figure 5.1 depicts the real-time setup for capturing images, and Fig. 5.2 presents the samples.

5.3.3 *Image Labeling and Annotations*

The proposed method uses deep learning-based object detection models for mango fruit defect detection and maturity detection prediction. The models identified for the detection of the defect and ripening stage include a custom-generated model using roboflow and the YOLOv7 model. The objective is to label each fruit in terms of the characteristics categorized into bruises and bacterial black spots within fruit region textures categorization followed by fruit level categories indicated as unripe, partially ripe, ripe, and rotten images, thus considering a total of 4 categories during the labeling and annotation process. The labeling and annotation involve farmers' knowledge to understand the different types of texture variations during the naturally progressive ripening stages. Figure 5.3 depicts the samples of annotations and labeling carried out within an overall fruit level.

The object detection models assume an input image of dimension 640X640 has the feature extraction based on CNN deep learning framework required a

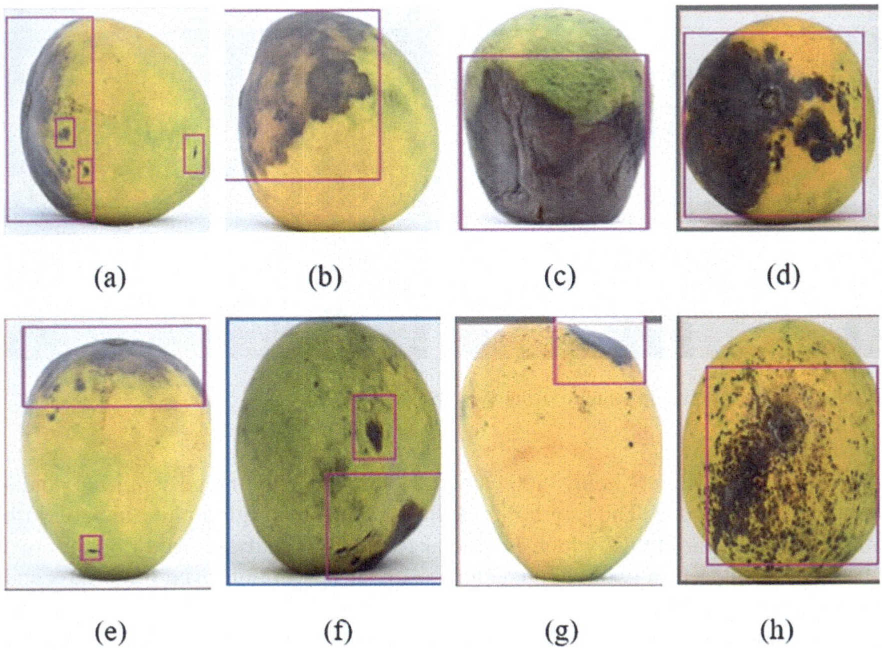

Fig. 5.3 Visual representation of annotated fruit samples (**a–d**) within fruit annotations (**g–h**) overall fruit labeling and annotations

squared shape spatial resolutions. Thus, the input image acquired is resized to 640x640 pixels while keeping the aspect ratio constant. The custom Roboflow and YOLOV7 models consider the input image resolution of 640X640 pixels. A series of preprocessing techniques and image augmentations are applied before training the custom deep object detection model using Roboflow API and the YOLO V7 model. The preprocessing operations include automatic orientation correction of mango fruit.

In addition to data preprocessing, image augmentation is also applied to enhance the effectiveness of the object detection model. The image augmentation operation includes vertical flip, 90°rotation, hue, brightness, and saturation variations in the range of −25° to +25°, and blur shear transformations. Thus, a comprehensive set of preprocessing and augmentation operations are applied to create a training dataset with diversity in fruit and image acquisition factors to achieve the model's generalisability and robustness. Table 5.2 presents the annotations and labeling details from the number of samples and regions affected within each sample.

As per Table 5.2, the number of annotations is carried out for each fruit sample where each fruit region is annotated with rectangular bounding boxes around the affected regions in terms of bruises, Bacterial Bacterial Spots (BBS), Rotten, unripe, partially ripe, and ripe. The number of samples from which the annotations are made

Table 5.2 Details of annotations and labeling—self-built dataset

Class label	No. of annotations	Number of image samples
Bruises	606	359
Bacterial black spots	690	483
Unripe	335	335
Partial ripe	382	382
Ripe	395	395
Rotten	336	305

includes the count of instances, as each fruit sample may comprise more than one region with BBS and bruises. Most of the samples in the datasets are affected with BBS infections, leading to rotting at a later stage.

5.3.4 Proposed Custom YOLO Model—Mango Fruit Defect Detection

The proposed model for defect detection in mango fruit comprises an input layer, backbone YOLO-head, detection head, post-processing, and output layer. An input RGB image of spatial resolution 640x640 pixels is initially considered for defect detection regarding bruises, bacteria back spots, rotten, and maturity stage analysis via dark net backbone. In the backbone layer, the image is explored to capture the hierarchical features through a series of convolution layers and darknet blocks, producing a feature map of spatial features in a high-level encoded format. Following this, the feature map obtained for the backbone layer is processed via the YOLO head block, which consists of 3 consecutive convolution layers. These layers refined the higher-level features by reducing the dimensionality of the feature map, achieving more abstract representations. Then, the YOLO head block output is passed through the detection head block to obtain the final prediction via convolution layers to generate bounding box predictions and confidence scores. Finally, the obtained output tensor from the detection head is subject to post-processing via non-maximum suppression applied to filter out redundant and low-confidence predictions, producing a final output with a list of defective objects along with a class label and confidence score.

Figure 5.4 presents the block diagram of the proposed custom YOLO model for Mango Fruit Defect Detection, and Fig. 5.5 presents the detailed sequence of convolution operations associated with the darknet backbone, YOLO head, and detection head.

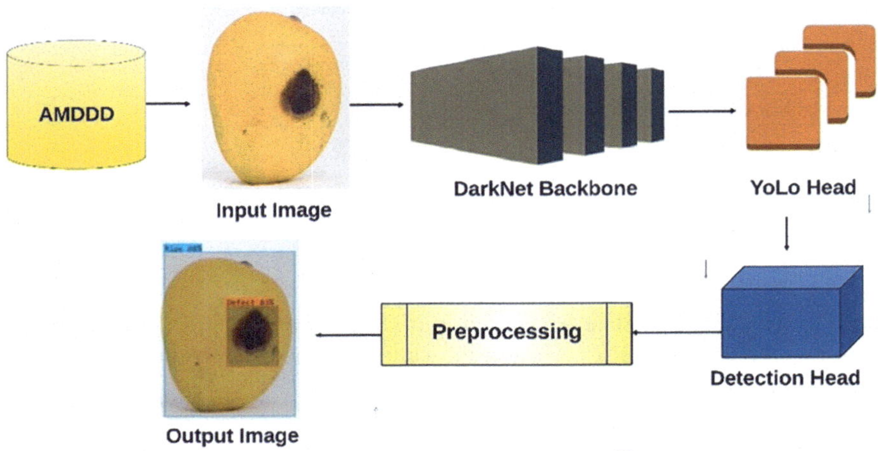

Fig. 5.4 Block diagram of mango fruit defect detection—Proposed custom YOLO model

5.3.4.1 Input Layer

The input layer I of dimensions $R \times C$ with d input channels. The input I is subject to 2 D convolution operation with kernel size k, stride length s with padding followed by batch normalization layer batchnorm2d. The normalized input tensor is regularised using a leaky ReLU activation function with a negative slope of 0.1.

5.3.4.2 Darknet Backbone

The darknet backbone acts as a backbone in the custom YOLO model, which represents the residual sequence of connections between convolution layers and darknet residual blocks. The input tensor obtained from the input layer is processed via two consecutive convolution layers, *Conv* 1 and *Conv* 2. The *Conv* 1 layer considers three input channels and produces 32 output channels via the convolution layer with 3×3 kernel size, stride length $s = 1$ with padding. Following this, *Conv* 2 processes the 32 input channel feature map and produces 64 output channels feature map with 3×3 kernel size, stride length $s = 2$ with padding. The connection between *Conv* 1 and *Conv* 2 represents the residual network structure that helps overcome the vanishing gradient problem during training. The convolution operation performed by *Conv* 1 and *Conv* 2 layers for an input image I with $m \times n$ and row index i and column index j is given by (5.1).

$$I(i, j, d) = \sum_{m=0}^{2}\sum_{n=0}^{2}\sum_{C=0}^{2} I(i + m - 1, j + n - 1, c) . F(m, n, c, k) \tag{5.1}$$

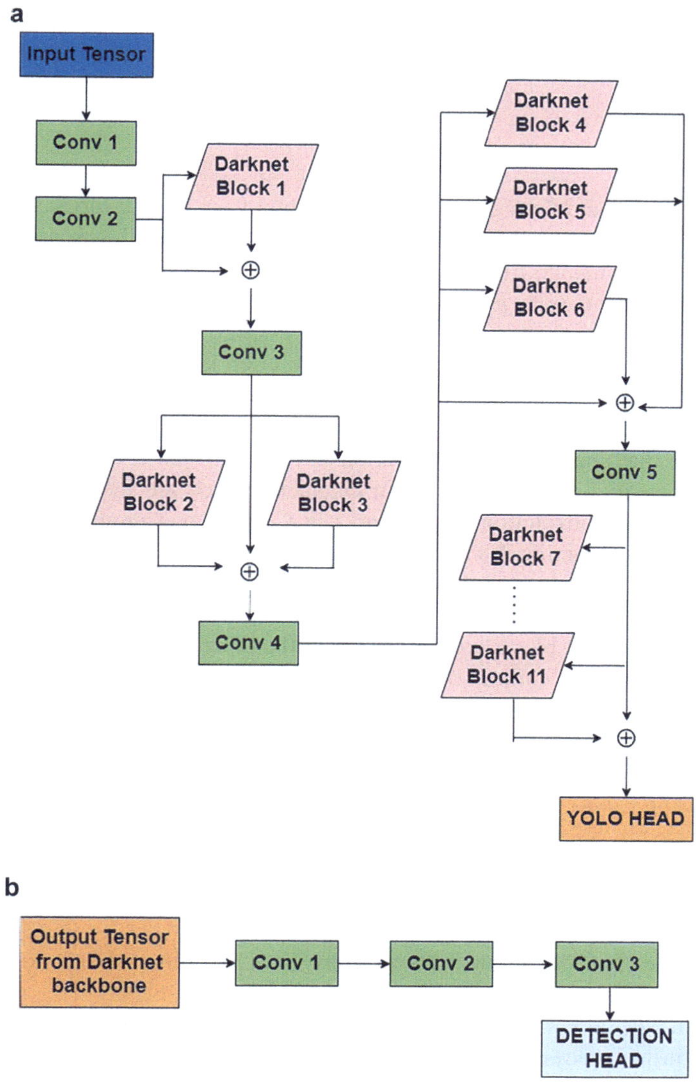

Fig. 5.5 Architecture of DarkNet backbone, YOLO head, and detection head

Where F is the convolution kernel, in (1), m and n represent the spatial dimensions of convolution kernel F from 0 to 2, *and* c represents the number of channels. The number of channels c is 3 for input image I, therefore iterating from 0 to 2 over each channel of the input tensor. The convolution operation performs the dot product of input tensor I with convolution kernel F for each spatial position (i, j) and channel c. The positions $i + m - 1$ and $j + n - 1$ are the relative positions of convolution kernel F.

Generally, residual connection $'r'$ can be expressed as given by (5.2) and (5.3).

$$out = conv2\,(conv1(x)) + x \tag{5.2}$$

$$out = conv\,(i+1)\,(conv(i)(I)) + I \tag{5.3}$$

x is original input and *Conv* 2(*Conv* 1) is the output from *Conv* 2 block.

The overall processing pipeline of the darknet backbone of the proposed custom YOLO model for mango fruit defect detection is described as follows. Initially, the convolution layer $'Conv1'$ processes the input image I with three channels using 32 filters, producing 32 output channels with a stride of 1 and padding. The 32 output channels are processed via 3 × 3 convolution kernels with 64 filters using a stride of 2 and padding. Then, the 64 output channels obtained via *the Conv* 2 layer are subject to feature analysis through darknet block 1 which is residual connections that apply 1 × 1 convolution to reduce 64 to 32 channels, followed by 3 × 3 convolutions with 64 output channels, which are then added with the output of second convolution layer *Conv* 2 in *Conv* 3 layer producing 128 output channels after undergoing 3 × 3 convolutions with stride of 2 and following which the 128 output channels are subject to processing by darknet block 2 producing 64 output channels after applying convolutions with 1 × 1 followed by 3 × 3 kernels. The output of darknet block two is added with the input from *Conv* 3 via a residual connection. Similarly, darknet block three repeats the same operations as darknet block 2.

Subsequently, the convolution layer *Conv* 4 processes 128 output channels using a 3 × 3 kernel with a stride of 2, producing 256 output channels. The obtained output channels from $'conv4'$ are processed via darknet block 4 using 1×1 and 3 × 3 kernel size producing 128 feature maps on darknet block four and darknet block 5, which has residual connections. The obtained 256 output channels from darknet block five are directed for processing by *Conv* 5 with 3 × 3 convolutions of stride 2, producing 512 feature maps.

Finally, the obtained output channels from *Conv* 5 are directed to darknet block 7 with residual connections by applying 1 × 1 convolutions, then 3 × 3 convolutions resulting in 512 output channels, which are subject forwarded to the YOLO head block for further processing. The YOLO head consists of 3 consecutive convolution layers, *Conv* 1, *Conv* 2, and *Conv* 3,that have 3 × 3 and 1×1 convolutions resulting in 256 output channels. The detection head finally predicts the bounding boxes with anchor box specifications with the labeling details of each region detected. The output layer presents the detection resulting with precise bounding box coordinates objectness score and class probabilities.

5.3.4.3 YOLO Head

The YOLO Head block is responsible for defect detection in the fruit region. It works by dividing an input image into a grid of two dimensions and identifying the bounding boxes with class membership probabilities based on the properties of the fruit texture within each grid cell. The properties in each grid cell are analyzed by exploring the convolution features in terms of gradient, texture, and shape-based features computed in the darknet backbone block.

The operations in the YOLO head block mainly comprise three convolution layers. Initially, the input tensors of 512 channels are assumed for processing in *the Conv* 1 layer that applies *a* 1×1 convolution kernel, producing an output tensor of 256 channels by reducing the dimensions through pooling. The output tensor concerning an output computed at position (x, y) concerning an index i of the output channel is given by (5.4)

$$out\ (, y, i) = \sum_{c=1}^{512} I\ (x, y, c) \times W\ (i, c) + b(i) \tag{5.4}$$

In (5.4), c represents the input channel index, W indicates the weight parameter associated with the convolution kernel, b is the bias corresponding to a learnable parameter, and out is an output tensor. Subsequently, the output tensor of 256 channels obtained from *Conv* 1 is directed to the *Conv* 2 layer by applying a 3×3 convolution kernel to the input tensor. Finally, the output tensor of 512 channels obtained from *Conv* 2 is repeatedly processed with 1×1 convolution in *Conv* 3, followed by max pooling, reducing the dimensions to 256 channels. The YOLO head block produces the final output predictions regarding bounding box coordinates and class probabilities for the properties explored and detected in the input tensor.

5.3.4.4 Detection Head and Output Layer

The detection head block of the custom YOLO model for mango defect detection is responsible for predicting the final defect detection outcomes based on the features extracted by the YOLO head block. In this block, a 1×1 convolution kernel is applied across the 2D grid cells to predict the bounding box coordinates, objectness scores, and class probabilities for each of the anchor box dimensions specified. The detection Head block produces the output tensor of 256 channels, which is then reshaped to represent the detection results for each anchor box. A confidence score indicating whether an object is present in the anchor box is obtained, called an objectness score, along with the likelihood of the object belonging to a particular class, which is predicted in class probabilities.

The anchor specifications comprise two categories in the proposed work for mango fruit defect detection and maturity stage analysis. One at the region level and the other at the fruit level; for the mango fruit level annotations comprising unripe, partial ripe, and ripe classes, the anchor box specifications are configured to capture the fruit level classes. The anchor box specifications for mango classes fruit level include width and height as (20, 26), (32, 60), and (66, 46) respectively. These specifications can be automatically adjusted per the training dataset specifications while prediction is in process. On the other hand, for defect detection within the fruit region that includes bruises, BBS, and rotten, the anchor box specifications are considered smaller sizes of (10, 13), (16, 30), and (33, 23). The anchor box specifications are optimized during the localization of region type while testing predictions are in process.

5.3.5 Custom YOLO Model Training

The proposed custom YOLO model for defect detection in mangoes comprises 6 distinct classes, including—bruises, Bacterial black spots, unripe, partially ripe and ripe, and rotten, for the training datasets sampled by adapting to random sampling by manually deciding the proportions of the count of several samples under training, validation, and testing. The manual split for proportions corresponding to training, validation, and testing is used because there is a dataset imbalance from one class to another. It is observed that the number of annotations related to bacterial black spot infections is very high compared to all other classes. Similarly, infections such as bruises and rot are found to be nearly 60% of the actual content of Bacterial black spots. On the other hand, the number of samples per fruit maturity in terms of unripe, partially ripe, and ripe classes and rotten is considered in terms of fruit level, which is less than 50% of annotations relating to bruises and BBS. Thus, the dataset is selected proportionate to 75%, 15%, and 10% by averaging the number of samples across each class; this involves eliminating fruit samples involving BBS and bruises. Table 5.3 presents the details of dataset sampling considered for training, custom YOLO model.

According to Table 5.3, the dataset covers a range of fruit conditions, from bruises, BBS, and rottenness to the maturity stage. The total training dataset includes

Table 5.3 Dataset sampling details

Class name	Train	Validation	Test	Total
Bruises	477	79	50	606
BBS	518	104	68	690
Unripe	276	35	24	335
Partial ripe	295	52	35	382
Ripe	322	45	28	395
Rotten	287	38	11	336

Table 5.4 Training parameter specifications of proposed custom YOLO

Parameter	Specifications
Optimizer	SGD
Loss Function	Focal Loss
Learning rate	0.01
Epochs	300
Batch size	8
Image Resolution	640 × 640 px
Weight decay	0.0001
Train, validation and test ratio	75%, 15%, 10%

Table 5.5 Hyperparameter specifications of the YOLOv7 model

Parameter	Specifications
Optimizer	SGD
Loss Function	Focal Loss
Tested learning rates	0.1, 0.01, 0.001
Momentum	0.997
Epochs	200
Batch size	8
Image Resolution	640 × 640 px
Weight decay	0.0001
Train ratio	75%

2175 samples, which is a substantial amount to learn and capture the defect-type characteristics of each class. The validation and test set also consists of 353 and 216 samples, which enables a comprehensive evaluation of the model's performance on unseen data, providing insights into its ability to generalize toward the unknown test samples. Table 5.4 specifies the custom YOLO model training specifications. Table 5.5 provides the specifications of the YOLO V7 model considered for comparison with the proposed model.

As per Table 5.4, the custom YOLO model training adapts stochastic gradient descent SGD) as the optimizer with a focal loss function. A learning rate 0.001 is evaluated while training the custom YOLO model with 300 epochs, batch size 8, and weight decay of 0.0001. The input tensor spatial resolution is maintained at 640 × 640 pixels. Figure 5.6 presents the view of training samples employed by the proposed custom YOLO model and YOLOv7 model.

To understand the effectiveness of the proposed model, the training is also conducted with the YOLO v7 model with three different learning rates of 0.1, 0.01, and 0. 001, respectively. Table 5.5 presents the hyperparameter specifications of the YOLOv7 model. The YOLOv7 model is trained with SGD optimizer, focal loss function by adapting to the momentum of 0.997, 200 epochs, batch size of 8 image resolution of 640 × 640, and weight decay of 0.0001. The training ratio is the same as the custom YOLO model.

Fig. 5.6 Samples of images used for model training/validation and testing—proposed dataset

5.4 Experimental Analysis

A comprehensive investigation is carried out to evaluate the performance of the proposed custom YOLO model for mango fruit defect detection and maturity stage analysis. The proposed model is evaluated on the dataset details provided in Table 5.4 using metrics such as mAP, precision, recall, and F1 score. The object detection models are usually evaluated with an mAP score that combines precision and recall at different confidence thresholds. In the proposed method, the confidence threshold is considered above 40%, which is above 0.4. The average precision across all classes is computed, and the outcome is reported as the mean of precisions across the classes. A higher mAP score signifies better performance and implies high precision and recall across multiple object classes. Next, the F1 Score is the harmonic mean of precision and recall that represents a balanced measure considering both false positives and false negatives. Finally, precision is the ratio of true positives to the sum of true positives and false positives, and recall is the ratio of true positives to the sum of true positives and false negatives. The higher precision, recall, and F1 scores indicate better performance, indicating that the model has a low false positive rate, representing an effective model. The performance evaluation of the present investigation is organized as follows.

1. The experimental evaluation is conducted on the proposed custom YOLO model for mango fruit defect detection, and result visualization is demonstrated.
2. The comparative analysis of the proposed model with the YOLOv7 model is carried out at various learning rates of 0.1, 0.01, and 0.001 with dataset augmentation and without dataset augmentation.
3. The study of generalizable ability of the proposed custom YOLO model towards the real-time datasets captured in an uncontrolled environment is illustrated through visualizations and mAP scores.

5.4.1 *Performance Evaluation Using the Proposed Custom YOLO Model*

The detailed performance evaluation of a proposed custom YOLO model for detecting defects in mango fruits is presented in this section to interpret the robustness and effectiveness. The quantitative evaluation uses mAP scores on validation and test sets. The training performance of the custom YOLO model is demonstrated through training plots using mAP versus a number of epochs and various loss graphs, indicating the learning performance in terms of box loss, object loss, and class loss. Figure 5.7a–d present the training performance evaluated for 300 epochs with batch size 8 and a learning rate of 0.01. Figures 5.8a–j depict the performance in terms of box loss, class, and object loss, along with the precision and recall curves on training and validation sets. The class-wise precision analysis for validation and test sets is presented in Table 5.6. The backbone and YOLO head majorly influence the performance of the object detection models, precisely the number of convolution layers and optimal aspect ratios considered for anchor box specifications.

The Darknet backbone adapted for defective region analysis as part of the custom YOLO model significantly contributed to achieving the mapping score of 64.3% with a confidence threshold more significant than 40%. The implication of eleven darknet blocks and five convolution layers using 3x3 and 1x1 convolution kernels reveals the proposed model's effectiveness in detecting mango fruit defects with moderately acceptable precision of more than 60%. The three convolution layers comprising the YOLO head demonstrate the effectiveness in computing features related to six different classes.

According to Fig. 5.8, the class loss, box loss, and Directional Feature Learning (DFL) loss are consistently decreasing, and it is noticed to be less than 1.5 on the training and validation set. The results suggest that the proposed model effectively obtains more accurate predictions. The consistent reduction in loss from one epoch to another generally indicates that the model is predicting the result in high proximity to the ground truth labels. Furthermore, it also implies that the convergence of the model is achieved after a significant number of epochs, resulting in a stable state in the training process. Additionally, the improvement in precision and recall measures, which is equal to the mAP scores, represents the decline in the number of false positives and false negatives as the training progresses.

Table 5.6 shows that the average precision demonstrating class-wise performance is presented in terms of six classes. About the class bruises, the model achieves an average precision value of 22% on the validation set and 29% on the test set, exhibiting relatively satisfactory performance. Then, towards BBS, the model demonstrates good performance, with an average precision of 61% on the validation set and 63% on the test set. On the classes unripe, partially ripe, and ripe, the average precision obtained is 58%, 88%, and 86% on the validation set. In comparison, it is 36%, 74%, and 91% on the test set, indicating overfitting issues in the unripe class. However, the performance of the proposed model towards partially ripe and ripe is

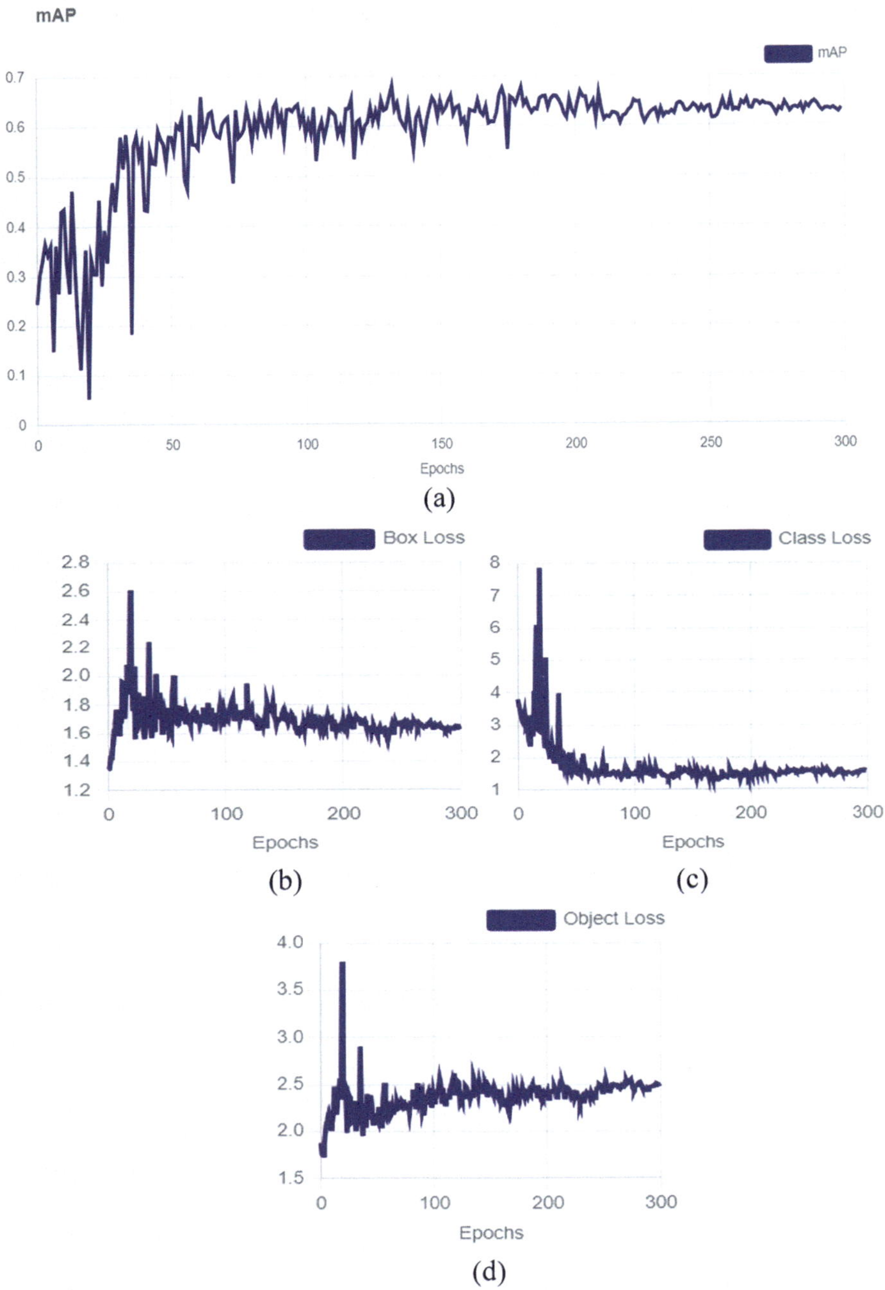

Fig. 5.7 Training performance by custom YOLO model (**a**) mAP score at confidence threshold >0.4 versus the number of epochs (**b**) Box loss versus the number of epochs (**c**) Class loss versus the number of epochs (**d**) Object loss versus the number of epochs

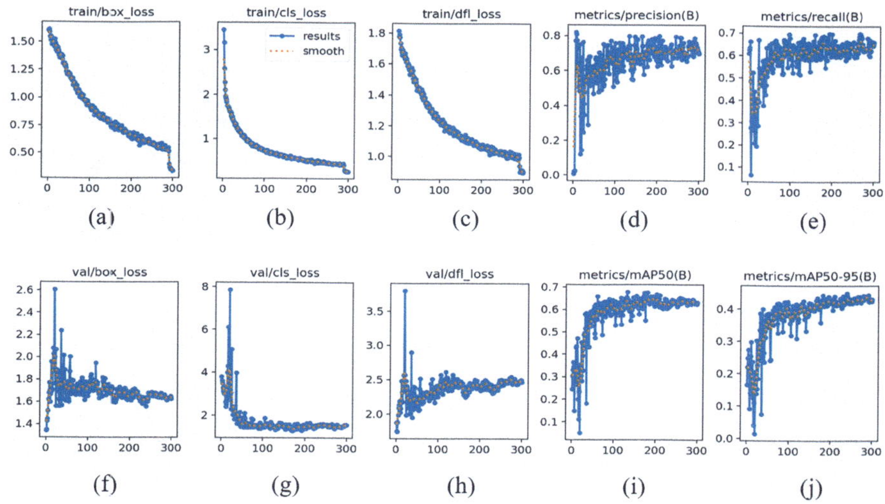

Fig. 5.8 Training graphs—Custom YOLO model for mango fruit defect detection

Table 5.6 Performance evaluation of training set and test set using average precision

Class labelling	Average precision-validation set (in %)	Average precision-test set (in %)
Bruises	22	29
BBS	61	63
Unripe	58	36
Partial ripe	88	74
Ripe	86	91
Rotten	71	52
Average precision across all classes	64.33	57.50

outstanding on validation as well as a test set. Finally, the model performs well in detecting rotten fruits, with average precision values of 71% on the validation and 52% on the test sets.

Further, the average precision across all classes is obtained as 64.33% on the validation set and 57.50% on the test set, respectively. The model performs well on four out of six classes, particularly partial ripe, ripe, BBS, and rotten. It is noticed that there is a generalization issue found towards the class's bruises and unripe, which is due to high similarities with other classes and also less trainable annotations compared to other classes. Figure 5.9 presents the visualization of defect detection results obtained using the proposed custom YOLO model.

The high-intensity markers denoting from no color to reddish in Fig. 5.10 indicate the measure of the F1 score from high to low as indicated in the scale in Fig. 5.10a, b. A no color indicates an F1 score of 1 in detecting the class type,

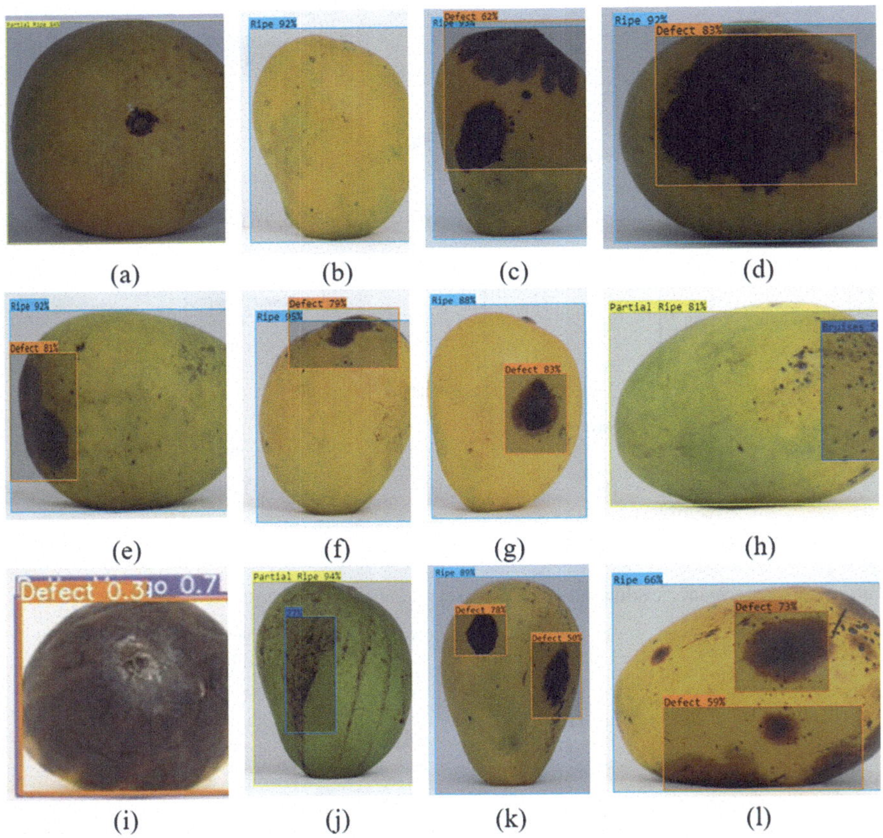

Fig. 5.9 Visualization of mango fruit defect detection outcomes on test set samples

whereas a slightly reddish indicates an F1 score of more than 0.80, and a little deeper red represents a decline in the F1 score. Each data point represents the mango fruit sample, as indicated in a few instances in Fig. 5.10d.

5.4.2 Performance Evaluation Using the YOLOv7 Model Using Different Learning Speeds

In the initial stage of analysis, the dataset is trained using the YOLO V7 model to understand the impact of higher to lower learning rates as 0.1, 0.01, and 0.001, respectively. The training is conducted in two ways: with and without dataset augmentation. Figure 5.11a–c present the outcome of the YOLO v7 model concerning its MAP score at 0.1, 0.01, and 0.001 on the pre-dataset augmentation.

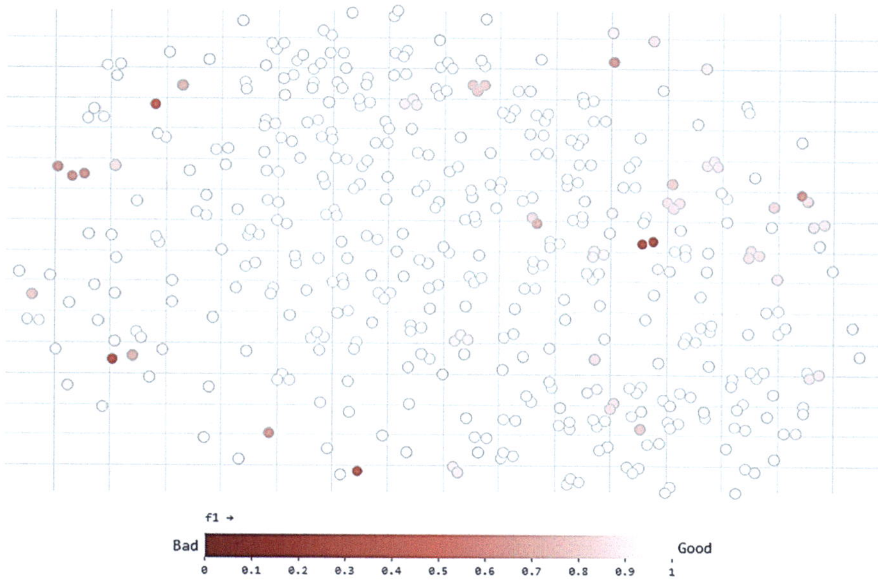

(a)

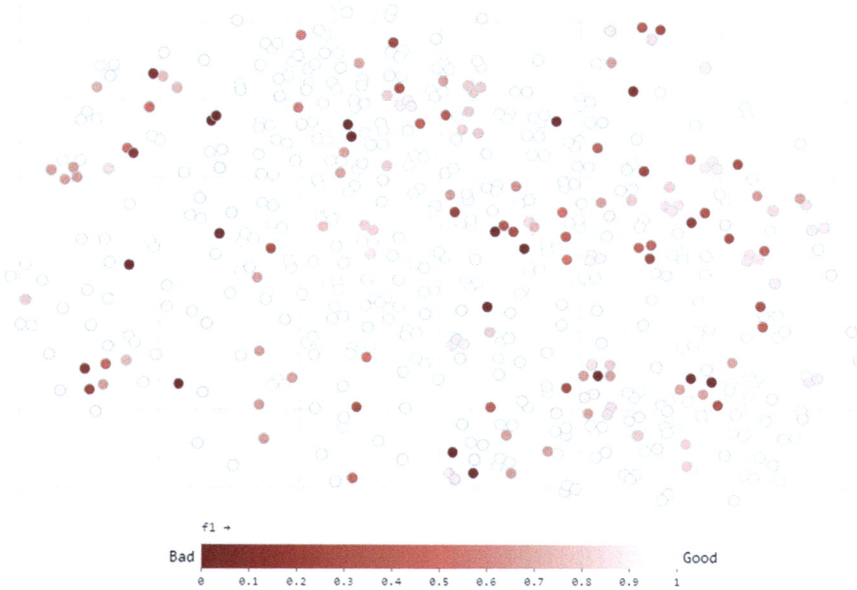

(b)

Fig. 5.10 (continued)

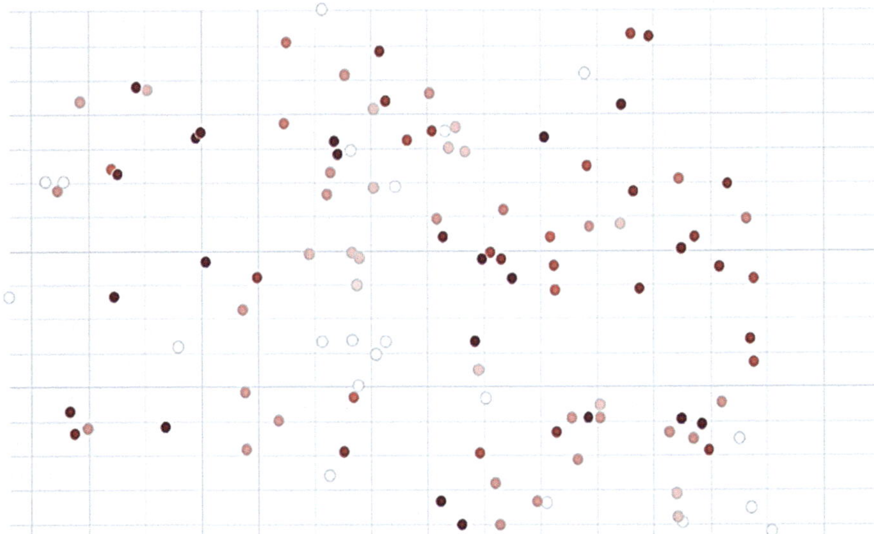

(c)

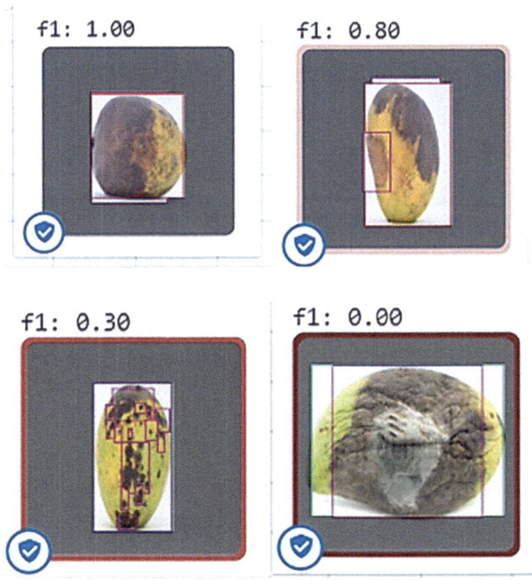

(d)

Fig. 5.10 Performance of custom YOLO model for Mango fruit defect detection (**a**) Scatter plot on training data (**b**) Scatter plot on validation set (**c**) Scatter plot on test set

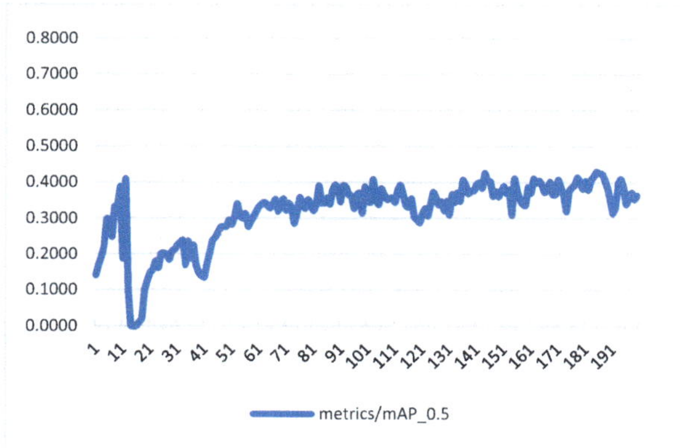

(a)

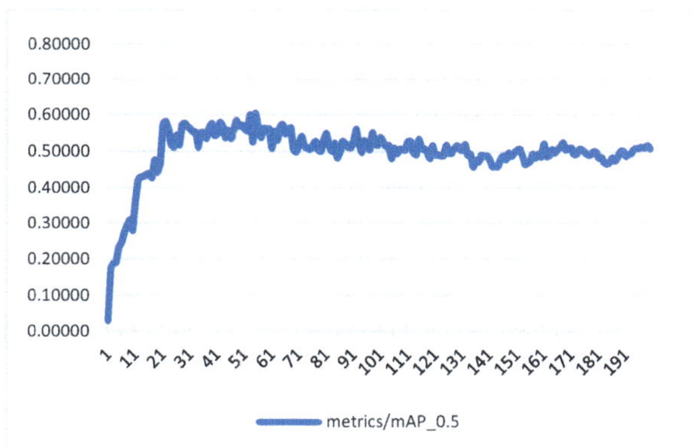

(b)

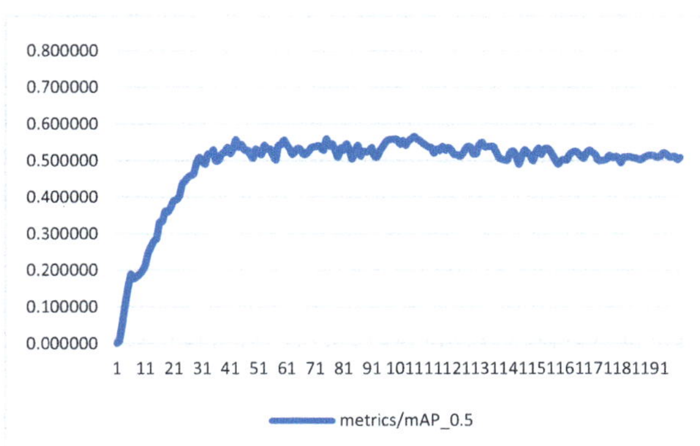

(c)

Fig. 5.11 Performance of YOLOv7 model on pre-augmentation dataset (**a**) At learning 0.1 (**b**) At learning rate 0.01 (**c**) At learning 0.001

Fig. 5.12 Performance of YOLOv7 model on post augmentation dataset (**a**) At learning 0.1 (**b**) At learning rate 0.01

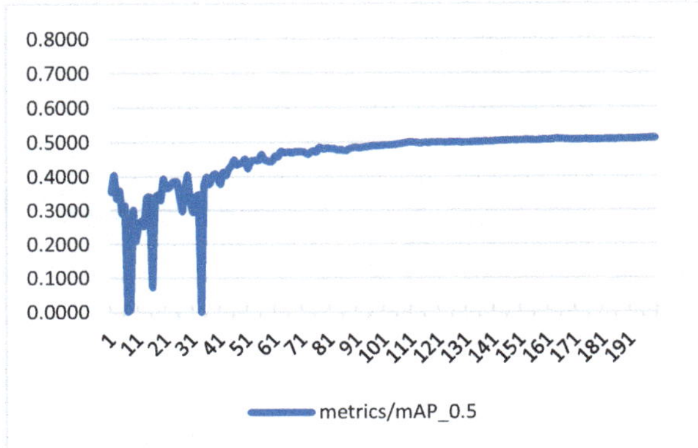

(a)

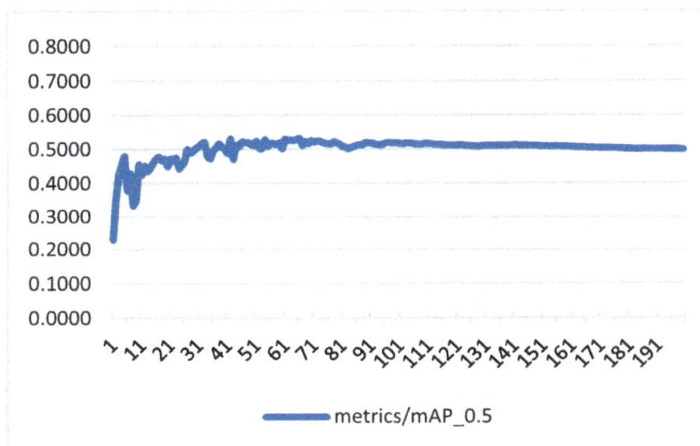

(b)

From the study, it is observed that the Map score of 61.3% is achieved on pre-augmented data at a learning rate of 0.01 toward the validation set. In the case of the test set, a MAP score of 62.1% is achieved with a learning rate of 0.01. A performance decline is observed concerning the learning rate 0.1 and 0.001 as it reports a validation MAP score of 44.2% and 41.8%, 55.7%, and 55.1% towards the validation set and test set, respectively.

A thorough analysis is conducted by augmenting the data and retraining the YOLO V7 model again at learning rates 0.1 and 0.01, and the results achieved towards the validation set are presented in Fig. 5.12a, b.

Figure 5.12a, b show a performance decline in mAP scores as the YOLO V7 model reports mAP scores of 51.3% and 53.3% towards validation set at learning rates 0.1 and 0.01, respectively. Similarly, the YOLO v7 model reflects the performance depreciation towards the test set by reporting 55.8% and 58.6% of the mAP score towards the test set concerning learning rates 0.1 and 0.01. The overall analysis with dataset augmentation and without dataset augmentation maintains an mAP threshold of above 0.5 to perform the defect detection toward validation and the test set.

Figure 5.13a, b present the confusion matrices obtained on the validation and test sets concerning the learning rate 0.001. The results represent the decline in performance due to the high rate of false positives noticed concerning class-wise performances. Based on the performances on validation and test sets, it is observed that only two out of six classes produce relatively satisfactory performance, indicating the poor generalizable ability of the model. Figure 5.14 presents the visualization of defect detection obtained by the YOLOv7 model with a learning rate 0.001.

As per the outcome of defect detection using the YOLOv7 model, the results, though visually appealing, exist misclassification with respect to the class bruises as defects. Some misclassifications are observed between the classes unripe as partially ripe and rotten as defects, leading to poor generalization and overfitting. Table 5.7 presents the results of performance evaluation on self-built datasets with augmentation using YOLOv5l model towards validation and test sets.

From Table 5.7, it is observed that the outcome table results depict the performance of the YOLOv5l model on the proposed mango defect detection dataset. The metrics such as precision recall and mAP at 0.5 for each class is quantified on both the validation and test datasets. The model shows comparatively equal performance with YOLOv7 in terms of precision and recall rates across classes. For Unripe class, the model achieves high precision and recall on both datasets. The overall average precision, recall, and mAP at 0.5 for all classes indicate the model's average performance. Thus, the propose custom YOLO model exhibits a better performance over the YOLOv7 and YOLOv5l.

According to Fig. 5.15, the performance of YOLO5l model towards training datasets reports an overall mAP score of 0.53 which is relatively low compared to proposed custom YOLO model. The performance of learning is though appreciable from epoch 0 to epoch 100, the mAP score begins to decline from 110th epoch. From overall performance towards training dataset, the proposed model proves to be reliable in understanding of complex relationships present in the dataset.

model.

5.4.3 Performance Evaluation Towards Publicly Available Datasets

About the investigation of the generalizable ability of the custom YOLO model towards mango fruit defect detection towards other publicly available datasets, in this section, a comprehensive evaluation is conducted on diverse publicly available datasets that include the mango fruit drop dataset [32] and Mangaa [33] from Roboflow application programming interface for computer vision model development. The samples are chosen according to the applicable classes per the

(a)

(b)

Fig. 5.13 Confusion matrices obtained by YOLOv7 model at learning rate 0.001 (**a**) Validation set (**b**) Test set

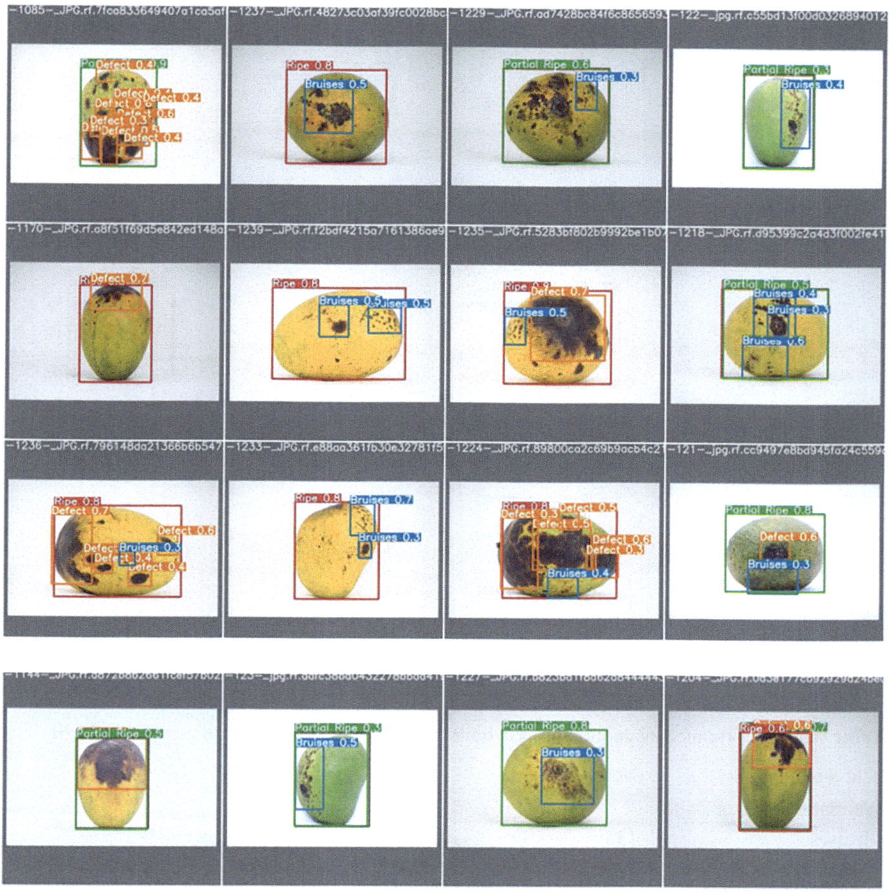

Fig. 5.14 (continued)

self-built datasets. The mango fruit drop dataset consists of samples collected in a controlled environment with three classes: ripe, unripe, partially ripe, and damaged, with 896 samples. At the same time, the fruit sample images considered part of the Mangaa dataset are all captured in an uncontrolled environment with various maturity stages and the defect types of multiple mango fruit varieties with 183 samples. Experimentations are conducted to test and visualize the defect regions along with the maturity stage with a custom YOLO model, and the results of predictions are presented in Figs. 5.15 and 5.16.

After subjectively analyzing the outcome of predictions, though we encounter a slight decline in the F1 score concerning the prediction obtained, the average F1 score is more significant than 42.3%, combining both datasets. Thus, the qualitative analysis conducted on two publicly available datasets assists us in providing

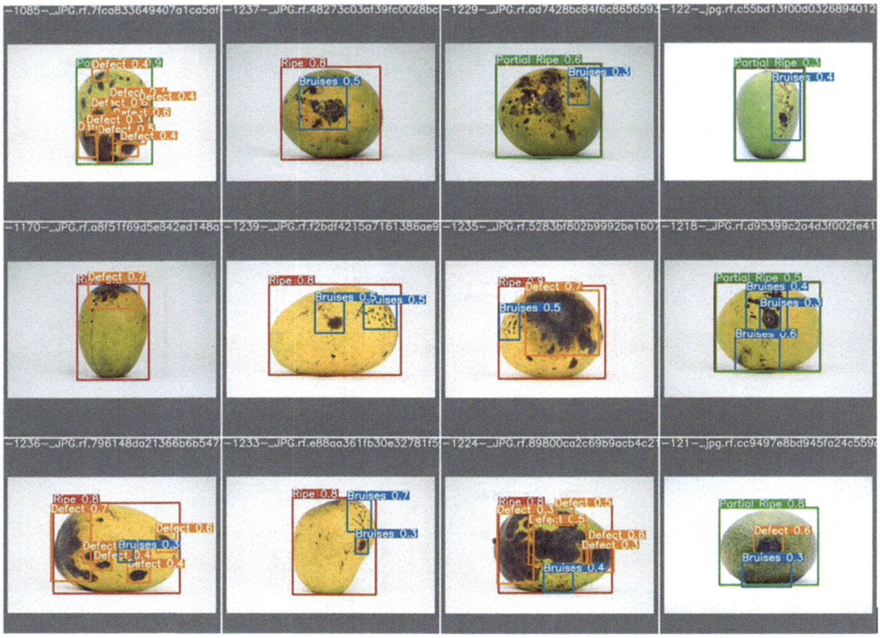

Fig. 5.14 Visualization of defect detection outcomes—YOLOv7 model with learning rate 0.001

Table 5.7 Performance evaluation on self-built datasets with augmentation using YOLOv5l

Class name	No of labels	Precision	Recall	mAP 0.5
Validation dataset				
Bruises	155	0.337	0.206	0.215
Defect	330	0.573	0.458	0.467
Partial ripe	166	0.68	0.88	0.767
Ripe	181	0.665	0.729	0.676
RottenMango	48	0.242	0.729	0.389
Unripe	61	0.552	0.754	0.721
All	941	0.508	0.626	0.539
Test dataset				
Bruises	115	0.57	0.148	0.201
Defect	199	0.606	0.452	0.498
Partial ripe	76	0.517	0.579	0.59
Ripe	173	0.73	0.799	0.793
RottenMango	25	0.37	0.8	0.528
Unripe	36	1	0.993	0.996
All	624	0.632	0.629	0.601

valuable insights into the model's ability to distinguish and accurately localize mango fruit defects in an uncontrolled environment.

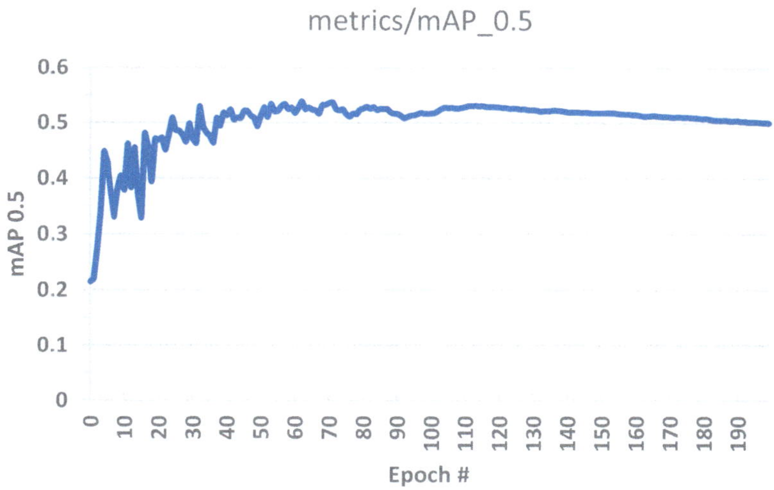

Fig. 5.15 Performance of YOLOv5l model towards training datasets

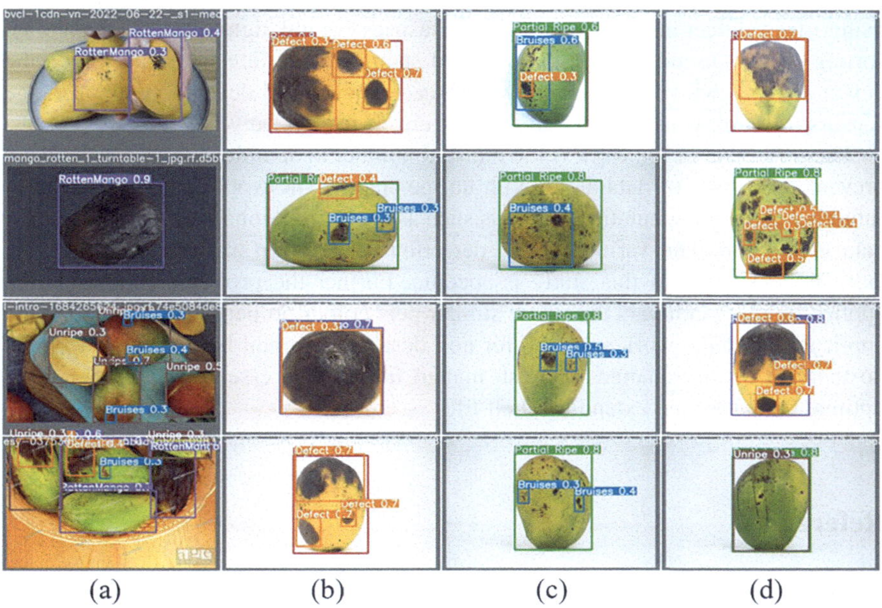

Fig. 5.16 Results of defect region prediction obtained using custom YOLO model, column (**a**) results of predictions from Mangaa datasets, column (**b**), (**c**) and (**d**) results of predictions from Mango fruit drop datasets

5.5 Conclusion

Part of the present investigation is inclined toward defect detection and maturity stage analysis of mango fruit samples at the fruit level and within fruit region analysis. The custom YOLO model, designed with a darknet backbone, can detect the defect types of bruises, BBS, rotten, unripe, partially ripe, and ripe, with relatively acceptable F1 scores. The model is also compared with the YOLOv7 model for understanding the efficiency, and it is noticed that the existing model is unable to capture the features that distinguish and localize the bruises vs. defects and unripe vs. partial ripe. Furthermore, the model is tested for its evaluation of publicly available datasets, proving that it can generalize satisfactorily towards datasets captured in an uncontrolled environment. In the future, the model must be finetuned concerning the exploration of specific features that help differentiate from one class of defect type to another in a highly accurate manner. It is also proposed that more fruit samples of bruises and other defect types at unripe or early stages be collected. Increasing the fruit samples for the classes to which there exists dataset imbalance would strengthen the proposed model in terms of its mAP scores, precision, and recall. However, the results of the present investigation, if integrated as part of the mango fruit defect analysis module in industries, would significantly enhance the sorting process to aid in the elimination of samples with defects. Furthermore, the defect analysis with fruit samples would lead to advanced developments of image sensors for intelligent postharvest applications of mango fruits.

The limitation of the work is the reduced number of samples for bruises that can prevent overfitting of data along with unripe stages. The work can be extended in future by using augmentation methods such as transformations along with synthetic data generation. The various object detection models can also be explored. The cultivar considered in this study is specific. Further the proposed model can be applied on more cultivars that share similar peel colour properties that illustrate the applicability of the work as a tool for non-destructive monitoring systems to track postharvest quality changes in fresh mango fruit that is essential for maintaining optimal freshness and extending shelf life.

References

1. Nturambirwe, J. F. I., & Opara, U. L. (2020). Machine learning applications to non-destructive defect detection in horticultural products. *Biosystems Engineering, 189*, 60–83.
2. Mditshwa, A., Magwaza, L. S., Tesfay, S. Z., & Mbili, N. (2017). Postharvest quality and composition of organically and conventionally produced fruits: A review. *Scientia Horticulturae, 216*, 148–159.
3. El-Ramady, H. R., Domokos-Szabolcsy, É., Abdalla, N. A., Taha, H. S., & Fári, M. (2015). Postharvest management of fruits and vegetables storage. In *Sustainable Agriculture Reviews: Volume 15* (pp. 65–152). Springer.

4. Gnanavel, S., Manohar, S., Sridhar, K. E., Sokkanarayanan, S., & Sathiyanarayanan, M. (2019). Quality detection of fresh fruits and vegetables to improve horticulture and agro-industries. In *2019 International Conference on Contemporary Computing and Informatics (IC3I)* (pp. 268–272).
5. Kader, A. A. (1983). Postharvest quality maintenance of fruits and vegetables in developing countries. In *Postharvest physiology and crop preservation* (pp. 455–470). Springer.
6. Tripathi, M. K., & Maktedar, D. D. (2020). A role of computer vision in fruits and vegetables among various horticulture products of agriculture fields: A survey. *Information Processing in Agriculture, 7*(2), 183–203.
7. Kundu, M., Krishnan, P., Kotnala, R. K., & Sumana, G. (2019). Recent developments in biosensors to combat agricultural challenges and their future prospects. *Trends in Food Science & Technology, 88*, 157–178.
8. Arakeri, M. P. (2016). Computer vision-based fruit grading system for quality evaluation of tomatoes in the agriculture industry. *Procedia Computer Science, 79*, 426–433.
9. Martinelli, F., Scalenghe, R., Davino, S., Panno, S., Scuderi, G., Ruisi, P., & Dandekar, A. M. (2015). Advanced methods of plant disease detection. *A review. Agronomy for Sustainable Development, 35*, 1–25.
10. Chakraborty, S. K., Chandel, N. S., Jat, D., Tiwari, M. K., Rajwade, Y. A., & Subeesh, A. (2022). Deep learning approaches and interventions for futuristic engineering in agriculture. *Neural Computing and Applications, 34*(23), 20539–20573.
11. Hewett, E. W. (1999). Chapter 3 fruits and vegetables, Part 3.2 Fruit and vegetable storage requirements. In *CIGR handbook of agricultural engineering, volume IV agro processing engineering*.
12. Singh, D., Sharma, R. R., & Kesharwani, A. K. (2021). Postharvest losses of horticultural produce. In *Postharvest handling and diseases of horticultural produce* (pp. 1–24). 33487–2742). CRC Press.
13. Sommer, N. F., Fortlage, R. J., & Edwards, D. C. (2002). The Pathogen. *Postharvest Technology of Horticultural Crops, 3311*, 197.
14. Hahn, F. (2009). Actual pathogen detection: sensors and algorithms-A review. *Algorithms, 2*(1), 301–338.
15. Sahu, D., & Potdar, R. M. (2017). Defect identification and maturity detection of mango fruits using image analysis. *American Journal of Artificial Intelligence, 1*(1), 5–14.
16. Mim, F. S., Galib, S. M., Hasan, M. F., & Jerin, S. A. (2018). Automatic detection of mango ripening stages–An application of information technology to botany. *Scientia Horticulturae, 237*, 156–163.
17. Nithya, R., Santhi, B., Manikandan, R., Rahimi, M., & Gandomi, A. H. (2022). Computer vision system for mango fruit defect detection using deep convolutional neural network. *Food, 11*(21), 3483.
18. Raghavendra, A., Guru, D. S., & Rao, M. K. (2021). Mango internal defect detection based on optimal wavelength selection method using NIR spectroscopy. *Artificial Intelligence in Agriculture, 5*, 43–51.
19. Patel, K. K., Kar, A., & Khan, M. A. (2019). Common external defect detection of mangoes using color computer vision. *Journal of The Institution of Engineers (India): Series A, 100*, 559–568.
20. Tiemtud, K., Saprasert, P., Tormo, T., & Chaturantabut, S. (2020). Automatic defect detection for mango fruit using non-extensive entropy with Gaussian gain. *Thai Journal of Mathematics*, 339–349.
21. Abbas, M. (2017). Image Analysis for Mango Fruit Defect Identification and Maturity Detection. *American Journal of Artificial Intelligence, 1*(1), 5–14.
22. Huang, T., Zheng, B., Zhang, J., Yi, C., Jiang, Y., Shui, Q., & Jian, H. (2021). Mango surface defect detection based on HALCON. In *2021 IEEE 5th advanced information technology, electronic and automation control conference (IAEAC)* (Vol. 5, pp. 2627–2631).
23. Gururaj, N., Vinod, V., & Vijayakumar, K. (2023). Deep grading of mangoes using convolutional neural network and computer vision. *Multimedia Tools and Applications, 82*(25), 39525–39550.

24. Vishwanath, M. (2023). *Image analysis for mango fruit defect identification and maturity detection.*
25. Li, B., Yao, C., Su, C. T., Zou, J. P., Wu, J., & Chen, N. (2023). Detection of skin defects on mangoes based on hyperspectral imaging combined with band ratio and improved Otsu method. *Microchemical Journal*, 109718.
26. Ashok, V., Bharathi, R. K., & Sheela, N. (2023). An Automatic Non-Destructive External and Internal Quality Evaluation of Mango Fruits based on Color and X-ray Imaging using Computer Vision Techniques. *Inteligencia Artificial, 26*(72), 223–243.
27. Velásquez, C., Aleixos, N., Gomez-Sanchis, J., Cubero, S., Prieto, F., & Blasco, J. (2024). Enhancing anthracnose detection in mango at early stages using hyperspectral imaging and machine learning. *Postharvest Biology and Technology, 209*, 112732.
28. Rungpichayapichet, P., Mahayothee, B., Nagle, M., Khuwijitjaru, P., & Müller, J. (2016). Robust NIRS models for non-destructive prediction of postharvest fruit ripeness and quality in mango. *Postharvest Biology and Technology, 111*, 31–40.
29. Rivera, N. V., Gómez-Sanchis, J., Chanona-Pérez, J., Carrasco, J. J., Millán-Giraldo, M., Lorente, D., Cubero, S., & Blasco, J. (2014). Early detection of mechanical damage in mango using NIR hyperspectral images and machine learning. *Biosystems Engineering, 122*, 91–98.
30. Ardila, C. E. C., Ramirez, L. A., & Ortiz, F. A. P. (2020). Spectral analysis for the early detection of anthracnose in fruits of Sugar Mango (Mangifera indica). *Computers and Electronics in Agriculture, 173*, 105357.
31. Gabriëls, S. H., Mishra, P., Mensink, M. G., Spoelstra, P., & Woltering, E. J. (2020). Non-destructive measurement of internal browning in mangoes using visible and near-infrared spectroscopy supported by artificial neural network analysis. *Postharvest Biology and Technology, 166*, 111206.
32. https://universe.roboflow.com/thesis-kflfx/mango-fruit-drop-xg5o0/dataset/2
33. https://universe.roboflow.com/search?q=like:thesis-kflfx%2Fmango-fruit-drop-xg5o0

Chapter 6
Machine Learning and Deep Learning for Cybersecurity in Smart Environments

Dietmar P. F. Möller

Abstract Artificial intelligence is considered as most breakthrough technology nowadays with primary subdivisions machine learning and deep learning. Artificial intelligence enabling digital entities not only to learn but also to gain and optimize knowledge to the manifold of possible applications in essential and important smart environmental domains. This includes, but is not limited to control and optimization of many kind of smart systems like cities, energy, financial, home, medical, traffic, and others with exiting solutions, never seen before. Unfortunately, an emerged growth can be seen for cybercrime, conducted by cyber-threat attacks based on AI-system applications, which has a negative endeavor due to cybersecurity risks. However, AI can also be used to defend against cybercrime activities, which has a positive endeavor making AI-based systems cyber-secure. Given this fact, the objective of this chapter is to introduce into both aspects, using AI methods to detect and defend against cybercrime. Finally, a practical example illustrates how AI can be successfully applied in the smart environment sector.

Keywords Artificial intelligence · Machine learning · Deep learning · Cybersecurity · Smart environments

6.1 Introduction to Artificial Intelligence

Today's technological development make new technologies available with manifold of options about their application capabilities. Artificial intelligence (AI) is considered as most technological upheaval that is going to impact everything in the near future being conceptualized, developed and deployed. This breakthrough technology goes back to Marvin Minsky and John McCarthy, which organized a conference at Dartmouth College in 1956 on artificial intelligence [1]. John

D. P. F. Möller (✉)
Clausthal University of Technology (TUC), Clausthal-Zellerfeld, Germany
e-mail: dietmar.moeller@tu-clausthal.de

N. E. M. Khalifa, M. H. N. Taha (eds.), *Empowering AI Applications in Smart Life and Environment*, https://doi.org/10.1007/978-3-031-78038-7_6

McCarthy coined the term "Artificial Intelligence" for the proposal to obtain funding for the conference. Together with Herbert Simon and Allen Newell they started AI laboratories at premier American research centers and universities. Although the name artificial intelligence had some controversies, it was accepted by the community [2]. AI as a new technology studies and develops theories, methods, techniques, and applications that simulate, expand and extend intelligent behavior. In this sense, AI seeks to gain knowledge in the essence of intelligence and set up a new type of intelligent machines that respond analog to human intelligence. Thus, AI research try to emulate the information process of human consciousness, but AI is not a human intelligence.

AI, can be defined as an entity with the capability to learn solve challenging problems, by using a set of computer algorithms and techniques ranging from speech recognition, pattern recognition, and others. As a research domain AI research evolving from reasoning, knowledge representation and storage to advanced approaches involving cognition, learning and decision making. Nowadays, AI support smart digital machines in different application domains with a high degree of complexity. A well-known example around is ChatGPT, an auto-generative pretrained AI chatbot system for online user support with the capability to summarize and reproduce knowledge in the shortest possible time. ChatGPT based on the Large Language Models (LLMs) concept that revolutionized natural language processing (NLP). LLMs are statistical models that assign a probability to a sequence of words, fundamental to many NLP tasks [3]. LLMs are very large model architectures with billions of parameters [4] trained on massive data sets, nearly a terabyte of e.g. English text [5].

This scaling increases the capability of LMMs to generate natural language outcome [6, 7], and to be applied to a plethora of other tasks [5, 8, 9], even without updating their parameters [4]. Given this fact, ChatGPT contains a transformer architecture that processes these very high number of data (terabytes), containing billions of words so that the chatbot can respond appropriately to questions and prompts. In this regard, the chatbot is a natural language processing system, that the user could go and talk to and ask questions. It has a knowledge base that it draws on answering questions. Hence, the chatbot can be understood as an "expert team member" to answer questions as users are trying to do an investigation. However, aggregation of such a technology significantly increases the complexity, vulnerability and expenditure required to set up the specific technology platforms. Hence, it is important to note that also a negative impact come into action through the rapid growth using these new specific technologies. This negative impact is conducted due to new types of cybercrime and the omnipresence connectivity of smart digital systems. These smart digital systems are increasingly used as an entrance for committing cyber-crimes, cybersecurity is a critical issue to cyber-secure usage of new technologies like AI, and part of the cyber-defense against cyber-attacks. In this regard, modern cybersecurity measures face many challenges to defend sophisticated cyber-attacks, executed in conjunction with the growing cyber-attack surface, data explosions, and increasing smart environment complexity that impact their ability to protect data, manage user access, and quickly detect and respond to cyber threat attacks [10]. Thus, specific approaches are required investigating and identifying anomalous behavior of AI based system operation. The regular methods behind are knowledge graphs, decay function, machine learning, deep learning, and others. Given this fact, a three-step AI approach is required that investigate, identify and report about the findings in case of cyber-attacks, e.g., malware and others. Investigating means representing information in conjunction with some kind of reasoning in order to do inference. Identifying refers to sorting the many log records to find out where are anomalous activities, where are the outliers. After a successful execution of the two steps, a report is essential to close the cybersecurity analysis cycle, complying with the regulation requirements. Therefore, the three-step sequence offers the way to find out what is the signature or pattern of the potentially intruded malware that interfere with regular system operation, based on which one can act to start with cyber-defense against the cybercriminal attack, for example the identified malware. Given this fact, it is clear that AI is increasingly important for prevention against cybersecurity risks through cyber threat attacks.

AI is the backbone of new developments in smart technological applications like intelligent manufacturing. Within AI as currently practiced, there are two primary subdivisions: Machine Learning (ML) and Deep Learning (DL), whereby both are also important to defend against potential cybersecurity risks. When it comes to cybersecurity threats and cyber-attack incidents, they are the biggest cybersecurity risk, because automation allows cybercriminals to reach a breadth and scale never seen before. ML focuses on classification and regression (see Fig. 6.1), based on previously learned features from the training data. In contrast DL based on learning

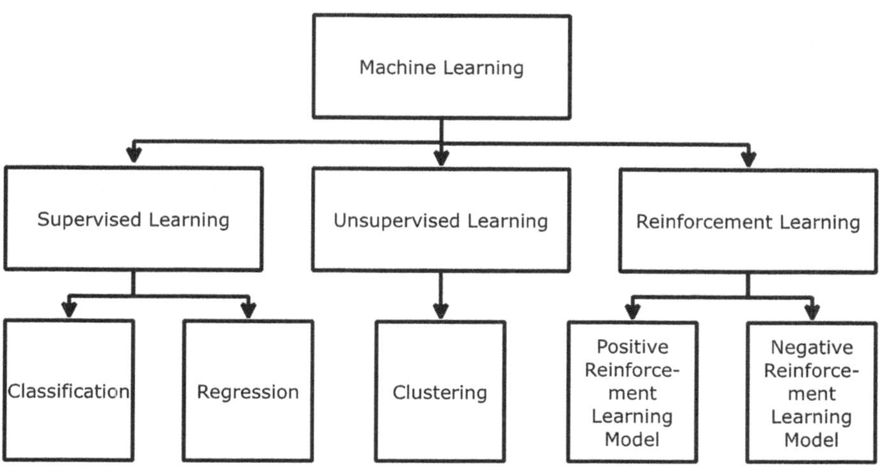

Fig. 6.1 Machine learning techniques

from data. Let's assume an image that can be described in a variety of ways, such as a vector of each pixel intensity value, or more abstract as a series of edges, a region of a particular shape, or the like. Furthermore, AI, and hence ML and DL, can analyze large amounts of data in almost less time, a capability when it comes to a cybersecurity risk problem, to detect cybersecurity risks, like malware, phishing, and others. On one hand, in case of a ML application, which is a pattern matching approach, multiple factors across multiple records can be analyzed, which can result in the conclusion that an outlier exist, or an anomalous pattern is detected, or another cybersecurity attack scenario has taken access to the system under investigation. However, specific differences between ML and DL exist [11]:

- Data Dependencies: DL do not perform good enough, if data volume is small. It requires large amount of data to interpret the data in a qualitative good manner. Conversely, ML algorithm use established rules to increase performance [12].
- Feature Processing: Feature Processing: Time-consuming process that requires specialized knowledge. ML performance depends upon accuracy of extracted features. Gaining high-level features directly from data is a major difference between DL and ML [13]. DL reduces the effort of designing a feature extractor for each problem.
- Problem Solving Method: ML breaks a problem down into multiple sub-problems and solves the sub-problems to obtain the final result. In contrast, DL advocates direct end-to-end problem solving.
- Execution Time: DL training takes time due to the many parameters. Hence, training step takes longer. ML training takes relatively little time. However, the test time is exactly the opposite. DL require less time to run during testing. Compared with ML, test time increases as amount of data increases, but this does not apply to all ML algorithms, because some ML algorithms have short test times.
- Interpretability: Crucially, interpretability is an important factor in comparing ML with DL [11].

It should be noted that the problem of detection of malicious malware code is not that simple as described, because cyber-criminals can modify their malicious malware code to evade detection. In this regard, ML is excellently suited for anti-malware protection since it can draw on data from previously detected malicious malware code to detect new variants. On the other hand, DL can be used for cybersecurity purpose to develop smart models for implementing malware classification and intrusion detection and threat intelligence sensing [14]. In this sense, AI-powered monitoring, using ML and DL, can track user behavior, detect anomalies, and react accordingly to make smart environments cyber-secure. Therefore, the following sections addresses the different important aspects of AI with regard to ML and DL, in the context of cybersecurity.

6.2 Introduction to Machine Learning

Machine learning (ML) enabling digital machines the capability of pattern recognition, continuously learning to accumulate knowledge, decision making based on data, or carry out decisions. For this purpose, ML process natural data in their raw form, to automatically identify relations essential in object detection of classification. Important relationships in ML are developed and the ML algorithm adapt to learn how to map them to a problem-oriented solution. Therefore, ML can be used to a variety of application domains, e.g. object identification in images, transcribing speech into text, and others. Furthermore, ML also enable to tackle tasks too difficult to solve with the traditional programming paradigms. Hence, ML also enables describing problems as collection of relations and characteristics, quantitatively measured at the object under investigation, e.g. a smart environment, the ML take over control. Typically, such a problem can be represented by a vector $\boldsymbol{x} \in \Re^{n}$, where each entry x_i of the vector is another relation or characteristic. For example, the relations or characteristics of an image are usually the values of pixels in the image. Thus, ML models be assumed as set of n input values $x_1, \ldots, x_n$ and associate them with an output y. These models learn a set of weights $w_1, \ldots, w_n$, and compute their output such as

$$f(x, w) = x_1 w_1 + \cdots + x_n w_n.$$

Given this fact, many problems be solved using ML algorithms. Some common ML application areas are [15]:

- Anomaly Detection: ML algorithm identify normal data, patterns and metrics and identifying e.g. data points that fall outside of an operation's normal behavior, and thus be anomalous. Therefore, ML algorithm sifts through a set of events, flags the ones being atypical or anomalous, and access the respective ML model, based on training data, which usually meet the required data instances that describe a set of attributes and associated labels. The attributes can be of different types such as categorical or continuous [16].
- Classification: Classification is a supervised ML method where the ML model tries to predict the correct label of given input data. Therefore, ML algorithm marks the k-categories some inputs belong to. Problem solving is done by generating a relationship f. For $y = f(\boldsymbol{x})$ the classification assigns an input vector $\boldsymbol{x}$ to a category identified by y.
- Denoising: Process of removing noise from objects, e.g. images. The noise present in images are practically hard to deal with. Therefore, the ML algorithm input use a corrupted problem vector $\boldsymbol{x_u} \in \Re^{n}$. The ML algorithm predict the regular problem vector $\boldsymbol{x_u}$ out of its corrupted problem vector $\boldsymbol{x_c}$, which means the ML algorithm predict the conditional probability distribution $p\ (\boldsymbol{x_u} \mid \boldsymbol{x_c})$.
- Density Estimation: Density estimation is a fundamental problem in statistics, e.g. density of high-dimensional data. In this context, ML algorithm has to learn

a function p: $\Re^n \rightarrow \Re$, where $p(\boldsymbol{x})$ be interpreted as a probability density function if x is continuous.

- Imputation of Missing Values: ML problem of missing data imputation, whereby the ML algorithm solve the problem vector $\boldsymbol{x} \in \Re^n$, although some entries $\boldsymbol{x}_i$ are missing. As problem solving approach the ML algorithm provides a prediction of the missing entries values.
- Machine Translation: Use classifiers that learn to distinguish human reference translations from machine translations, whereby the ML algorithm input include a sequence of symbols in one language that has to be converted into a sequence of symbols in another language.
- Regression: Regression in ML is used to capture the relationships between independent and dependent variables, predicting an outcome. Therefore, ML algorithm has to output a function f: $\Re^n \rightarrow \Re$.
- Synthesis and Sampling: ML algorithm generates new examples that are similar to those in the training data.
- Transcription: ML algorithm detect an unstructured representation of data and transcribes it into discrete or textual form.
- And others.

6.2.1 Types of Machine Learning

ML techniques are divided into different methods: Predictive or supervised method, descriptive or unsupervised method, and reinforcement method, as shown in Fig. 6.1.

The alignment of the first method, predictive or supervised learning ML, is to learn a mapping from inputs x into outputs y, given a labeled set of input-output as follows:

$$D = \{x_1.y_1\} \; \begin{matrix} N \\ i = 1 \end{matrix},$$

with D as training set, and N as number of training samples. For its simplest setting, each training input x is a D-dimensional vector of numbers (relations, attributes or covariates), stored in a $N = D$ design matrix, whereby x_i could be a complex structured object. Output y be anything, but most ML methods follow that y_i is a categorical or nominal variable from some finite set

$$y_i \in \{I, \ldots, Z\}$$

or a real value scalar. If y_i is categorical, ML yields classification or pattern recognition, and if y_i is real-valued, ML is yields regression [17].

The second method of ML is descriptive or unsupervised learning. Inputs, and the alignment of ML, is identifying relevant patterns in data, referring to some kind of knowledge discovery. Thus, unsupervised ML algorithms using datasets that contain many features to identify essential properties of the structure of the dataset.

The third method of machine learning is reinforcement learning. It interacts with the environment through a feedback loop between the ML system and human experiences exists. This method is suitable to learn how to act or behave for given occasional reward or punishment.

6.2.1.1 Supervised Machine Learning

Supervised Machine Learning (SML) is most common in ML, based on relations and characteristics associated with a label or target. SML algorithm investigate data set of objects of interest, classifying object features into different classes, based on their measurements, also known as density estimation. In SML y is usually tried to predict, which is equivalent make predictions or statements. The advantage of SML is obvious, smart environmental systems can be developed that precisely adapt to specific system task. Thus, they are not standard solutions, but rather highly specialized approaches for individual and specific tasks. However, their basic operational principle is always the same: A certain data set (input x) runs through a previously trained SML algorithm and at the end is the result (output y). As shown in Fig. 6.1, SML can be divided into classification models and regression models. Both types make use of different learning methods with the capability to learn under specific constraints. Some of the most important SML methods are:

- Classification Learning Method CLM): This method includes:
  - Linear Discriminant Analysis (LDA): Predictions estimating the probability that new inputs belong to each class under investigation,
  - Naive Bayes Method (NBM): Bayesian networks composed of directed acyclic graphs with a major entity that represent the unobserved mode, as well as several entities corresponding to observed nodes with strong assumption of independence against the entity nodes in the context of their major entity [18, 19],
  - Nearest Neighbor Method (NNM): Optimization problem identifying the point in a given data set closest to a given data point, the nearest neighbor [20, 21],
  - And others.
- Regression Learning Method (RLM): This method includes:
  - Decision Tree Method (DTM): Flowchart-like structure where each tree-node characterizes a test on features for which a decision is found. After evaluating all features, gained information of the corresponding leaf node represent the class label,
  - Ensemble Learning Methods (ELM): Represent prediction models that combine the strengths of a collection of simpler base models,
  - And others.

Against this background, SML enable predictions or statements. A problem example to be solved by SML is to calculate the ideal sales price for an innovative digital product in conjunction to the sales price of a competitor's sales price in the same product category. Another problem example solved by SML are cyber-attack problems, e.g., spam detection by using spam filters that create rules based on SML algorithms. Hereby, SML learn spam filters behavior to recognize junk mails and phishing messages by analyzing rules across a very huge number of similar cases. During the training phase, SML tries to approach the correct result.

6.2.1.2 Unsupervised Machine Learning

Unsupervised Machine Learning (UML) directive is to discover interesting structures in data of an object of interest, also known as knowledge discovery. Sometimes it is also called unconditional density estimation. UML is agreed more typical to human learning behavior, because it does not need a human expert to manually label data. As shown in Fig. 6.1, UML algorithms can be characterized as clustering models that are capable to learn as follows:

- Clustering Learning Method (CLM): This method includes:
  - Density-based Clustering Methods (DCM): Identify distinctive clusters in data, starting from the idea a cluster in a data space is a contiguous region of high data point density, however separated from others, like clusters with contiguous regions and low data point density,
  - Hierarchical Clustering Methods (HCM): Approach that groups similar objects into clusters,
  - Partitioning Clustering Methods (PtCM): Relocates instances moving them from one cluster into another, starting on an initial partitioning. Several algorithms used in partitioning clustering such as
    - K–means algorithm partitions data into K clusters (C_1, C_2, ..., C_K), represented by their centers of means,
    - K–medoids method is a partitioning to minimize the sum of squared error (SSE), and similar to the K–means algorithm,
    - K–mode clustering corresponds to a two-way CANDULUS model, if both ways corresponding to the data matrix modeled, via discrete parameters and a LFCS –norm based fitting function, where FCS is infinitesimally small [22],
    - K–medians clustering is a special case of the two-way CANDULUS model, if S, a matrix from the general elements, correspond to N-way data arrays [22],
  - Probability-based Clustering Methods (PbCM): Assumes that a cluster is a parameterized distribution,
  - Fuzzy C-Means (FCM): Allows one piece of data to belong to two or more clusters,

- And others.

To conclude: UML models including methods such as data analysis, factor analysis, hidden Markov models, K-means clustering, and others. They are mainly used in applications such as automation, classification, maintenance, and others. A good overview on UML can be found in [23]. Furthermore, UML models can be used defending cyber threat attacks with different degrees in sophistication and success in the smart environments to discover new potential ways to entities that could possibly be attacked in the near future.

6.2.1.3 Reinforcement Machine Learning

Reinforcement Machine Learning (RML) is a ML method to learn how to interact or behave given occasional reward or punishment signals [17]. This is considered how software agents take actions in environments. RML is also considered as part of deep learning to maximize some portion of cumulative reward, but is somewhat less used. The two kinds of RML methods are:

- Positive Reinforcement Learning (PRL): Interact due to a specific behavior,
- Negative Reinforcement Learning (NRL): Strengthening of a behavior due to negative condition that should stop or avoided.

Implementing reinforcement algorithms three approaches are possible:

- Value-based Reinforcement Learning Algorithm (VRLA): Maximize a value function *V(s)*.
- Policy-based Reinforcement Learning Algorithm (PRLA): Comes up with a policy to perform support to gain maximum reward in the future. There are two types of policy-based approaches:
    - Deterministic: For any circumstance the same action is created by policy π.
    - Stochastic: Every action taken has a certain probability, determined by a stochastic policy equation

$$n\,\{a\backslash s) = P\backslash A, = a\backslash S, = S\Big]$$

- Model-based Reinforcement Learning Algorithm (MRLA): Creates a virtual model for each environment for which an agent learns to perform in. There are two learning models available:
    - Markov Decision Process (MDP): Mathematical approach used for modeling decision-making problems where outcomes are partly random and partly controllable,

  - Q Learning (QL): Mathematical approach that finds an optimal action-selection policy for any finite Markov decision process (MDP), which means supplying information to inform which action an agent should take,
- And others.

6.2.1.4 Comparison of Machine Learning Methods

The different ML methods perform complex processing tasks, based on different characteristic algorithms, whereby each of which have advantages and disadvantages to the application domain used for. Table 6.1 summarize the advantages and disadvantages in SML.

Table 6.2 summarize the advantages and disadvantages in UML.

Table 6.3 summarize the advantages and disadvantages in RML.

Table 6.4 illustrate a comparison for supervised, versus unsupervised and versus reinforcement ML, based on same evaluation criteria to identify pros and cons of ML models.

From Table 6.4 it can be concluded:

- SML: Learning model learns from labeled data set with guidance.

Table 6.1 Advantages and disadvantages in SML

Supervised machine learning	
Advantages	Disadvantages
Define classes; trains classifier for perfect decisions; distinguish differentiate classes accurately,	Decision boundary can over trained; training set may not include class examples if no correct class labels achieved after training,
Determine how many classes needed,	If input is not from classes, classification can show wrong class label,
Mathematical decision boundary for classifying future inputs.	Requires good examples from each class for training classifier, Training requires computation time for classification.

Table 6.2 Advantages and disadvantages in unsupervised machine learning

Unsupervised machine learning (K-means)	
Advantages	Disadvantages
Easy to implement,	Difficult to predict number of clusters (K-values),
Larger number of variables, K-means compute fast,	Initial variables have strong impact on final outputs,
K-means generate tight clusters,	Order of data has impact on final output.
If centroids are recomputed, cluster instance change.	

Table 6.3 Advantages and disadvantages in reinforcement machine learning

Reinforcement machine learning	
Advantages	Disadvantages
Solve complex problems that cannot be solved by conventional techniques,	Not preferable to use solving simple problems,
Learning model similar to human learning; better perfection,	Can lead to overload of states that diminish output,
Create perfect model to solve a particular problem,	Needs many data and much computation,
In absence of training data, learns from experience.	Dimensionality, Dimensionality limits usage of real physical systems, Achieve long-term outputs hard to achieve.

Table 6.4 Supervised learning versus unsupervised learning versus reinforcement learning

Evaluation criteria	Supervised machine learning	Unsupervised machine learning	Reinforcement machine learning
Machine learning model:	Learn labeled data set with guidance,	Trained unlabeled data without any guidance,	Interacts with environment performing actions and learn from errors or rewards,
Problem types solved:	Regression and classification,	Association and clustering,	Reward based,
Data type required:	Labeled data,	Unlabeled data,	No predefined data,
Training method:	External supervision,	No supervision,	No supervision,
Machine learning method:	Maps labeled inputs to known outputs,	Understand pattern and discovers output,	Follow trial and error method,
Computational complexity:	Computationally simple,	Computationally complex,	Depends on usefulness of samples,
Accuracy:	Highly accurate and trustworthy method,	Less accurate and trustworthy method,	Uncertainty reduces predictability,
Best suited for:	Interactive software system or applications,	Automation and classification,	Supports and work in AI, human interaction,
Cybersecurity applications:	Find function or model to explain completely labeled data sets to detect intrusions, anomalies, malware and others.	Find patterns, structures, knowledge in unlabeled data sets to detect intrusions, anomalies, DDoS, unauthorized access, and others.	Labeling data sets during acquisition to detect intrusions of cyber threat attacks, and others

- UML: Learning model needs training based on unlabeled data without any guidance.
- RML: Agent interact with environment, performing actions and learns from errors or rewards.

Against this background, ML methods can also be applied to detect and defend cyber risk, whereby ML execute actions required for cybersecurity, e.g., scan large data volumes fast and analyzing them using statistical methods. Hence, ML is a powerful method to use to cyber-secure smart environments, as it can be seen from Table 6.4.

6.3 Introduction to Deep Learning

Machine Learning (ML) was introduced as specific type of practically implemented Artificial Intelligence (AI). Deep Learning (DL) is the subset of ML, using algorithms to imitate human thinking as faithfully as possible. In this regard, DL is a method composed of multiple processing layers to enable representations of data with multiple feature levels. These features levels automatically discovered and composed in various levels to produce outputs. Each level represents abstract features that are identified form features in the previous level. This allow DL obtaining simpler, but non-linear models, each transform the representation at one level, e.g. instance raw input data, into a representation at higher, slightly abstract level, solving real world problems. Therefore, DL enable extract patterns from data using neural networks. Neural networks date back decades based on artificial neurons. In DL, an articial neuron is a perceptron, the structural building block of deep learning. The perceptron itself is a forward propagation, described as follows:

$$y = g\left(\sum_{1=1}^{m} x_i w_i\right)$$

with y as perceptron output, g as non-linear activation function of the perceptron, x_i are perceptron inputs, and w_i are perceptron weights, rewritten as

$$y = g\left(X^T W\right)$$

with

$$X = \begin{bmatrix} x_1 \\ \dots \\ x_m \end{bmatrix}$$

and

$$\boldsymbol{W} = \begin{bmatrix} \boldsymbol{w_1} \\ \dots \\ \boldsymbol{w_m} \end{bmatrix}$$

Activation functions g be sigmoid functions, hyperbolic tangent, as well as the rectified linear units. Purpose of activation functions is introducing non-linearity into the DL neural network. Linear activation functions generate linear decisions, no matter the neural network size. In contrast non-linear activation functions allow to approximate arbitrarily complex functions. Let's assume that

$$\boldsymbol{W} = \begin{bmatrix} \mathbf{6} \\ -\mathbf{4} \end{bmatrix}$$

Then.

$$y = g\left(X^T W\right) = g\left(\begin{bmatrix} x_1 \\ x_2 \end{bmatrix}^T \begin{bmatrix} 6 \\ -4 \end{bmatrix}\right) = \mathrm{g}\,(6x_1 - 4x_{2.})$$

which represent a 2D space graph.

6.3.1 *Classification of Deep Learning*

Deep learning algorithms be classified into subgroups that depend on the fact whether algorithms are trained to yield the expected results or not. The most natural way to perform this is to use generative models such as directed, undirected and mixed [24].

6.3.1.1 Deep Directed Network

Deep Directed Network (DDN) contains at the bottom level the observed patterns and emaining layers are hidden. DDN in general is trained in three steps: Pertaining one layer in time in a greedy way, using UML at each layer in a way that preserves information form the input and disentangles factors of variation, fine-tuning the whole network with regard to the criterion of interest [24].

6.3.1.2 Deep Belief Network

Deep Belief Network (DBN) is a generative graphical model, or a class of deep neural network, composed of multiple layers of latent variables (hidden units) with connections between the layers but not between units within each layer. Unsupervised fast greedy layer-by-layer training suppose upper layers to represent more abstract concepts that explain input observation x, whereas the lower layers extract low level features from x. The fast-greedy algorithm advocates deep directed belief networks one layer at a time, is derived, provided the top two layers form an undirected associative memory [24]. DBN solve optimization problems in deep multi-layer structure learning by using space relative relationship, reducing the number of parameters to improve training performance. For a case with three hidden layers the model can be defined as follows [14]

$$p\,(h_1, h_2, h_3, v|\theta)$$

where h_i are the hidden layers, v is the visible mode, and $\boldsymbol{\theta} = (\boldsymbol{w_0}, \boldsymbol{w_1}, \boldsymbol{w_2}, \boldsymbol{w_3})$ are all the parameters in the model.

6.3.1.3 Restricted Boltzmann Machine

Restricted Boltzmann Machine (RBM) is an algorithm useful for dimensionality reduction, classification, regression, collaborative filtering, feature learning and others. RBMs are shallow, two-layer neural nets that constitute the building blocks of deep-belief networks. The first layer of the RBM is called the visible, or input, layer, and the second is the hidden layer, whereby the visible and the hidden layer are used to express a random network and a random environment. The learning model expresses the correlation between layers by weighting [25]. In this regard the RBM defines a probability distribution p on data vectors v as follows:

$$p(v) = \sum_h \frac{e^{-E(v,h)}}{\sum_{u,g} e^{-E(u,g)}}$$

where v is the input variable, and the variable h corresponds to observed features, which can be thought of as hidden causes not available in the original data set [26]. Thus, RBM describes a joint probability on the observed and unobserved variables which are referred to as visible and hidden layers respectively, to measure the distance between its estimated probability distribution and the ground-truth of the input. The distribution is marginalized over the hidden layers to give a distribution over the visible layers, and the probability distribution be defined by an energy function E [27].

6.3.1.4 Deep Bayesian Neural Network

Deep Bayesian Neural Network (DBNN) is a model that combine Bayesian Networks that employ probabilistic relationships and Neural Networks that rely on learning patterns in data through complex, neuron-like structures. Thus, DBNN add uncertainty to handle in models. Instead of having deterministic weights to learn, it is all to learn the parameters of a random variable used to sample weights during forward propagation. To learn the parameters, backpropagation is used that sometimes require adoption to make parameters differentiable. In this context in

DBNN the probability of, e.g., incident I, if the evidence E is given, which can be written as follows:

$$p\,(I|E) = \frac{p\,(E|I)\,p(I)}{p(E)}$$

with $p(I)$ as a priori probability of I, which is equivalent to a probability of an incident before the evidence is known, and $p(I|\,E)$ as a posterior probability of I, which is equivalent to a probability of an incident after the evidence is known.

6.4 Smart Environments

Smart environments are ecosystems of communicating and interacting entities with the capability to self-organize, coordinate, provide services, control data and others, gathered from sensors, actuators, information devices, and other connected entities [28]. In this context, the physical part of smart environments is some kind of an intelligent entity, which benefits from interacting with devices connected with, and the alignment to enhance self-organization, control, services and others to the smart environments. To create a smart environment, at least three technological domains must converge: ubiquitous computing, intelligent systems, and context awareness:

- Ubiquitous Computing: Describes how innovative technologies like smart objects with some kind of attachment, embedment, blending of computers, sensors, actuators, sensor-actuator-networks, tight integration, ubiquitous networking, and others relate to and support a computing vision for greater availability and range of digital systems, used in a greater scope of smart environments, such as smart manufacturing environments.
- Intelligent Systems: Refers to technologically advanced machines that operate in environments with other objects. It gathers analyses and respond to the data it collects from its surrounding environment. Major features are to process cognitive abilities such as perception, action control, reasoning and others and follows behavioral principles, based on rationality and norms, and has the capacity to learn from experience and adapt through learning according to current data.
- Context-awareness: Describes the possibility that digital entities can both senses, and react to their environment. These entities can gather information about facts that enable them to operate based on rules, or intelligent interaction, to react accordingly.

Given the fact of the three technologies foregoing mentioned, the smooth incorporation into smart environment applications must be easy, unproblematic, and understandable, to enable a smooth interaction between ambient systems and their users. Therefore, smart environment use intelligent apps that include methods like data mining, statistical analysis, machine learning, optimization, and others, to enable a smooth behavior. Furthermore, contextual knowledge in smart environments needs and benefits from environmental adaptation, which is important in perception and management of contexts that changes demands. Smart environments are manifold such as Smart City, Smart Communications, Smart Grid, Smart Health, Smart Home, Smart Manufacturing, Smart Meter, Smart Mobility, but not limited to. Furthermore, smart environments refer to a variety of possible forms of use as described by [29]:

- Virtual Digital Environments: Enable smart devices access pertinent services anywhere and anytime.
- Physical Environments: Embedded in a variety of smart entities of different types including tags, sensors and controllers with different form factors ranging from nano- to micro- to macro sized.
- Human Environments: Humans form a smart environment. Humans can be accompanied by smart devices such as smartphones, smart watches, and wearable smart devices that sense and control. Wearable smart devices especially useful for applications that require more computational support. Thus, wearable smart devices are a research topic of several specific application domains like medicine, space and others. A specific topic therefore includes user interface design, augmented reality, pattern recognition, and others.

A general requirement for all smart environments is that they are cyber-secure from cybersecurity threats and/or or cyber-attack incidents, which means at least the CIA Triad must be fulfilled. The elements of the CIA Triad considered as most crucial characteristics of security, confidentiality, integrity, and availability:

- Confidentiality: If likelihood of a cybersecurity threat and/or a cyber-attack is higher than low, e.g., an unauthorized person tries getting access to sensitive data or assets of a crucial smart environment or a smart system entity, and cybersecurity risk(s) occur, then immediately cybersecurity incident response is required, defending the unauthorized access in real-time.
- Integrity: Involves maintaining consistency, accuracy, and trustworthiness of data and assets over its entire life cycle, which considers the essential topics of data integrity and system integrity. Data integrity is the requirement that data and assets are changed only in a specified and authorized manner, while system integrity refers to the requirement that a smart environment or smart system performs its intended function in an unimpaired manner, free from deliberate or inadvertent unauthorized manipulation.
- Availability: If likelihood of a cybersecurity threat and/or a cyber-attack incident is higher than low means that a potential cybersecurity threat and/or cyber-attack can cause a
    - Denial of Services (DoS) attack to a crucial smart environment or smart system;
    - Malfunction of data and assets of a crucial crucial smart environment or smart system;

If likelihood of a cybersecurity threat and/or a cyber-attack incident is higher than moderate, e.g., a service is unavailable for a period of time that happens not more than for example once for every month, then the incident behavior should be monitored for further decision.

6.4.1 Smart Manufacturing Environment Use Case

The primary objective of manufacturing environments is to manufacture goods that can be sold to customers. Therefore, equipment is designed and build up to accomplish this goal. Hence, appropriate product layouts are designed for a specific product, referred to as flow lines, since manufacturing equipment is designed so that the product can flow from the first machine or workstation to the second, from the second to the third, and so on down the manufacturing environment line. In this regard raw material enters the front line of the manufacturing environment. Completing processing the product at the final machine or workstation, the raw material has been fully converted into the product of the manufacturing environment line. However, processing at a workstation remove raw material that must be disposed. Therefore, manufacturing environment lines have effective arrangements for manufacturing process and embedded disposal zones. Furthermore, the design of the production line considers how machines be located and maintained, how parts are batched and dispatched, and how performance can be measured, to realize optimal manufacturing environment performance.

Smart manufacturing environments are the future concept in manufacturing, merging the virtual and the physical worlds through Cyber-Physical Systems (CPS) [30] as well as embedding technical and business processes. This leads to a new form of manufacturing environments, introduced as smart manufacturing environment, synonymous Industry 4.0 or Intelligent Manufacturing. The term I4.0 refers to the mix of traditional manufacturing and industrial practices embedding technological innovations, including advanced analytics, cloud computing, CPS, industrial internet of things (IIoT), artificial intelligence (AI), seamless connectivity, and others. These advances are the backbone of I4.0 to achieve fully integrated, automated intelligent or smart manufacturing environments, leading to greater efficiencies. Thus, smart manufacturing environments represents a manufacturing revolution in terms of innovation, cost and time savings as well as a bottom-up manufacturing model with advanced networking capability. This include:

- Smart manufacturing environment processes like CPS-optimized units that enable identifying and determining the area of activity, configuration options and manufacturing conditions as well as omnipresent connectivity and wireless communication with other smart units.
- Optimized and individualized manufacturing processes through advanced compilation of smart manufacturing environment units, which account product

properties, costs, logistics, and security, reliability, time, and sustainability considerations.
- Resource efficient smart manufacturing environments achieved through tailored adjustments with regard to the human workforce so that the manufacturing machine adapts to the human work cycle as well as to enhance circular economy.

A core element in smart manufacturing environments is the fully interconnectedness of partially autonomous and smart entities, which situationally enable controlling themselves, even configure sensor-based and distributed manufacturing resources like manufacturing machines, robots, conveying and storage systems, utilities, including their planning and control systems. Against this background, a smart manufacturing environment refers to a consistent engineering approach that embeds the manufacturing process and the manufactured product, whereby the cyber and the physical components seamless interlock into each other. Hence, the smart manufacturing environment is a peer-to-peer information and communication interaction between manufactured products, systems, and machines. In this regard, a smart manufacturing environment allow manufacturing products, which are able to control their manufacturing processes themselves by sharing the appropriate use of machines through their product code, showing essential requirements like next processing steps and others. Henceforth, a smart manufacturing environment comprises the vision that CPS is a enabling technology beside AI, IIoT and others, which bring the virtual and the physical components together in manufacturing, whereby the IIoT be used as infrastructure resource collecting information and controls and others required in the physical domain. Given that fact, Cyber-Physical Manufacturing System (CPMS) enable synergy among the objects of the virtual and the physical domain, by integrating middleware and cyber-ware on the digital components of smart manufacturing environments. Thus, smart manufacturing environments control and optimize them self, because manufactured products communicate with each other and with the machines on the manufacturing floor shop to adapt or clarify their production steps sequences if required. Beyond that, smart manufacturing environments also schedule manufacturing priorities on demand as well as urgency requirements of products in the manufacturing line, supported by advanced AI algorithm, software-based agents, who are autonomously executing AI programs, enabling monitoring the requisite processes to ensure that production rules are respected or adapted on demand. Furthermore, smart manufacturing environments can manufacture individually products without become uneconomical, whereby manufacturing machines monitor themselves and in case of predicted failures autonomously activate the necessary repair procedure to eliminate the fault on demand. Moreover, company's internal cloud will enable to merge worldwide distributed smart manufacturing environments operating data. This allow identifying and better coordinating required supply chains, repairs and others, enabling an efficient utilization of natural and preprocessed resources. Ultimately, individual smart manufacturing environmental locations can also control themselves through suitable AI based algorithms (apps), deposited in the cloud.

Beside all the positive technological impacts of smart manufacturing environments, CIO and CISO must be conscious and aware about hidden associated cybersecurity risks and hazards, because the severity of the increasing prevalence of cybercrime is seriously be worried. In this context, the ever increasing complex and interdependent smart manufacturing environment technology could lead to new forms of cybersecurity threat and/or cyber-attack incidents, with an ever-intrinsic threatening potential. Therefore, proactive defend methods required, without compromising the opportunities of smart manufacturing environments.

6.5 Cybersecurity in Smart Environments

Cybersecurity is the body of knowledge, technologies, processes, practices and others, to protect smart environments data, assets, networks, and others from cybersecurity threats, and cyber-attack incidents, unauthorized access, and others. Hence, in a smart manufacturing environment for example someone can access remote, and hijacks various features of the manufacturing floor shop which then have tremendous malicious influence of the manufacturing process such as manipulating the whole manufacturing line or cancelling assembly steps or changing the sequence of assembling steps and others. These are some relevant reasons which illustrate that cybersecurity is essential for coordinated efforts throughout a smart manufacturing environment process. In regard to these possible interferences cybersecurity should address respective activity requires like [31]:

- Application security planning,
- Business continuity planning
- Data security planning,
- Disaster recovery planning
- Information security planning,
- Network security planning,
- And others.

One of the most important problematic impact to cybersecurity is the fast and constantly evolving sophisticated cybersecurity risk. From a general perspective, a cybersecurity risk is any identified anomalous event detected, e.g., in a smart manufacturing environment. Therefore, anomaly detection is required to identify cybersecurity threats and/or cyber-attack incidents of smart manufacturing environment. Anomaly detection is a powerful method to identify malicious cyber incident in real time, analyses possible effects of intrusion and possibilities for mitigation [32]. Hence, anomaly detection classifies deviations from normal (regular) of smart environments that indicate the presence of accomplished cybersecurity threats and/or cyber-attack incidents, cybercriminal fraud, and others. Methods for executing anomaly detection for cybersecurity purposes are AI based ML and DL algorithms, which continuously monitor smart manufacturing environments and detect potential threats or signs of compromise in real time [16]. Hence, AI based

ML and DL algorithms enable detection and tracking various types of anomalies such as unsuccessful logon attempts in accordance with time and frequency and destructive modifications to files and can automate actions taken in response to anomalies. These measures can block malicious traffic, isolate devices, or send alerts to save valuable time and minimize the amount of data at risk, which is vital to the protection against cybersecurity threats and/or cyber-attack incidents in smart manufacturing environments shop floor components or subsystems. Given that fact, the process of anomaly detection, if a suspicious incident suspected, create an alarm of possible attack-forms to potentially attacked component(s) or subsystem of the smart manufacturing environment, to avoid the cyber-attacker attempting to attack, is put on lock. Therefore, anomaly detection has gained a broad attention and become an important field for research, and still being a subject of widespread interest in the manifold of applications.

To conquer cyber-attack risks, cybersecurity standards have been developed and used for detection, prevention or mitigating cybersecurity threats and/or cyber-attack incidents, to protect that sensitive data and assets can unauthorized accessed in the ubiquitous networking smart manufacturing environment. One cybersecurity standard is the ISO/IEC 27 K family, an information security management system (ISMS) standard, which specifies specific actions taken for developing an ISMS to get information security under explicit management control. Moreover, advantages are given obtaining cybersecurity certification including the ability to get cybersecurity insurance.

6.5.1 Machine Learning Application to Intrusion Detection in Smart Manufacturing Environments

Machine learning (ML) is the ability of a digital machine to learn without being explicitly programmed. ML is represented by different types of learning methods as supervised machine learning (SML), unsupervised machine learning (UML), and reinforcement learning (RML). All learning methods use specific mathematical methods to create ML models for predictions on input data. In this context, ML detect patterns in input data that be compared with measured data, predicting whether these data are applicable as expected or not, whereby the latter case indicating that cyber-risk incidents are present. The identified incident(s) can gain a negative impact on the regular operational state of a smart environment shop floor, which result in a certain degree of uncertainty. Hence, ML analyze detected potential cyber-risky events to respond on them quickly in an automated way. Therefore, ML is a method to deal with uncertainty to gain a clear decision making. Given this fact, ML is an important method to perform in decision making under uncertainty in case of detecting potential cybersecurity threats and/or cyber-attack incidents. Consequently, ML techniques be applied to a variety of cyber risk problems, as discussed in [23]:

- Anomaly detection,
- Biometric recognition,
- Denial-of-Service (DoS) and Distributed Denial-of-Service (DDoS) Attack Detection,
- Detection of Advanced Persistent Threats (APT),
- Detection of hidden channels,
- Detection of identity theft,
- Detection of information leakage,
- Detection of software vulnerabilities,
- Malware detection and identification,
- Misuse detection,
- Spam mail and phishing page detection,
- User identification and authentication,
- And others.

ML based detection of cybersecurity threats and/or cyber-attack incidents lies in their intrinsic methodology based on training and testing, in connection with the following steps [33]:

- Identify class attributes and classes of training data or patterns,
- Identify a subset of the attributes necessary for classification,
- Learn model using training data or patterns,
- Use trained model to classify the unknown data or patterns.

Therefore, ML based cybersecurity measures applied to smart manufacturing environments, for both, detecting and preventing cybersecurity threats and/or cyber-attack incidents in data or assets. Therefore, the used ML methods can broadly be assigned to misuse detection and anomaly detection, whereby misuse detection methods are intended to recognize known patterns, described by rules, while anomaly detection focusses on detection of inacceptable activity patterns in observed data. If the problem of anomaly detection is ill-posed, makes it hard to decide what an anomaly is.

In misuse detection training, each misuse class is learned by using appropriate scenarios from the training data set. During test, data or patterns gathered from the smart environment under investigation through the ML, and thereafter classified as to whether they belong to one of the misuse classes or not. In case the data or patterns does not belong to any of the misuse classes from the training set, it is classified as normal.

In anomaly detection normal traffic patterns are defined during training, and thereafter learned pattern applied to pattern, gained from the smart environment. Finally, every inacceptable measured pattern is classified as anomalous in correlation to the test pattern.

Given this fact, ML methods becoming an essential approach in cyber intrusion detection in smart manufacturing environments. Cyber intrusion detection is the process of monitoring dynamically events occurring in a smart manufacturing environment and analyzed for signs of possible cyber threat events to interdict the unauthorized access [30]. This is typically accomplished by collecting data from a variety of smart environments sources, and thereafter analyzing this data or patterns for possible cybersecurity problems. Thus, data or pattern is of great importance for ML to learn from available data sets or patterns, because these data or patterns of a smart manufacturing environment application have to be cyber-secure. Consequently, the main task of an intrusion detection system architecture (IDSA) is detect data, patterns or signatures of potential cybersecurity breaches, when monitored operating the smart manufacturing environment factory shop floor. Monitoring means track data flow or packets in smart manufacturing environments, and analyze them for suspicious data, patterns or signatures activities, and finally report detected cybersecurity breaches to the organization's cybersecurity team, responsible for further action to defend or mitigate the danger. Therefore, IDSA designed and applied to deter potential damage or mitigate the damage caused by cyber-attackers [30].

A practical cybersecurity ML-based intrusion detection application, illustrating the scenario and the capability to monitor and protect a smart manufacturing environment factory against cybersecurity threats and/or cyber-attack incidents, is shown in Fig. 6.2.

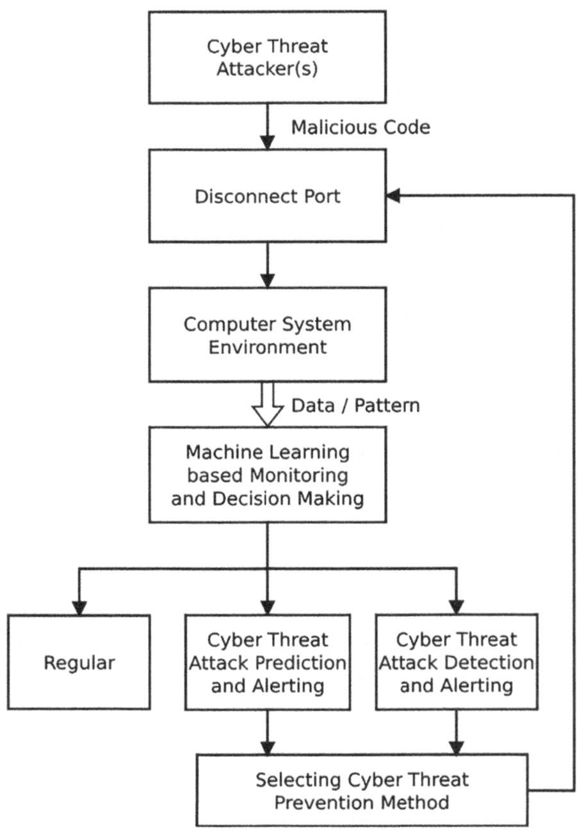

Fig. 6.2 ML in intrusion detection in smart manufacturing environment [31]

Table 6.5 Cyber threat risk level and related security model

Cyber threat risk level	Security model
Known knowns (KK)	Information security (IS)
Known unknowns (KU)	Cybersecurity (CS)
Unknown unknowns (UU)	Cyber resilience (CR)

The ML-based cyber-risk intrusion detection architecture in Fig. 6.2 use data exploration, a data analysis technique in which data analysts use different techniques to describe dataset characterization's, in order to better understand the nature of the data. With regard to cybersecurity data exploration is used to learn about regular and not regular behavior of smart manufacturing environment facilities interaction with one another within smart system environments. Based on the obtained results, malicious cyber threat attacks can be detected at early stages and output alerting, or to detect malicious cyber threat attacks and decide how to prevent becoming successful or mitigate them. Henceforth, this learning approach refers to learning based on experience.

Moreover, ML is a method capable to decide between known and cyber threat attack types not known. The later are introduced as unknown. In this context, ML algorithms comparing whether detected cyber threat attacks belong to the cyber threat attack category known knowns or not. In case of not known cyber threat-attack types the cyber treat risk level belong to the attack category known unknowns, because its known that it is not known, as illustrated in Table 6.5 [30, 31].

Known-knowns in Table 6.5 belong to the group cyber threat attacks, which corresponds with the CIA Triad, based on cyber threat event information methods used to characterize information security. Risks considered as known-knowns are risks that happened, and documented as facts. Detecting known-knowns describe being aware about all known risks, since identified, and defenders are certain about, and have solutions that best defend or allay those risks.

Risks that don't fit this category represent known-unknowns, which refer to objects known, and the one not known yet belong to unknowns. Thus, known-unknowns describes a case due to yet not known, referred to as unknown, known to as existing, but there is not enough known about what the unknown is.

Finally, unknown-unknowns characterize a dangerous risk situation while not clear whether a risk appears or not. Thus, unknown-unknowns refers to cyber threat attack not identified yet by anyone, stated as unforeseeable or unpredictable, and require ongoing exploration. For this type of risk, no one know how to find out is a risk intruded or not, because there is not enough knowledge to ask the right questions to identify and close the existing knowledge gap to risks. Therefore, unknown-unknowns are risks that may be real, but no one know how it will show up. Thus, now this cyber threat attack level is believed as impossible to understand or imagine it in advance. Cyber threat attacks at this level are assumed as highly dangerous and risky, because no identification and defense strategy exists. A probable attempt to address this problem is attempting to identify as many risks as possible to turn as many unknown-unknowns into known-knowns. While this be a worthwhile endeavor, it does not address a fundamental approach how to identify unknowability.

The goal of measures of known-knowns cyber security threats and cyber-attack incident attacks is to protect and defend data and assets of smart manufacturing environments resources against known cyber threat attacks. This can be achieved applying the CIA triad and the Cyber Threat Intelligence (CTI) approach.

The CIA triad is a widely accepted information security approach, consisting of three core elements: confidentiality, integrity and availability. In this respect, information security is a compliance that requires policies, processes and procedures protecting against cybersecurity risks, and acting to changing cyber threat attack possibilities, to withstand or recover rapidly from cybercriminal attacks. However, an effective information security needs a strategic approach to benefit, because a holistic plan how to achieve and sustain a desired level of cybersecurity maturity is required.

CTI is an information-based knowledge model, gathered from a variety of sources about current known or potential cyber risks against smart environments. The knowledge obtained is analyzed, redefined and arranged with the intention to minimize or mitigate cyber risks. This method is required since CTI is evidence-based knowledge, including context, mechanisms, indicators, implications and actionable advice about an existing or emerging cyber risk to assets. Therefore, well-written documentation how to mitigate cyber risks must be available. In some cases, specific configured mitigation approaches enable detecting and even mitigating cyber risk automatically. Beyond that, a detected cybersecurity threat and/or cyber-attack incident is automatically identified as new cyber riskt of attack category known unknowns. Bearing in mind this fact requires that the smart environments must have beside a secure communication between its smart environment devices and networks, a cybersecurity-specific intelligence with a focus on ML-capabilities, which is especially the case when it comes to category known unknown cyber risk attacks. Maintaining the security requirements against the manifold of attack vectors to the cyber and physical components in smart manufacturing systems it is challenging to meet these comprehensive cybersecurity requirements [34, 35]. In order to achieve the desired security requirements, the cybersecurity solution has to consider holistic considerations with regard to the distributed access point's connectivity in smart manufacturing environments.

Another promising approach in ML based intrusion detection combines the outputs of classification methods as collective output and enhance classification performance. In this context, ensemble learning method enables to combine heterogeneous homogeneous multi-classifiers to obtain good classification results [36, 37]. The ensemble learning method use different ML methods to reduce variance and is robust to over-fitting [38]. In Table 6.6 the potential of two ML methods, to secure smart manufacturing environments, is given.

Table 6.6 Machine learning models for securing smart manufacturing environments

ML model	Working principle	Advantages	Disadvantages	Application(s)
Associated rule-based learning method	Investigates relationships between variables in training data sets	Simple algorithms that are easy to use	Execution time of algorithm is high due to complexity	Intrusion detection Cyber risk detection and protection
Ensemble learning method	Combines concepts of different classification methods	Robust algorithm that adapt better as single classifier-based methods	Execution time of algorithm is high due to complexity	Intrusion detection, anomaly detection, Malware detection

6.5.2 *Machine Learning Application to Anomaly Detection in Smart Manufacturing Environments*

Anomaly detection is a specific method examining data and detecting rare occurrences that seem suspicious because they are different from the expected pattern of behaviors, also named outliers. Anomaly detection is not a new approach. However, as data volume increases manual data tracking becomes impractical. The main models of anomaly detection techniques are: supervised, unsupervised, and semi-supervised machine learning models.

Supervised Machine Learning (SML) algorithms are trained by human intervention to generate SML datasets that contain examples of both, normal data pattern and anomalies. SML anomaly detection runs with unbalanced classes and common outliers. However, the trained data fed to the SML algorithm is pre-labeled and categorized, and therefore, SML can only categorize new data if they are already be known in a pre-learned example. This makes SML unsuitable for the detection of unknown outliers (anomalies).

The most common version of anomaly detection model uses Unsupervised Learning (USL), which is trained to fit to the normal behavior using an unlabeled test set of data based on the intrinsic characteristics of each value rather than any pre-determined example of normalcy. This enables USL algorithms to detect previously unseen outliers (anomalies).

Semi-supervised Machine Learning (SSML) provides a ML system with a labeled training data set devoid of anomalies, used to establish a model for normal behavior. The SSML function is that if the algorithm knows what a normal dataset looks like, it will be able to detect any anomalies that crop up.

In cybersecurity risks, three anomalies outliers' types are of interest:

- Global Outliers: Value that exists far outside of the data set it exists within. Thus, they are simple and easily identifiable as anomalous. They often refer to hacking or fraud incidents.

- Contextual Outliers: Data point significantly differs from the other data points in the same sample. This anomaly commonly is found in time-series data analysis as the context is usually temporal.
- Collective Outliers: Subset of data points that deviate significantly from the whole dataset, but individually appear not anomalous on either a global or contextual level.

In summary, this means that an outlier is a statistical observation markedly different in value from the others of the sample.

Unsupervised Machine Leaning (UML) algorithm used in anomaly detection detect so far unseen rare events without any prior knowledge about. Assume anomalies are rare and unknown to the user at training time, then anomaly detection in most cases comes down to the problem to model the normal data distribution and defining a measure in order to classify samples as anomalous or normal. Thus, the anomalous detection is to compare input data streams to the reference test data, to decide whether or not they both represent the same behavior, or one is anomalous, an outlier. For this purpose, a number of possible methods exist for measuring the similarity of the two data sequences. The most straight-forward is the equality function, which yields TRUE when both sequences match in every position in the data space, and FALSE otherwise, which indicate an anomalous behavior (outlier).

A UML method in anomaly detection is based on K-nearest Neighbors (k-NN) to identify global anomalies by finding the k-NN. In this case, the anomaly score of a data point be calculated in different ways. One option is using the distance to *k*th nearest neighbor [39, 40]. In this regard, data points that are sparse and further away compared to other data points have a greater distance to *k*th nearest neighbor, and thus are more likely being an outlier (anomalous behavior). Another possibility is using average distances to its k-nearest-neighbors. This approach has the benefit also considering the local density of the points [39, 41].

6.5.3 Deep Learning Application to Intrusion Detection in Smart Manufacturing Environments

Deep Learning (DL) is a method composed of multiple processing layers to describe representations of data with multiple levels of features. DL methods are applicable for cybersecurity applications in smart manufacturing environments. In DL different methods are applied like Deep Belief Network (DBN), Restricted Boltzmann Machine (RBM), Deep Learning Network (DLN) that have been applied to anomaly detection, intrusion detection, malware detection, and others

A Deep Belief Network (DBN) is a generative model, composed of multiple layers of stochastic and hidden variables [42, 43], with connections between the layers but not between variables within each layer. DBN based on an unsupervised fast greedy layer-by-layer training algorithm. Upper layers are supposed to represent more abstract concepts that explain the input observation x, and lower layers extract

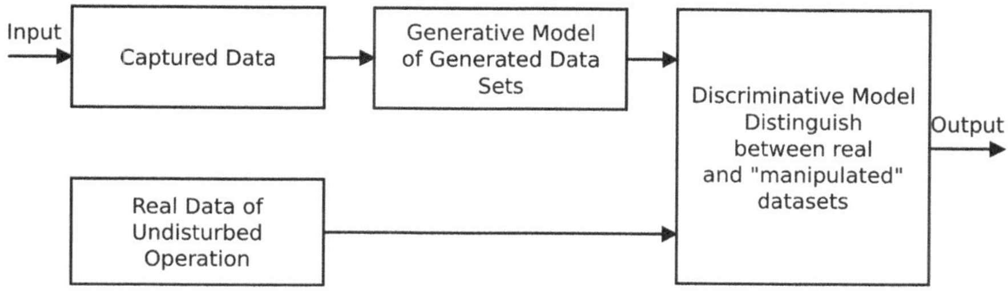

Fig. 6.3 Generative adversarial network

low level features from x. Ding et al. [43] applied DBN in a study to detect malware as opcode sequences by using unlabeled data to pretrain the DBN.

Restricted Boltzmann Machine (RBM) and DBN are interrelated, because composing and stacking a number of RBMs enables hidden layers to train data effectively through activations of an RBM for further training stage. This is an important issue to smart manufacturing environment intrusion detection, based on experiments showing the feasibility of a DL approach to smart manufacturing environments network traffic analysis.

Another type of Deep Learning Network (DLN) is the Generative Adversarial Network (GAN) that provide a way to learn deep representations without extensively annotated training data. The GAN block-diagram architecture is shown in Fig. 6.3, representing a framework for estimating generative models through an adversarial process in which simultaneously two models are trained, a generative model that captures the data set distribution, and a discriminative model that estimates the probability that a sample came from the training data set rather than the generative model. This model was developed by Goodfellow et al. [44, 45] in which the training procedure for the generative model is to maximize the probability of discriminative model making a mistake. The framework model corresponds to a minimax two-player game. In the space of arbitrary functions of the generative model and the discriminative model, a unique solution exists, with the generative model recovering the training data set distribution and the discriminative model to 0.5 everywhere [31]. In case the generative model and the discriminative model are defined by multilayer perceptron's, the entire system can be trained by Backpropagation (BP). As described in [44]. The algorithm back propagates derivatives through generative processes using the observation that

$$\min_{\sigma \to 0} \nabla_x E_{0 \sim N(0, \sigma_2 I)} f\,(x+) = \nabla_x f(x).$$

When training is finished, the generator is capable generating data that is not distinguishable [41].

Since Goodfellow's proposal of GAN [44], a number of GAN variants have been created. The major innovative points include model structure improvement, theoretical extension, novel applications, and others. An interesting book bridges the application areas of Deep Learning and Cybersecurity, providing Deep Learning tools and frameworks to allow users to quickly develop workable and advanced prototypes, which is referenced to in [46]. It also introduces into advances in the fields of intrusion detection, malicious code analysis, and forensic identification and shows how DL methods can be used to handle complex cybersecurity objectives, including incident detection, intrusion modeling, monitoring and analysis as well as defense against the various types of cyber threats. In [47] the performance of Deep Neural Network (DNN) for cybersecurity application is evaluated, which also includes the use cases of malware classification, incident detection, and fraud detection (FD).

6.6 Conclusion

The creation and use of AI-based methods like ML and DL posed new challenges for the different applications in smart environments like smart manufacturing environments. However, ensuring information security of smart environments is one of the most complex problems to be solved in regard to the wide range of defence possibilities against cybersecurity threat and cyber-attack incidents. Therefore, the chapter analyse and classify cybersecurity methods of AI based approaches in smart environment applications, which will become a game changer. Therefore, the main methodological concepts are described in detail and developments of ML and DL applications of cybersecurity in smart manufacturing environments is introduced, and new research directions are considered.

References

1. McCarthy, J., Minsky, M. L., Rochester, L., & Shannon, C. E. (2006). A proposal for the Dartmouth summer research project on artificial intelligence. *AI Magazine, 27*(4), 122.
2. Akhilesh, K. B., & Moller, D. P. F. (Eds.). (2020). *Smart technologie – Scope and applications* (pp. 1–16). Springer Nature Publication.
3. Carlini, N., Tramer, F., Wallace, E., Jagielski, M., Herbert-Voss, A., Lee, K., Roberts, A., Brown, T., Song, D., Erlingsson, U., Oprea, A., & Raffe, C. (2021). Extracting training data from large language models. In: 30th USENIX security symposium (pp. 2633–2650).
4. Brown, T. B., Mann, B., Ryder, N., Subbiah, M., Japlan, J., Dhariwal, P., Neelakantan, A., Shyam, P., Sastry, G., & Askeli, A. (2020). Language models are few-shot learners. arXiv preprint arXiv:2005.14165
5. Raffel, C., Shazeer, N., Roberts, A., Lee, K., Narang, S., Matena, M., Zhou, Y., Li, W., & Liu, P. J. (2020). Exploring the limits of transfer learning with a unified text-to-text transformer. *Journal of Machine Learning Research, 21*(140), 1–67.
6. Radford, A., Wu, J., Amodei, D., Amodei, D., Clark, J., Brubdage, M., & Sutsjkever, I. (2019). *Better language models and their implications*. OpenAI Blog.
7. Zhang, Y., Sun, S., Galley, M., Chen, Y. -C., Brocken, C., Gao, X., Gao, J., Liu, J., & Dolan, B. (2020). DialoGPT: Large-scale generative pre-training for conversational response generation. In ACL Demo Track.

8. Hoang, A., Bosselut, A., Celikyilmaz, A., & Choi, A. (2019). Efficient adaptation of pretrained trans-formers for abstractive summarization. arXiv preprint arXiv:1906.00138.
9. Liu, Y., Oti, M., Goyal, N., Du, J., Joshi, M., Chen, D., Levy, O., Lewis, M., Zettlemeyer, L., & Stoyanov, V. (2021). RoBERTa: A robustly optimized BERT pretraining approach. arXiv preprint arXiv:1907.11692
10. Gordon, S., & Ford, R. (2006). On the definition of classification of cybercrime. *Journal in Computer Virology, 2*(1), 13–20.
11. Xin, Y., Kong, L., Liu, Z., Chen, Y., Li, Y., Zhu, H., Gao, M., Hou, H., & Wang, C. (2018). Machine learning and deep learning: Methods for cybersecurity. *IEEE Access, 6*, 35365–35381.
12. Lecua, Y., Berigo, Y., & Hinton, G. (2015). Deep learning. *Nature, 521*(7553), 436–444.
13. Deng, L., & Yu, D. (2017). Deep learning: Methods and applications. *Foundations and Trends® in Signal Processing, 7*(3), 197–387.
14. Li, J.-H. (2018). Cyber security meets artificial intelligence: A survey. *Frontiers of Information Technology & Electronic Engineering, 19*(12), 1462–1474. https://doi.org/10.1631/FITEE.1800573
15. Möller, D. P. (2020). Cybersecurity in digital transformation. In *Guide to cybersecurity in digital transformation: Trends, methods, technologies, applications and best practices* (pp. 1–70). Springer Nature Switzerland.
16. Omar, S., Ngadi, A., & Jebur, H. (2013). Machine learning techniques for anomaly detection: An overview. *International Journal of Computer Applications, 79*(2), 33–41.
17. Murphy, K. P. (2012). *Machine learning – A probabilistic perspective*. MIT Press.
18. Good, I. J. (1950). *Probability and the weighting of evidence*. Charles Grin Publ.
19. An, A., & Cerone, N. (1999). Discretization of continuous attributes for learning classification rules. In *3rd Pacific Asia conference of methodologies for knowledge discovery and data mining* (pp. 509–514). Springer Berlin Heidelberg.
20. Biau, G., & Devroy, L. (2015). *Lectures on the nearest neighbor method*. Springer Publ.
21. Greenspan, M., & Godin, G. (2001). A nearest neighbor method for efficient ICP. In *Proceedings 3rd international conference on 3-D digital imaging and modeling* (pp. 161–168). https://doi.org/10.1109/IM.2001.924426
22. Carroll, J. D., Chaturvedi, A., & Green, P. E. (1994). K-means, and K-modes: Special cases of partitioning multiway data. In *Proceedings annual meeting of the classification society North America* (Vol. 11).
23. Khanum, M., Mahboob, T., Imitaz, W., Ghafoor, H. A., & Sehar, R. (2015). A survey on unsupervised machine learning algorithms for automation, classification, and maintenance. *International Journal of Computer Applications, 119*(13), 34–39.
24. Du, K. L., & Swamy, M. N. S. (2014). *Neural networks and statistical learning*. Springer Publ.
25. Xin, Y., Kong, L., Liu, Z., Chen, Y., Li, Y., Zhu, H., Gao, M., Hou, H., & Wang, C. (2018). Machine learning methods for cybersecurity. *IEEE Access, 6*, 35365–35381.
26. Ghahramani, Z. (2004). Unsupervised learning. In *Advanced lectures in machine learning* (pp. 72–112). Springer Berlin Heidelberg.
27. Arnold, A., Rebecchi, S., Chevallier, S., & Paugam-Moisy, H. (2011). An introduction to deep learning. In *Proceeding European symposium on artificial networks.*
28. Styliaras, G., Koukopoulos, D., & Lazarinis, F. (2011). *Handbook of research and technologies and cultural heritage: Applications and environments*. IGI Global.
29. Poslad, S. (2009). *Ubiquitous computing: Smart devices, environments and interactions*. Wiley.
30. Möller, D. P. F. (2016). *Guide to computing fundamentals in cyber-physical systems: Concepts, design methods, and applications*. Springer International.
31. Möller, D. P. F. (2023). *Guide to cybersecurity in digital transformation: Trends, methods, technologies*. Applications and Best Practices.
32. Ten, C., Hong, J., & Liu, C. (2011). Anomaly detection for cybersecurity of the substations. *IEEE Transactions of Smart Grids., 2*(4), 865–873.

33. Dempster, A., Laird, N., & Rubin, D. (1977). Maximum likelihood estimation from incomplete data via EM algorithm. *Journal Royal Statistical Society, Series B, 39*(1), 1–38.
34. Mavroeidis, V., & Bromander, S. (2017). Cyber threat intelligence model: An evaluation of taxonomies, sharing standards, and ontologies within cyber threat intelligence. In *Proceedings European intelligence and security informatics conference* (pp. 91–98).
35. Casey, T. (2015). *Underfstanding cyber threat motivations to improve defense*. Intel White Paper.
36. Wozniak, M., Grana, M., & Corchado, E. (2014). A survey of multiple classifier systems and hybrid systems. *Information Fusion, 16*, 3–17.
37. Domingos, P. (2012). A few useful things to know about machine learning. *Communications of the ACM, 55*(10), 78–87.
38. Zhang, Z., & Ma, Y. (2012). *Ensemble machine learning methods and applications*. Springer Publ.
39. Iivari, A. (2022). *Anomaly detection techniques for unsupervised machine learning*. Bachelor thesis. Umea University.
40. Ramaswamy, S., Rastogi, R., & Shim, K. (2000). Efficient algorithms for mining outliers from large data sets. In *Proceedings of the 2000 ACM SIGMOD international conference on management of data* (pp. 427–438).
41. Angiuuli, F., & Pizzuti, C. (2002). Fast outlier detection in high dimensional spaces. In *European conference on principles of data mining and knowledge discovery* (pp. 15–27). Springer Publ.
42. Imamverdiyev, Y. N., & Abdullayeva, F. (2020). Deep learning in cybersecurity: Challenges and approaches. *International Journal of Cyber Warfare and Terrorism, 10*(2), 82–205.
43. Ding, Y., Chen, S., & Xu, J. (2016). Application of deep belief networks for opcode based malware detection. In *International joint conference of neural networks* (pp. 3901–3908).
44. Goodfellow, I., Pouget-Abadie, J., Mirza, M., Xu, B., Warde-Farley, D., Ozair, S., Courville, A., & Benhio, Y. (2014). Generative adversarial nets. *Advances in Neural Information Processing Systems, 27*, 2672–2680.
45. Goodfellow, I., Bengio, Y., & Courvillee, A. (2016). *Deep learning*. MIT Press.
46. Alazab, M., & Tang, M. J. (2019). *Deep learning applications for cybersecurity*. Springer Publ.
47. Vinayakumar, R., Barathi Ganesh, H.B., Prabaharan, P., Anand Kumar, M., Soman, K. P. (2018) Deep-net: Deep neural network for cybersecurity use cases.

Part II
AI in Smart Healthcare and Sustainability

Chapter 7
Deep Learning-Based Multi-class Skin Disease Diagnosis Toward Sustainable Healthcare

Youssef M. Nassar, Marwan Makhlouf, Mohammed Hassan El-tohamy, Wafaa Abdelgawad, Esraa Darwish, Hady Abdalla, and Gehad Ismail Sayed

Abstract Timely and precise identification of skin conditions is essential for patient outcomes and efficient treatment. Conventional techniques frequently depend on dermatologists' subjective and time-consuming visual evaluation. This chapter introduces a deep learning-based multi-class skin disease diagnosis model. The proposed model supports Sustainable Development Goal 3 by improving access to accurate and efficient skin disease diagnoses, thereby enhancing overall health and timely treatment. Image classification and data preprocessing phases make up the suggested model. Data preprocessing incorporates image resizing for uniformity and data augmentation techniques to improve the ability of the model to manage variances in images. Image classification phase builds upon a pre-trained ResNet50 architecture, which efficiently extracts high-level features from input images. To enhance the model's discrimination between five specific skin disease categories, the classification stage leverages additional processing layers to refine the high-level features extracted by the ResNet50 network, ultimately enhancing the model's ability to discriminate between different disease categories. The evaluation of a comprehensive dataset demonstrates the model's effectiveness. The suggested ResNet model attains 90.74% accuracy, 87.78% precision, 86.84% sensitivity, and 87.04% F1-score. The findings illustrate how competitive the suggested model is since it performs better than the state-of-the-art model currently in use.

Keywords Skin disease diagnosis · Sustainable development goals · Deep-learning architecture · Multi-class classification

Y. M. Nassar · M. Makhlouf · M. H. El-tohamy · W. Abdelgawad · E. Darwish · H. Abdalla · G. I. Sayed (✉)
School of Computer Science, Canadian International College (CIC), Cairo, Egypt
e-mail: gehad_sayed@cic-cairo.com

N. E. M. Khalifa, M. H. N. Taha (eds.), *Empowering AI Applications in Smart Life and Environment*, https://doi.org/10.1007/978-3-031-78038-7_7

7.1 Introduction

Providing high-quality health care is one of the great challenges that humanity faces. The quality of health care impacts society and individuals in tremendous ways. As it directly affects the overall economics of society, according to research published in 2020, there is a direct proportion between spending on developing the healthcare system and the increase of the Gross Domestic Product (GDP) of the nation [1]. Recognizing the significant impact of health care, the United Nations (UN) put health care in the third rank in its Sustainable Development Goals (SDG) [2].

One of the major problems facing the world healthcare system is the long waiting times in hospitals. People may have to wait days or even months to visit a specialized health expert, as demonstrated by new research by the Organization for Economic Co-operation and Development (OECD) [3]. The study conducted in 2022 in various countries (Chile, Costa Rica, Estonia, Hungary, Italy, Lithuania, Netherlands, New Zealand, Portugal, Spain, and Sweden) revealed an average waiting time of 106 days for professional treatment [3]. In contrast, a study by the Fraser Institute in Canada [4] showed a median waiting time of 88.2 days between a General Practitioner (GP) referral and specialist consultation. The median waiting time from a specialist appointment to treatment averages 103.6 days [4]. The median wait from GP referral to treatment in Canada reaches an average of 191.4 days [4]. These extended waiting periods result in longer suffering for individuals dealing with illnesses. For instance, skin diseases, even the non-life-threatening types, can significantly impact patients' lives. According to the British Skin Foundation's 2021 report [5], 35% of people state that their skin conditions affect their mental health [5]. So, not receiving the right and immediate treatment could affect how individuals interact with society. For instance, individuals with untreated urticaria may avoid social events due to the unpredictability of flare-ups and visible hives. Those with lupus might withdraw from social interactions due to fatigue and the stigma associated with facial rashes. People with untreated skin cancer could experience social isolation because of changes in appearance or scars from lesions, while individuals with burn scars may face self-consciousness and reduced self-esteem, leading them to limit their social engagements. The extensive waiting times contribute to individuals seeking alternative and often unreliable sources of treatment, particularly in the case of skin diseases.

This reliance on cultural remedies has become more prominent in African and Middle Eastern countries like Egypt due to the need for more awareness. Also, there is a misleading conception that skin diseases are cosmetic diseases that don't pose a real threat to patients while in reality, this is not true. According to the World the World Health Organization (WHO), 0.04% of total deaths in Egypt were related to skin diseases [6]. Furthermore, it results in a limited number of individuals seeking regular consultations with dermatologists; even people who seek professional consultation still retain a percentage of incorrect diagnoses by dermatologists due to lack of experience in a certain case, according to a study published in 2022, 333 dermatological reports (years 2004–2018) were allocated to three five-year intervals [7]. 104 of those reports dealt with diagnostic error which is 31.2% [7]. To avoid all of these problems, Artificial Intelligence (AI) has been used to diagnose skin diseases. AI, throughout the years, has proved its efficiency and accuracy. So, this chapter proposes a solution by utilizing AI to solve the problem of long waits in hospitals to get information from a reliable source and the problem of accurately diagnosing skin diseases.

Early detection of skin diseases can reduce rates associated with certain conditions. For example, skin cancer has a higher survival rate when detected early and treated immediately [8]. Skin diseases that are not diagnosed and treated can lead to complications that may increase mortality risk. Serious infections or neglected skin problems, for example, might have effects on other organs. Early detection reduces the effect on healthcare systems, increasing their sustainability [9]. When diseases are identified early, they are often easier and less expensive to treat compared to advanced stages, when there may be a need for large actions [10, 11]. Preventive techniques, like routine skin checkups, can identify problems early and stop them from getting worse and require complex and expensive treatments. This is an example of a sustainable healthcare practice.

Skin disease detection and treatment might be completely transformed by machine learning. Big data analysis, pattern recognition, and very accurate prediction are all capabilities of machine learning algorithms [12]. In the field of dermatology, ML can be used to analyze images of skin conditions and provide accurate diagnoses. Compared to conventional techniques, machine learning-powered diagnostic tools provide several benefits, such as increased efficiency, improved accuracy, and improved patient experience. One branch of AI called deep learning (DL) is very useful for jobs involving image processing. Convolutional neural networks (CNN) are used by DL algorithms to examine images and find patterns [13]. Skin condition images may be analyzed using DL algorithms, which can be taught to deliver precise diagnoses in dermatology. DL has several advantages over traditional machine learning methods, including automated feature extraction, improved accuracy, and increased efficiency.

In this chapter, a deep learning-based multi-class skin disease detection model is developed. The suggested model consists of pre-processing and classification phases. To enhance the model's capacity to handle image fluctuations, data preprocessing applies image scaling and data augmentation techniques. The classification step is based on a pre-trained ResNet50 architecture. The chapter's primary contribution can be summed up as follows:

1. A new model for multi-class skin disease diagnosis is proposed.
2. The significance of each component of the proposed model is evaluated.
3. Several evaluation metrics are employed.

The rest of the chapter is organized as follows: A review of earlier research on the classification of skin conditions is provided in Sect. 7.2. An overview of the selected dataset can be found in Sect. 7.3. The suggested multi-class kin disease diagnostic model is shown in Sect. 7.4. The experimental findings and a discussion of them are presented in Sect. 7.5. An overview of the major findings and suggestions for further research are provided in Sect. 7.6.

7.2 Literature Survey

The section will identify important obstacles and possibilities in the identification of skin diseases. It shows areas that may benefit from more study and where current methods or technology may not work effectively. By collecting current information, it may gain important insights into the possibilities and difficulties in the skin disease identification's field.

A model for skin disease diagnosis is proposed in [14]. The authors are mainly focused on hive skin disease. The authors utilized different YOLO deep learning architectures. The authors evaluated their model with 353 images. According to the findings, the suggested model had a 62.4% overall F1-score, 68.1% accuracy, and 57.8% recall. CNN model built on the ResNet-50 was presented by the authors in [15]. Their analysis produced impressive findings, with the suggested model having an overall accuracy of 91.4% and a precision of 89.8%. The assessment was carried out on 24,736 images, comprising 18,647 images of patients with rosacea and 6089 images of patients with other skin conditions. The authors in [16] introduced an automated skin disease diagnosis model with a primary focus on rosacea.They evaluated 41 face image datasets using several deep learning architectures, such as ResNet-v2, Inception, and ResNet-101, which were all adapted to extract rosacea traits from facial images. The efficacy of the model yielded weighted average Dice coefficients of 89.8% and 87.8% with ResNet-v2, and ResNet-101, respectively.

In [17], the authors proposed a model for skin disease diagnosis. The authors are mainly focused on hive skin disease. The authors utilized different YOLO deep-learning architectures. The authors evaluated their model with 353 images. According to the findings, the suggested model had a 62.4% overall F1-score, 68.1% accuracy, and 57.8% recall. The authors introduced a diagnostic model for automatically evaluating the severity of skin diseases, with a specific emphasis on eczema, which comprises four distinct levels [18]. Employing a model, the authors augmented the existing Eczemanet1 model to develop Eczemanet2, a deep-learning architecture tailored for this purpose. A thorough analysis of the suggested model was carried out with a dataset of 271 images. The findings underscored the model's effectiveness, revealing an overall F1-score and precision of 60%. In [19], the authors explored the field of automated skin disease diagnosis with a focus on multiple skin disease detection in a clinical setting. With Google's EfficientNet-b4 with pre-trained weights on ImageNet serving as the foundation for deep learning architectures, their model underwent extensive testing using a sizable dataset made up of 13,603 images representing 14 distinct disease types. The model produced results with an overall accuracy of 94.8%, a sensitivity of 93.4%, and a specificity of 95.0%. Focusing on acne image analysis, the authors proposed a novel perspective by employing CNN-Recurrent Neural Networks (RNN) [20].

Simultaneously addressing image grading and lesion counting, their model attains a test accuracy of 84% on 1457 images across 4 classes. The precision value is reported as 84.37%.

7.3 Dataset Description

This adopted skin disease dataset provides images and associated for different skin diseases, as shown in Fig. 7.1. These diseases are urticaria, cancer, burns, lupus, and normal skin. The Demnet database, Kaggle, the Google search engine, and other reliable sources have all been thoughtfully selected to provide a range of data from many sources in the dataset. As depicted in Fig. 7.1, the majority of samples fall within the normal and burn classes, highlighting a notable class imbalance issue.

Figure 7.2 provides visual representations of samples from the adopted dataset, on skin disease images sourced from different sources. Fig. 7.2a shows examples of lupus images. There is a lack of standardized imaging protocols for capturing lupus-specific skin manifestations. Variations in imaging techniques, such as lighting, camera settings, and image resolution. Figure 7.2b presents samples of Urticaria images. The limited features of urticaria make it challenging to capture images at the exact moment of occurrence, as the lesions may have resolved or changed by the time the image is taken. This can result in a lack of representative images of active urticaria. Figure 7.2c displays samples of cancer images. Skin cancer can manifest in various forms, textures, colors, and sizes. Lesions can differ significantly across individuals, making it challenging to create a strong classification model capable

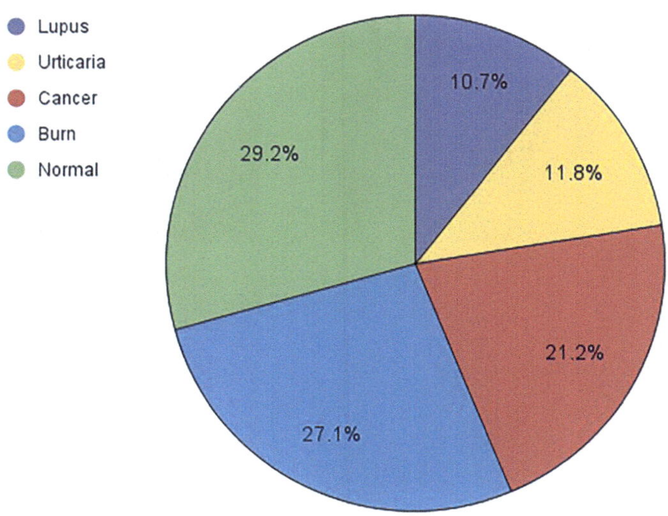

Fig. 7.1 The adopted dataset's class distribution

(a)
(b)
(c)
(d)
(e)

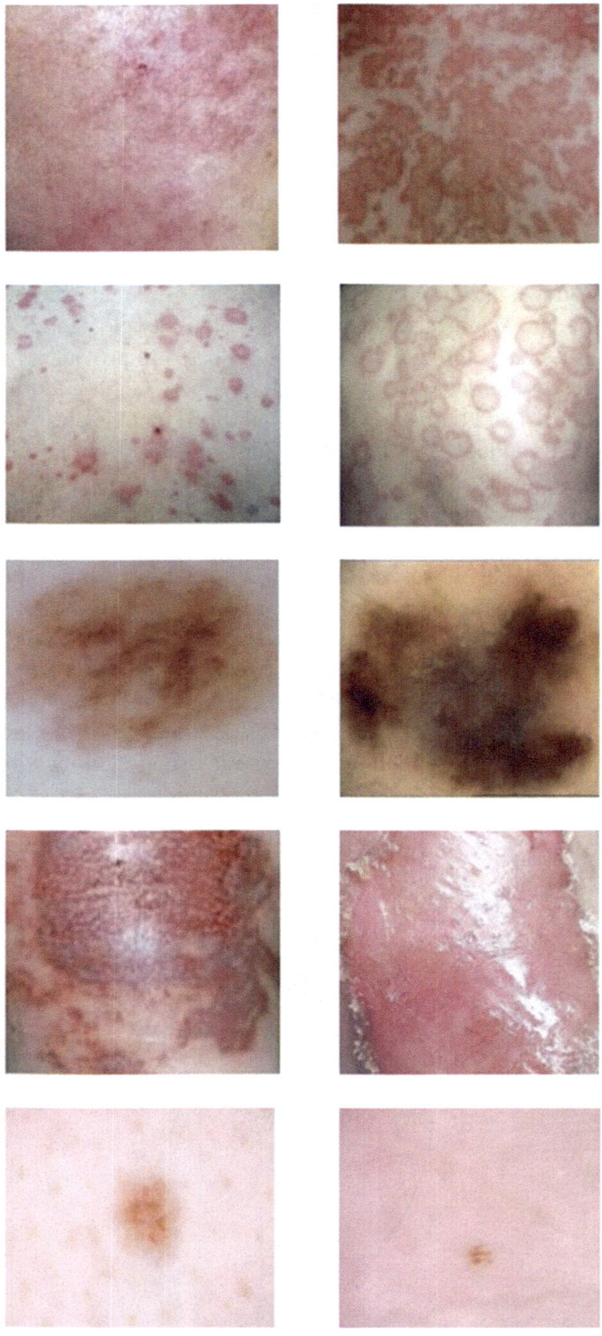

Fig. 7.2 Samples of the adopted dataset; (**a**) Lupes images; (**b**) Urticaria images, (**c**) Cancer images; (**d**) Burn images; and (**e**) Normal images

of precisely identifying various forms of skin conditions. Figure 7.2d showcases examples of burn images. Some images may be blurry, heavily pixelated, or taken under challenging circumstances, making it difficult to extract meaningful features for classification and variability in burn types and degrees. Figure 7.2e The normal skin class serves as a reference or baseline category, representing healthy skin. Including normal skin images in the dataset allows the classification model to learn the characteristics and patterns of healthy skin, enabling it to differentiate between normal and abnormal conditions. From this figure, it can be observed the complexity of skin lesions present in the collected dataset.

7.4 The Proposed Deep Learning-Based Multi-class Skin Disease Diagnosis Model

In order to multi-classify skin disorders, this chapter provides a deep learning based model. It utilizes a pre-trained ResNet50 model, which is modified by freezing the weights in the ResNet50 layers and adding additional layers for classification. The model takes as input RGB images of size $224 \times 224 \times 3$ [21]. High-level features are extracted from the input images using the pre-trained ResNet50 model [22]. These features are then passed through a global average pooling layer to produce a fixed-length feature vector. The feature vector is supplied into a fully connected dense layer with 256 units with a ReLU activation function. A fully connected dense layer with 5 units and a softmax activation function is the final layer of the model, which outputs a probability distribution over the five categories of skin disorders. The model is trained with an Adam optimizer and a categorical cross-entropy loss function. To reduce the loss function, the model is trained by feeding it labeled images and adjusting its weights. The model is assessed on a validation set using measures such as F1-score and accuracy. A sample of images from a collected dataset was used to classify skin lesions. The ideal hyperparameters for the model were determined by carefully evaluating various combinations of learning rates, such as 0.001, 0.01, and 0.1, and batch sizes, such as 16, 32, and 64. These hyperparameters can significantly impact the proposed multi-class skin disease diagnosis model [10, 11]. This iterative procedure entailed training and assessing the model with various hyperparameter combinations before deciding on the configuration that produced the best results. To enhance the training process, the proposed model incorporates data augmentation. The data augmentation parameters are carefully chosen to ensure that the transformed images are still realistic and representative of the original dataset [23]. The rotation range is set to 6 degrees to prevent the images from becoming distorted or unrecognizable. The width and height shift ranges are set to 13.4% of the image width and height, respectively, to simulate small variations in the camera position. The shear range is configured to 0.1 radians to avoid introducing unrealistic distortions. The zoom range is configured to [0.8, 1.2] to simulate variations in the distance between the camera and the subject. The horizontal and vertical flip transformations are applied to help the model learn features that are invariant to the orientation of the image. The fill mode is set to 'reflect' to prevent the introduction of artifacts at the edges of the transformed images.

Figure 7.3 illustrates a comprehensive flow detailing the various stages involved in training a deep learning model. The process begins with data collection, where a dataset of skin images is gathered for analysis. The collected data then undergoes preprocessing, which involves cleaning, normalizing, and preparing the data for further processing. Following data preprocessing, the diagram showcases the steps of data augmentation. This process involves generating additional training samples by applying transformations or modifications to the existing data. Data augmentation helps increase the diversity and variability of the dataset. This increases the model's capacity to generalize and perform well on previously unknown data. Moving forward, the diagram depicts the training phase, where the deep learning model is trained through the preprocessed and augmented data. A number of layers make up the model, including an input layer to receive the skin images, hidden layers where the model learns intricate patterns and features, and an output layer that provides the classification results. The training process can be divided into different stages, as illustrated in the diagram. Initially, the model undergoes an initial training phase to learn the basic patterns and features present in the skin images. Subsequently, the model goes through a fine-tuning stage where it refines its learned parameters and adapts to specific characteristics of the skin image dataset.

Finally, the figure depicts the testing and validation phases. Utilizing a different set of skin images not utilized during training, the trained model is assessed. The model's efficacy, precision, and capacity to accurately categorize the skin pictures are evaluated with the aid of this assessment. The output of the model classification is divided into three categories: normal, lupus, or cancer, providing valuable insights into the skin condition.

Figure 7.4 illustrates the workflow of a deep-learning model for skin disease classification. The figure consists of interconnected boxes that depict the different stages of the process. Starting with the "Input Data" box, it suggests that the model takes in a dataset or input images for analysis. The data then flows into the "ResNet50 Feature Extraction" box, indicating that a ResNet50 model, a popular deep learning architecture, is employed to extract relevant features from the input images. These extracted features are then passed on to the "Classification" box, where a classification algorithm is applied to assign labels or classes to the images according to the characteristics that were retrieved. The process's sequential nature is highlighted by the diagram, with arrows indicating the flow of information from one stage to another. Finally, the "Predicted Labels" box represents the output of the classification process, showing the predicted classes assigned to the input images by the model. a visual representation of the deep learning workflow for skin disease classification, highlighting the key steps involved in the analysis and classification of input images.

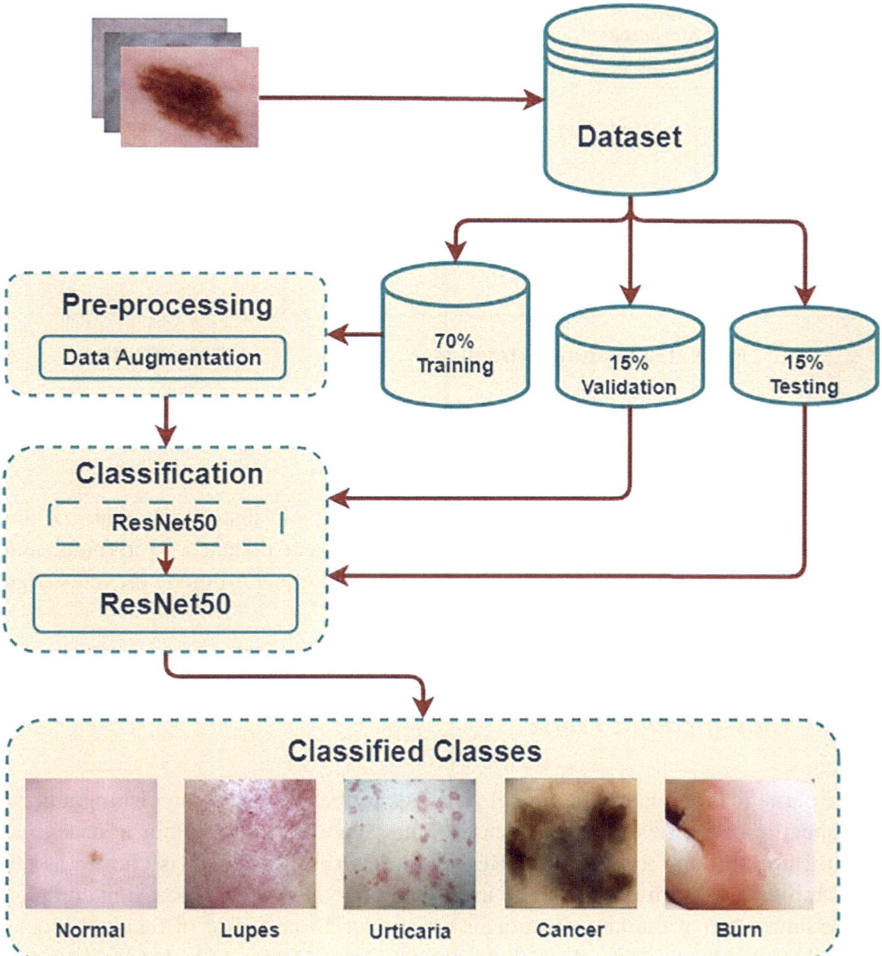

Fig. 7.3 The suggested multi-class skin disease diagnosis model's block diagram

7.4.1 Data Preprocessing Phase

Image resizing and data augmentation are two important tasks carried out during the preprocessing phase. Firstly, image resizing ensures uniformity in dimensions, typically 224 × 224 pixels, to meet the model's input requirements. Secondly, data augmentation enriches the dataset by applying various transformations while ensuring the authenticity and representative of the augmented images.

Carefully selected parameters govern these transformations to maintain realism and fidelity to the original dataset. Specifically, a rotation range of 6 degrees prevents distortion, while width and height shifts of 13.4% simulate minor changes in camera

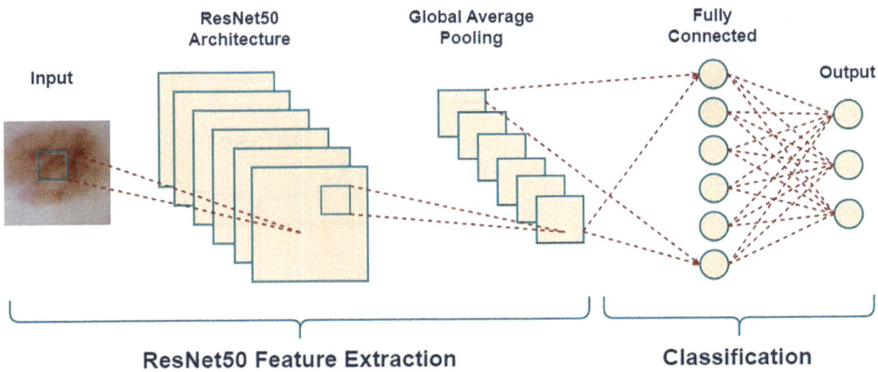

Fig. 7.4 The Workflow of the utilized deep learning model for multi-class skin disease classification

position. A shear range of 0.1 radians avoids unrealistic distortions, and a zoom range of [0.8, 1.2] mimics changes in camera-subject distance. Horizontal and vertical flips aid in invariant feature learning, while a reflect fill mode prevents edge artifacts.

7.4.2 Classification Phase

In the classification phase, the model proceeds to the task of distinguishing among five specific categories of skin diseases. This stage operates within a structured architecture utilizing a pre-trained ResNet50 network. ResNet50 is chosen as the core architecture in this study due to its proven effectiveness in processing complex image data. One of the key advantages of ResNet-50 is its use of residual blocks This allows for the training of much deeper networks, leading to better performance in learning complex features. ResNet50's design, featuring residual connections, enables the training of deep neural networks without suffering from the vanishing gradient problem that can hinder deeper architectures like VGG [24]. While VGG architectures are straightforward and widely used, their absence of residual connections may limit their ability to efficiently learn intricate features from medical images, potentially impacting diagnostic accuracy in dermatological applications [25]. Additionally, ResNet50 has fewer parameters than very deep models like VGG, making it less prone to overfitting and requiring less computational power and memory. Inception models, with their multiple filter sizes and parallel paths within the same layer, introduce a lot of complexity, making implementation and tuning more challenging. EfficientNet, known for its scalable model structure through compound scaling, offers compelling advantages in terms of performance optimization across various computational resources [26]. However, its complexity and the extensive tuning required for different datasets and tasks can present practical challenges in the context of medical image analysis, where robustness and interpretability are crucial [27].

Additional layers are integrated into the architecture to complement the ResNet50 model for skin disease classification. These added layers refine the features extracted by the ResNet50 network, enhancing the model's discriminatory abilities. Upon receiving input images, the pre-trained ResNet50 efficiently extracts high-level features relevant to skin diseases. These features undergo further processing stages, resulting in a refined representation suitable for classification. Following this processing, the refined features are formatted for categorical discrimination. A fully connected dense layer with 256 units, utilizing a ReLU activation function, further refines the feature vector, extracting subtle distinctions essential for classification. Lastly, the model's classification process is executed through a final layer comprising five units, each corresponding to one of the five distinct skin disease classes. This layer creates a probability distribution across the classes using a softmax activation function, which shows how likely it is for an input image to fall into each category.

7.5 Results and Discussion

The effectiveness of the model in classifying various skin conditions was assessed by a number of tests carried out. The proposed deep-learning-based multi-class skin disease diagnosis model is implemented in the Python programming language with Google Colab. The performance of the suggested deep-learning-based multi-class skin disease diagnostic model is evaluated using a number of assessment indicators. The f1-score, accuracy, precision, and sensitivity are these assessment measures. The mathematical definitions of each are shown in the following equations.

$$Accuracy = \frac{TN + TP}{FP + TP + FN + TN} \tag{7.1}$$

$$Precision = \frac{TP}{FP + TP} \tag{7.2}$$

$$Sensitivity\ (Recall) = \frac{TP}{FN + TP} \tag{7.3}$$

$$F1 - Score = \frac{TP}{TP + \frac{1}{2}(FP + FN)} \tag{7.4}$$

Table 7.1 The proposed model's performance evaluation before each component was applied

	Accuracy (%)	F1-Score (%)	Sensitivity (%)	Precision (%)
Before (augmentation)	64.81	82.98	55.69	49.34
After (augmentation)	90.74	87.04	68.84	87.78

Table 7.2 The F1-score values of different combinations of batch size and learning rate

Batch size	Learning rate	F1-score
32	0.001	0.8704
16	0.001	0.8534
64	0.01	0.8281
64	0.001	0.8218
32	0.01	0.7564
32	0.1	0.7513
16	0.01	0.7109
64	0.1	0.4449
16	0.1	0.3630

where *FP* denotes the false positive samples, *FN* denotes the false negative samples, *TP* denotes the true positive samples, and *TN* denotes the true negative samples.

The performance of the suggested model is shown in Table 7.1 both before and after augmentation was applied. The model's performance is demonstrated in the table by the accuracy, F1-score, sensitivity, and precision measurements. Before the application of augmentation, the model achieved an accuracy of 64.81%. This indicates that the initial model correctly predicts around 64.81% of the instances in the dataset. Additionally, the F1-score, which measures the balance between precision and recall, is at 82.98%. This score indicates that the model minimizes false positives and false negatives while accurately detecting positive samples. The model's sensitivity, which measures how well it can identify positive cases, is 55.69%. Lastly, the precision, indicating the model's ability to provide accurate positive predictions, is at 49.34%. After the application of augmentation, the model's performance significantly improved. The accuracy rises to 90.74%, indicating a substantial increase in correct predictions. The F1-score improves to 87.04%, demonstrating an improved recall and accuracy ratio. The sensitivity shows a notable improvement, reaching 68.84%, indicating an enhanced ability to accurately identify positive instances. The precision also improves significantly to 87.78%, reflecting a reduction in false positives.

Table 7.2 compares the F1-score values for different combinations of batch size and learning rate. The F1-scores range from 0.3630 to 0.8704, depending on the specific batch size and learning rate used. Notably, a batch size of 32 with a learning rate of 0.001 achieves the highest F1-score of 0.8704, while a batch size of 64 with a learning rate of 0.1 yields the lowest F1-score of 0.3630. These results indicate that the choice of batch size and learning rate can significantly impact the model's performance in skin disease classification. The overall results and discussion reveal that the proposed ResNet model performs well in skin disease classification, especially in light of other deep learning architectures such as Inception, DensNet, and

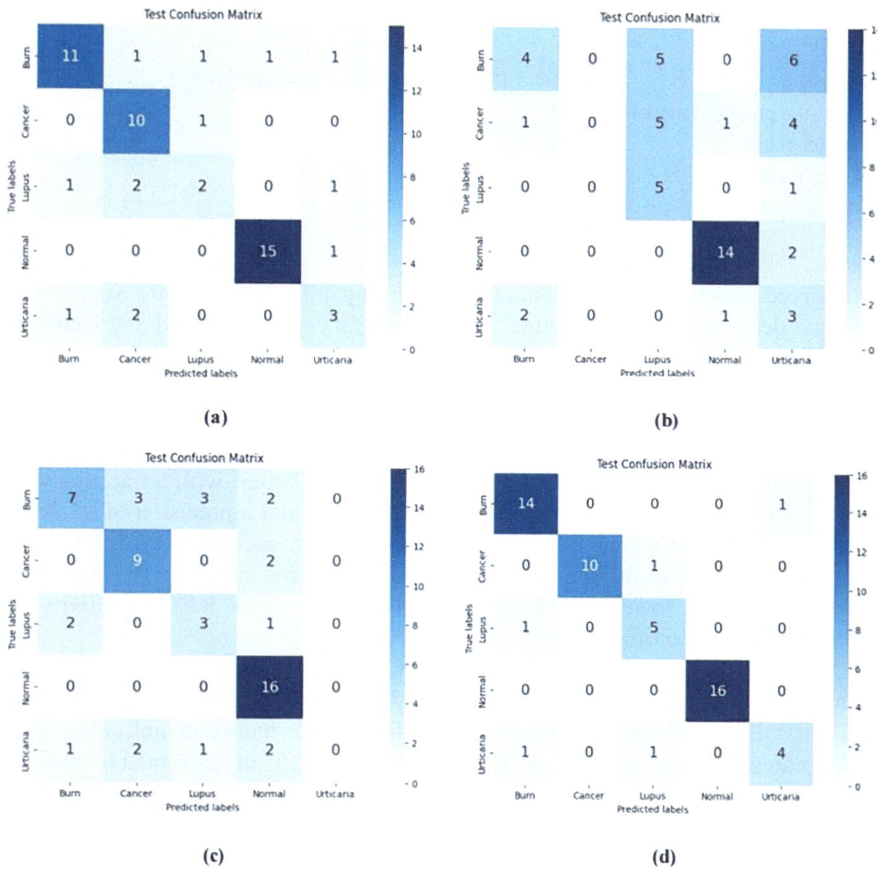

Fig. 7.5 The confusion matrix for different deep learning architecture (**a**) DensNet, (**b**) Xception, (**c**) Inception, (**d**) ResNet50

Xception. Moreover, it turns out that enhancing the model's sensitivity, precision, F1-score, and accuracy requires data augmentation. In addition, the decision of batch size and learning rate affects the model's performance. These results offer useful data for enhancing the deep learning model's effectiveness in tasks involving the categorization of skin diseases.

Figure 7.5 compares the confusion metrics for the proposed model based on ResNet50 with three other deep-learning architectures on the collected dataset. These architectures are Inception, Xception, and DenseNet. The suggested multi-class skin disease classification model's performance is visually represented by the confusion matrix. It offers insightful information on how well the model can categorize various skin disease types. The matrix is divided into different quadrants, with each quadrant representing specific classification outcomes. As can

Table 7.3 Comparison of accuracy, sensitivity, precision, and f1-score with various deep learning architectures

	Accuracy (%)	F1-score (%)	Sensitivity (%)	Precision (%)
ResNet (the proposed model)	90.74	87.04	86.84	87.78
Inception model	64.81	51.24	55.69	49.34
DensNet model	75.92	67.84	68.28	69
Xception model	48.14	87	49.5	39.34

be observed, ResNet50 is the optimal deep-learning architecture, while Xception is the worst deep-learning architecture. Additionally, it can be observed that DensNet is in second place.

Table 7.3 compares the accuracy, F1-score, sensitivity, and precision of different deep learning architectures. The proposed ResNet model achieves an accuracy of 90.74%, an F1-score of 87.04%, a sensitivity of 86.84%, and a precision of 87.78%. In comparison, the Inception model performs slightly better, with an accuracy of 94.17%, F1-score of 93.93%, a sensitivity of 93.76%, and a precision of 94.28%. The DensNet model shows lower performance with an accuracy of 75.92%, F1-score of 67.84% a sensitivity of 68.28%, and a precision of 69%. The Xception model exhibits the lowest accuracy of 48.14%, F1-score of 87%, sensitivity of 49.5%, and precision of 39.34%.

The receiver operating characteristic (ROC) of the suggested multi-class skin disease classification model based on deep learning is shown in Fig. 7.6. The ROC curve is a graphical depiction of a classifier's performance in multi-class skin disease categorization. In this case, the classifier is specifically designed to classify five different classes: burn, cancer, lupus, urticaria, and normal. Provided states that the ROC curve for each class has a different Area Under the Curve (AUC) value. The classifier's overall performance is assessed using the AUC metric. Better performance is indicated by a higher value, which goes from 0 to 1. The ROC curve and the corresponding AUC values demonstrate the classifier's effectiveness in the multi-class classification of skin diseases.

The performance of the suggested model and the state-of-the-art models are compared in Table 7.4. Each table entry represents a state-of-the-art study and includes details on the number of classes, the public or private status of the dataset used, and the balance or imbalance of the dataset, and performance metrics such as F1-score, accuracy, specificity, recall, and precision. The performance metrics provide insights into the accuracy and effectiveness of the models proposed in each study. Metrics like recall, specificity, accuracy, precision, and F1-score are frequently employed to assess how well disease detection models work. This table shows that the suggested multi-class model has great competitiveness.

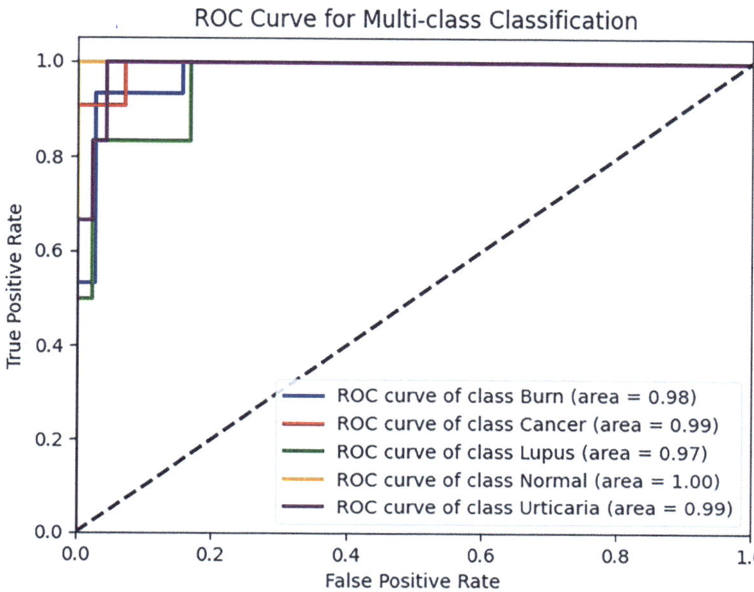

Fig. 7.6 The suggested deep-learning-based multi-class skin disease diagnosis model's ROC curve

7.6 Conclusion

This chapter explored the potential of deep learning for categorizing four different skin diseases using a ResNet50 architecture. These skin diseases are urticaria, cancer, burns, lupus, and normal skin. The results revealed that the proposed model based on the utilized ResNet50 achieved an accuracy of 90.74%, along with a precision of 87.78%, sensitivity of 86.84%, and F1-score of 87.04%. Furthermore, the outcomes showed that when compared to DenseNet, Inception, and Xception, the suggested model based on ResNet50 produced better classification results. Furthermore, the outcomes showed that the suggested model before augmentation, the model's accuracy was only 64.81%, demonstrating the crucial role of data augmentation in enhancing the model's ability to handle image variations and achieve robust classification. In addition, the outcomes demonstrated how competitive the suggested model is when compared to the state-of-the-art models.

Future work can explore further refinements to the model and investigate its generalizability across diverse clinical settings. By addressing these considerations, deep learning architecture models have the potential to revolutionize skin disease diagnosis, offering a more objective, efficient, and accessible solution for healthcare professionals.

Table 7.4 The suggested model compared to the state-of-art models

Reference	Model	Balanced or not	No. of classes	Public or private	Accuracy	Recall	Precision	F1-score
Bassel et al. [28]	CNN/SVM	Not balanced	–	Private	0.818	0.816	–	0.787
Suha and Sanam [29]	CNN/SVM/CNN WITHVGG16	Not balanced	3	Private	0.958	0.960	0.960	0.950
Zhang and Ma [30]	VGG16, R-FCN, ResNet50, (localization – YOLOv5)	Not balanced	3	Public	0.739	–	–	–
Quattrini et al. [31]	VGG-19(binary) – DenseNet121(multi-class)	Not balanced	5	Public	0.670	0.631	0.598	0.608
Huynh et al. [32]	Faster R-CNN with the ResNet50	Not balanced	5	Private	0.850	0.756	0.732	0.740
Mac Carthy et al. [17]	Different versions of yoloo	Not balanced	2	Private	–	0.578	0.681	0.624
Sazzadul Islam Prottasha et al. [14]	Inception ResNet-v2	Balanced	2	Public	0.935	0.950	0.955	
Attar et al. [18]	EczemaNet2 (ROI detection)	Balanced	4	Private	–	–	0.600	0.600
	The proposed model (ResNet50)	Not balanced	5	Private	0.907	0.868	0.877	0.870

References

1. Raghupathi, V., & Raghupathi, W. (2020). Healthcare expenditure and economic performance: Insights from the United States data. *Frontiers in Public Health, 8*, 156. https://doi.org/10.3389/fpubh.2020.00156
2. Fong, B. Y. (2022). Impacts of sustainable development goal 3 and health systems. In *Systems thinking and sustainable healthcare delivery* (pp. 18–33). Routledge.
3. Siciliani, L. (2023). A review of policies to reduce waiting times for health services across OECD countries: Waiting times for health services. *Nordic Journal of Health Economics, 6*(1), 162–181. https://doi.org/10.5617/njhe.10214
4. Moir, M., & Barua, B. (2022). *Waiting your turn: Wait times for health care in Canada, 2022 report*. Fraser Institute.
5. Harris, G. (2022). Optimising the management of skin conditions: Physiological and psychological approaches. *British Journal of Healthcare Management, 28*(3), 78–81. https://doi.org/10.12968/bjhc.2022.0027
6. World Health Organization (2024) Skin diseases. WHO mortality database. Retrieved January 5, 2024, from https://platform.who.int/mortality/themes/theme-details/topics/topic-details/MDB/skin-diseases#:~:text=Skin%20diseases%20include%20dermatitis%20and,as%20pressure%20ulcer%20or%20bedsores
7. Lehmann, L., Appelbaum, S., Ostermann, T., Weber, B., & Hofmann, S. C. (2022). Medical error analysis in dermatology according to the reports of the North Rhine medical association from 2004 to 2018. *Journal of the German Society of Dermatology, 20*(12), 1603–1611. https://doi.org/10.1111/ddg.14899
8. Aijaz, S. F., et al. (2022). Deep learning application for effective classification of different types of psoriasis. *Journal of Healthcare Engineering, 2022*, 7541583. https://doi.org/10.1155/2022/7541583
9. Shetty, B., et al. (2022). Skin lesion classification of dermoscopic images using machine learning and convolutional neural network. *Scientific Reports, 12*(1), 18134. https://doi.org/10.1038/s41598-022-22644-9
10. Sayed, G. I., et al. (2024a). Intelligent and sustainable waste classification model based on multi-objective beluga whale optimization and deep learning. *Environmental Science and Pollution Research, 31*, 31492–31510. https://doi.org/10.1007/s11356-024-33233-w
11. Sayed, G. I., Khoriba, G., & Haggag, M. H. (2024b). The novel multi-swarm coyote optimization algorithm for automatic skin lesion segmentation. *Evolutionary Intelligence, 17*(2), 679–711. https://doi.org/10.1007/s12065-020-00450-4
12. Abbas, M., et al. (2022). Skin diseases diagnosis system based on machine learning. *Journal of Computing & Biomedical Informatics, 4*(01), 37–53. https://doi.org/10.1016/j.health.2022.100122
13. Sayed, G. I., Soliman, M. M., & Hassanien, A. E. (2021). A novel melanoma prediction model for imbalanced data using optimized SqueezeNet by bald eagle search optimization. *Computers in Biology and Medicine, 136*, 104712. https://doi.org/10.1016/j.compbiomed.2021.104712
14. Sazzadul Islam Prottasha, M., Mahjabin Farin, S., Bulbul Ahmed, M., Zihadur Rahman, M., Kabir Hossain, A. B. M., & Shamim Kaiser, M. (2023). Deep learning-based skin disease detection using convolutional neural networks (CNN). In M. S. Hossain, S. P. Majumder, N. Siddique, & M. S. Hossain (Eds.), *The fourth industrial revolution and beyond* (Vol. 980, pp. 551–564). Springer. https://doi.org/10.1007/978-981-19-8032-9_39
15. Zhao, Z., et al. (2021). A novel convolutional neural network for the diagnosis and classification of rosacea: Usability study. *JMIR Medical Informatics, 9*(3), e23415. https://doi.org/10.2196/23415
16. Binol, H., et al. (2020). Ros-NET: A deep convolutional neural network for automatic identification of rosacea lesions. *Skin Research and Technology, 26*(3), 413–421. https://doi.org/10.1111/srt.12817

17. Mac Carthy, T., et al. (2023). Automatic Urticaria activity score (AUAS): Deep learning-based automatic hive counting for Urticaria severity assessment. *JID Innovations, 4*(1), 100218. https://doi.org/10.1016/j.xjidi.2023.100218
18. Attar, R., et al. (2023). Reliable detection of eczema areas for fully automated assessment of eczema severity from digital camera images. *JID Innovations, 3*(5), 100213. https://doi.org/10.1016/j.xjidi.2023.100213
19. Zhu, C. Y., et al. (2021). A deep learning based framework for diagnosing multiple skin diseases in a clinical environment. *Frontiers in Medicine, 8*, 626369. https://doi.org/10.3389/fmed.2021.626369
20. Wu, X., et al. (2019). Joint acne image grading and counting via label distribution learning. In *Proceedings of the IEEE/CVF international conference on computer vision* (pp. 10642–10651). https://doi.org/10.1109/ICCV.2019.01074
21. Omer, Z. T., & Abbas, A. H. (2022). Image anomalies detection using transfer learning of ResNet-50 convolutional neural network. *Indonesian Journal of Electrical Engineering and Computer Science, 27*(1), 198–205. https://doi.org/10.11591/ijeecs.v27.i1.pp198-205
22. Huang, Z., et al. (2022). Fusion of MRI images and PET images based on ResNet50. In *2022 IEEE 5th advanced information management, communicates, electronic and automation control conference (IMCEC)* (Vol. 5, pp. 904–910). IEEE. https://doi.org/10.1109/IMCEC55388.2022.10019936
23. AdlinLayola, J. A., & MuraliBhaskharan, V. (2021). Data set preparation using the method of data augmentation for classification of skin diseases. In *Smart intelligent computing and communication technology* (pp. 234–240). IOS Press. https://doi.org/10.3233/APC210043
24. He, K., et al. (2016). Deep residual learning for image recognition. In *Proceedings of the IEEE conference on computer vision and pattern recognition* (pp. 770–778).
25. Shah, S. R., et al. (2023). Comparing inception V3, VGG 16, VGG 19, CNN, and ResNet 50: A case study on early detection of a rice disease. *Agronomy, 13*(6), 1633. https://doi.org/10.3390/agronomy13061633
26. Ali, N. H., et al. (2023). Brain cone beam computed tomography image analysis using ResNet50 for collateral circulation classification. *International Journal of Electrical & Computer Engineering, 13*(5), 5843. https://doi.org/10.11591/ijece.v13i5.pp5843-5852
27. Karki, M. V., & Inamdar, S. (2022). Skin cancer classification using deep networks. In *2022 4th international conference on circuits, control, communication and computing (I4C)* (pp. 1–5). IEEE. https://doi.org/10.1109/I4C57141.2022.10057868
28. Bassel, A., et al. (2022). Automatic malignant and benign skin cancer classification using a hybrid deep learning approach. *Diagnostics, 12*(10), 2472. https://doi.org/10.3390/diagnostics12102472
29. Suha, S. A., & Sanam, T. F. (2022). A deep convolutional neural network-based approach for detecting burn severity from skin burn images. *Machine Learning with Applications, 9*, 100371. https://doi.org/10.1016/j.mlwa.2022.100371
30. Zhang, H., & Ma, T. (2022). Acne detection by ensemble neural networks. *Sensors, 22*(18), 6828. https://doi.org/10.3390/s22186828
31. Quattrini, A., et al. (2022). A deep learning-based facial acne classification system. In *Clinical, cosmetic and investigational dermatology* (Vol. 15, pp. 851–857). https://doi.org/10.2147/CCID.S360450
32. Huynh, Q. T., et al. (2022). Automatic acne object detection and acne severity grading using smartphone images and artificial intelligence. *Diagnostics, 12*(8), 1879. https://doi.org/10.3390/diagnostics12081879

Chapter 8
AI Integration Acceptance in Elderly Care Institutions: A Step Toward a Smarter Life

Andrea Sell and Cecilia Colloseus

Abstract In the context of integrating artificial intelligence (AI) into elderly care institutions, this article explores the importance of participatory research and the acceptance of technological innovations. It focuses on the development and implementation of technologies tailored for non-technical areas, particularly nursing homes. Through collaborative workshops involving the nursing staff, the research aims to identify and address specific needs in the caregiving environment. The article emphasizes the significance of building trust and understanding among all involved parties (care workers, residents, developers). Furthermore, the research outlines a methodological approach that prioritizes human-centered design principles and iterative feedback loops. By engaging end-users throughout the development process, the study aims to ensure that AI technologies meet the practical needs of care workers. It illustrates how the digitization of work processes forms the foundation for AI integration in caregiving settings. The research acknowledges the importance of considering the readiness of institutions and the practical limitations of current infrastructures and advocates for a balanced approach to AI integration, prioritizing the digitization of work processes before implementing AI-controlled systems. By aligning technological advancements with the real-world needs and capabilities of care facilities, the research seeks to promote acceptance and meaningful adoption of AI in elderly care institutions.

8.1 Introduction

Elderly care homes in Germany are grappling with a significant challenge: a persistent staff shortage exacerbated by an escalating number of elderly individuals requiring care. This shortage is compounded by the increasing time pressure on existing staff, who are often burdened with numerous care-unrelated tasks that detract from their primary caregiving responsibilities, with studies indicating that

A. Sell (✉) · C. Colloseus
Aalen University, Aalen, Germany
e-mail: andrea.sell@hs-aalen.de; cecilia.colloseus@hs-aalen.de

N. E. M. Khalifa, M. H. N. Taha (eds.), *Empowering AI Applications in Smart Life and Environment*, https://doi.org/10.1007/978-3-031-78038-7_8

nurses spend approximately between 30% and 40% of their working time on administrative duties [3]. Amidst this growing crisis, the integration of artificial intelligence (AI) into care facilities emerges as a promising solution. By automating administrative duties and streamlining operational workflows, AI can potentially alleviate the workload on nurses, allowing them to focus more on direct patient care and improving overall service quality. This paper explores the multifaceted challenges posed by staff shortages in German elderly care homes and examines how AI implementation can play a pivotal role in addressing these issues, utilizing a participatory research approach that actively involves the nursing staff to ensure practical and effective solutions. It presents the results from an exemplary field lab conducted in a selected elderly care home in Germany.

8.2 Literature Review

The healthcare sector is increasingly leveraging AI to improve efficiency and support healthcare professionals. One significant area of focus is the use of AI to assist nurses with administrative tasks. This literature review explores how participatory research and design methodologies are being applied to develop AI systems that help nurses manage their administrative responsibilities, thereby allowing them to focus more on patient care. Ma et al. conducted an extensive scoping review [12] examining the intersection of elderly care and AI. Their review provides a comprehensive overview of current AI applications in the sector, highlighting how these technologies are being used to support caregivers and improve care outcomes. The study categorizes various AI tools, ranging from automated administrative systems to advanced patient monitoring solutions, and assesses their effectiveness in easing the workload of nursing staff. Ma et al.'s findings underscore the transformative potential of AI in elderly care, offering valuable insights into both current practices and future possibilities for integrating AI to enhance care delivery and operational efficiency. Despite the promising potential of AI in elderly care, there remains a notable gap in the literature regarding participatory research and design involving AI technologies in this field. While numerous studies explore the technical and operational benefits of AI, few focus on involving nursing staff and other stakeholders in the development and implementation processes [11, 13]. This lack of participatory research is a significant oversight, as involving those who are directly impacted by these technologies is crucial for ensuring their practical applicability and acceptance. Engaging caregivers in the design and deployment of AI tools can lead to more user-friendly and effective solutions, ultimately enhancing the quality of care. This paper aims to address this gap by incorporating a participatory research approach, ensuring that the perspectives and insights of nursing staff are integral to our study.

8.3 Socio-Technical Systems and Their Investigation

The retirement center where the field research was (and is still being) conducted is run by a Catholic welfare association and was rebuilt for the third time in 2005 [17]. It consists of four residential areas with space for a total of 100 residents. Around 60 employees (nursing staff, nursing assistants, care staff) are working here in nursing care. In addition, there are social care and housekeeping staff whose joint task is to care for the people in need of care living here [10]. The facility consists of two buildings connected by so-called "bridges"—meaning long corridors, "bridges of encounter". These buildings house the so-called living areas where the residents have their quarters, mainly single bedrooms, and the occasional shared bedroom for two residents, mostly shared by married couples. The atmosphere is relaxed and friendly. The friendliness inside the retirement home is carried to the outside in the two inner courtyards: a "sensory garden" with flowering plants, seating and raised beds, colorfully painted wooden stakes and walking paths create space to pass the time. It is apparent what is in the focus of everyday life here: The care and needs of aging people, creating a dignified and pleasant evening of life. One would not associate this place with high-end technological solutions, as it is quite "undigitized". However, our task at the retirement center is to examine it as a so-called socio-technical system against the backdrop of a larger AI research project which will be elaborated on later in the text. A socio-technical system refers to an integrated system where social and technical elements interact to achieve specific goals or functions. In simpler terms, it is a system where people and technology work together within a particular environment [1, 7]. This concept recognizes that both social and technical factors are intertwined and influence each other within a given system. In the retirement home where we are conducting our research, we are trying to get a grasp on how the implementation of digitized technological solutions can be managed so that the socio-technical system is regarded and respected as a whole. By understanding the complex interactions between social and technical components, researchers and practitioners can better design, implement, and manage systems to achieve desired outcomes while considering human factors, organizational dynamics, and technological capabilities. Socio-technical systems represent a pivotal concept in contemporary scientific discourse, encapsulating the intricate interplay between social and technical elements within complex systems [7]. Rooted in the understanding that technological advancements and social structures are inherently interconnected, our research delves into the dynamic relationships between technology, individuals, organizations, and the broader societal context. By recognizing the mutual shaping of technology and society, the analysis of socio-technical systems transcends traditional disciplinary boundaries, offering profound insights into how technological innovations emerge, evolve, and impact various facets of human life. Through an interdisciplinary lens, we investigate the socio-cultural, economic, political, and ethical dimensions of technological systems, shedding light on emergent phenomena, unintended consequences, and opportunities for sustainable development and societal progress.

8.4 The Project Idea: AI-Cockpit and Use Case “Elderly Care”

A research project that, in the broader sense, deals with the analysis of said socio-technical systems is the project “AI cockpit”, funded by the German Ministry of Labor. The aim of the project is to create user interfaces that intuitively and effectively support human monitoring and control of AI systems. The “AI cockpit” is not only intended for high-risk applications but can also be extended to applications with moderate or minimal risk. The aim of the project is to develop and test an open-source AI cockpit as a digital control unit. This empirically tested and scientifically supported cockpit represents our response to the “human oversight” required by the EU’s AI Act (Art. 14) and supports the productive cooperation between humans and machines by allowing users to oversee, control, and influence the decisions of the system. The ideal of man and machine working hand in hand is already a reality in many places. Intelligent machines have been playing a central role for decades, for example as autopilots in aviation. When these systems were introduced, there were also discussions about the degree of automation and how tasks should be divided between man and machine. Research into autonomous driving is based on similar principles. The research project will investigate whether these principles can also be applied to the use of AI in various fields of work.

The AI cockpit is being developed and tested in three use cases: In the “Human Resources” field lab, for instance, researchers are working on the integration of such regulatory mechanisms into an existing job-matching software. The “Smart City” field lab takes a different perspective. Here, traffic management planning and parking space management are at the center of an AI cockpit development. In this article, however, the focus is on the third field lab: “Elderly Care”. In the above-mentioned care center for the elderly, we want to develop technical solution strategies in order to relieve care staff in their day-to-day work, focusing on tasks that are unrelated to actual hands-on care, such as care documentation and administration. Eventually, this technological solution is to be equipped with a custom-made cockpit.

The general system model of an AI cockpit is shown in Fig. 8.1. The process begins with the AI algorithm, which works within the specified parameters (step 0). The generated data is then first transferred to the AI cockpit in a human-in-the-loop

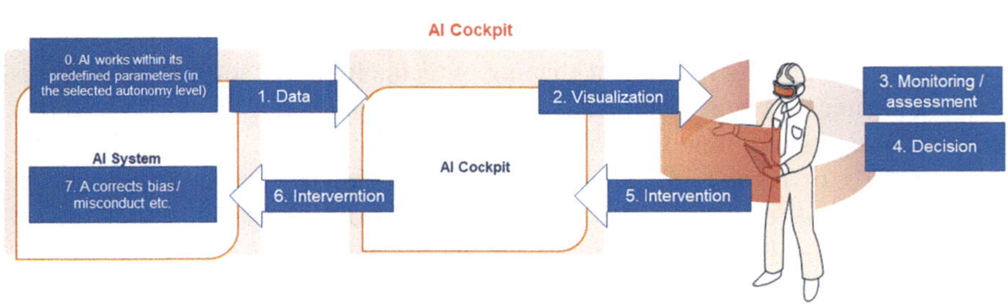

Fig. 8.1 Schematic overview of the AI Cockpit

approach (step 1) and then visualized and forwarded to the human (step 2). There, the human takes on a monitoring and evaluation function by critically assessing the actions of the algorithm (step 3). If the human decides that an intervention is necessary (step 4), this can be carried out via the interface of the AI cockpit (step 5). The human input is translated into algorithmic adjustments (step 6), which then have an effect on the original system (step 7). Adapted behavior can be, for example, the transfer to another autonomy level in which the human decides directly, or the retraining of the AI system based on the decisions made in step 4. How the cockpit will work in the care use case can only be answered when the respective AI system has been developed.

8.4.1 Participatory Technology Development to Relieve the Burden of Day-to-Day Elderly Care

Germany will be faced with the problem of an ever-increasing number of people in need of care in a few years' time, and there will be a shortage of skilled workers to care for them. Nursing staff is already facing precarious conditions in their day-to-day work, which makes a rethink necessary.

> The recent demographic changes in Europe, combined with increasing life expectancy and falling birth rates, will have a serious impact on age structures; at the same time, the availability of labor in the professional care sector will decrease (European Commission 2015 [Background Paper: Growing the European Silvereconomy]). Information and communication technology (ICT) is seen as having great potential to mitigate the associated negative effects [19]. [Translation: DeepL]

One possible scenario could be to alleviate the time pressure and overload on nursing staff by using artificial intelligence (AI) which is the subject of the project presented in this article. The key research question here is: Which technical developments can provide meaningful support for care staff in their daily work? The following sections describe our research process to show the path from an ethnographic needs assessment to the implementation of new technology.

8.5 Methodology

8.5.1 Premises of Cultural Anthropological Research

> From a social and cultural studies perspective on everyday life, science, technology and society [...] are inextricably linked [14].

The central field of research of ST studies is to examine the entanglement of science, technology, and society in everyday life [14]. Research into technological innovations in the working environment is therefore based on the fundamental assumption that technologies are always to be understood in the context of [their, author's note] production and use practices [14]. Technology is interpreted as a social and cultural construct. Suppose we cultural anthropologists are now entrusted with the task of conducting a needs assessment among nursing staff. In that case, we find ourselves in the field of work culture research which uses ethnographic methods and puts a special focus on the actors and their practices and self-perceptions.

The guiding methodological principle of *ethnographic cultural analysis* encompasses approaches to the research field that can be used to gain insights into past and present everyday orders. Field research is regarded here as a qualitative empirical survey procedure consisting of several methodological steps [6]. When researching everyday phenomena, experience is the source and basis of knowledge [6]. The research process is therefore not only about getting to know and understand the experiences of the field actors, but also about gathering one's own experiences in the research process itself. In order to counteract the problem of intersubjectivity, this always includes in-depth reflection on the researcher's role. Our individual case analyses do not follow any laws or contain exactly repeatable modules, as we know them from the natural sciences or the quantitatively arguing social and behavioral sciences. Ambivalences are part of everyday cultural research and must always be taken into account [6]. We ask about the meaning and significance that actors ascribe to their daily practice, we ask about values and patterns of action. Getting to know the institution and the people who live and work in it is of fundamental importance. The aim is to understand the day-to-day work processes in the care of people in need of help.

8.5.2 Participatory Observations and Interviews

In our case, we therefore opted for participant observation and semi-structured interviews. As interns in nursing scrubs, we gained insight into the work processes in the residential areas during the morning shift of the nursing staff. The importance of this "going along as a method" [15] can hardly be underestimated. While interview situations can quickly reach the limits of what can be told,

> the method of the go-along [. . .] describes situations in which field researchers accompany informants on "natural outings" and - by asking questions, listening and observing - actively try to understand the flow of their experiences and actions [15].

During our stay, we gained insights into how people interact with each other and the general atmosphere that prevails at the senior center. In addition to ideas about the layout of the rooms, being there is a decisive advantage over simply listening, because it creates the basis for understanding everyday work processes.

Participant observers are guided by their viewing habits when watching and experiencing. In addition, people only perceive selectively in order to reduce complexity and process what they see. We sort, order, and categorize to recognize patterns of action and behavior. At the same time, we are constantly confronted with rebalancing the relationship between closeness and distance to the research field - as a first-person narrator from a bird's eye view. Social and emotional involvement in the events at the retirement home were recorded in memory logs and so-called field research diaries, evaluated, and used as a basis for new procedural strategies [6]. As researchers, for example, it was particularly important to us from the outset not to be seen as academically educated scientists, but to be perceived as part of the project group, which was not outwardly different from the nurses as project partners. We deliberately chose jeans and sweaters as our everyday clothing so that we became a homogeneous unit in the workshops, creating a sense of "belonging" that has a major effect on participatory research processes.

A fundamental insight from the hours we spent with the nursing staff in their care and administrative activities in the residential areas was that we had completely different experiences. Participatory observations, which are announced, elaborately planned and therefore only take place selectively, also only show excerpts of what everyday life on a nursing ward can mean. We must always be aware of this, as we are presented with a possible range of interpretations whose claim to truth remains relative. On the other hand, the data collected was rather limited in terms of what it could tell us about possible technical innovations. The experience of having to take care of the personal hygiene of people in need of care or taking part in the singing and playing of the social care services was too far removed from our actual research assignment, so conducting interviews and, in a central position, joint research work with care staff seemed more effective to us. Nonetheless, the insights we gained have become the moments we will remember, because

> you can't actually write to anyone straight away and say that's how it works. It's too complex for that. And the plans we have are simply far too long to just read through. [Transcription Workshop preparation for prototype development, own source]

In addition to our observations, we conducted interviews with the management of the retirement home, nursing staff, social care representatives, and residents. Casual conversations in the corridors were usually no less meaningful than planned interviews in quiet environments. These brief exchanges, while all the interviewees were actually pursuing a different goal, showed us how we ourselves are ethnographed as research subjects on site. The outside view of us as AI scientists, "who might bring care robots into the facility", clearly showed us the fears with which our project is met. As a rule, we conducted interviews as two-way conversations, guided by a structure that was only mentally present. All interviews were transcribed using the MAXQDA analysis software and included in the analysis for evaluation. We interviewed workshop participants and employees who declared themselves willing to talk by chance or were recommended to us by the facility management. In this way, we were able to make further contacts according to a kind of snowball principle. The analysis of the interview recordings revealed the following focal points: Motivation for taking up a nursing profession, work processes in everyday nursing care, wishes, hopes, fears, and criticism. The discussion of these topics in the individual interview situations, but also within the workshops, provided us with a basis for comparison, on the foundation of which both the dimensions and the ambiguity of individual problem areas became apparent.

8.5.3 Participatory Research

However, the core of our research work consists of workshops that we conducted as researchers together with representatives of the nursing staff. Three long-standing local female employees and a male care manager from a neighboring facility were temporarily released from their regular professional duties to take part in our workshops. In addition to getting to know the facility and understanding the daily work processes at the care center, mutual trust is of great importance in the joint project work. In the beginning, explaining our objectives was no less important than emphasizing what we did not want to do. The fear of care robots seems to be great and once again shows the widespread lack of understanding and knowledge in connection with artificial intelligence systems. We have been increasingly confronted with fears fueled by the media, expressed in robot-run care homes in which activities performed by humans have become worthless. The recurring emphasis on our research premises has ultimately created the basis for a trusting collaboration: Our research is open-ended. A thematic focus on technical aspects of day-to-day care should direct the view, but not lead it. And: the nursing staff are the experts in their day-to-day work. Without their input, improvements cannot be implemented effectively. Participatory research is a research style and not a clearly definable method. The fundamental objective is to understand people as a central element of research in order to make reality in its complexity more tangible, to understand it, and, above all, to change it [18]. The approach of developing software in a participatory manner originates from Norwegian technology projects in the 1970s [19].

> The Scandinavian approach follows three core principles that still characterize participatory design today: 1. democratization, 2. emancipation, and 3. product quality [19].

The focus here is therefore on equal cooperation between academic researchers and local specialists, which includes both shared control and shared power. The necessary goal of our cooperation is the development of skills to be able to work independently with—in our case—technological innovations [18]. The will to reflect together, to form so-called "epistemic partnerships" [4] also requires finding a common language. We have met these requirements for collaborative work and the ability to co-design in our workshops.

8.5.4 Insights from the Workshops

At these work meetings, usually with coffee and cake, we got to know and understand each other in a relaxed atmosphere. An important realization in this context was that we had to give the nursing staff time and space to become able to speak, i.e. to put their experiences into words and think about formulations for their daily work routine. It is not part of their regular work tasks to present their own thoughts on a flipchart, to speak in front of a group of people, some of whom are strangers, and to have to muster the courage to contribute creatively. Getting involved in the project, and growing together as a research team, requires patience and empathy. Above all, however, it requires an atmosphere that expresses appreciation of the other person and mutual respect. We used playful methods as the basis for designing the workshops.

> Through the theoretical lens of play, cultural-scientific argumentation can be conducted that allows a more precise understanding of communities, their contexts of meaning, value systems, and cultural and social dynamics [9].

Because "homo ludens" experiences in play that they can master situations [9], this methodological approach is suitable for analyzing certain work cultures and the social relationships that prevail in them. Games arouse emotions and bring moods to light [9].

On the basis of the so-called photo-voice method, for example, we asked the workshop participants to take a tour of the retirement center, which was linked to the task of identifying places and rooms where they feel comfortable and enjoy spending time and, in turn, to photograph the places that they dislike. Our aim was to see the facility through the eyes of the people who work there and to understand where they look and how rooms are categorically sorted when the only options available are good or bad. The most important result in this context was the change in attitude among the employees after we had looked at and discussed the photographs together. The feeling of insecurity, the fear of speechlessness, and a lack of creativity had given way to the realization that there were no "wrong answers". Based on the photographs, we were able to clearly identify areas in need of change as we continued to work together.

The task of assessing the need for technical infrastructure must not be limited to a collaborative workspace. The need to walk through the retirement center together and understand the spatial conditions must be seen as the basis for being able to change the room equipment. If work processes and therefore also work paths are unclear, technology cannot be implemented in a meaningful way. Using the popular scavenger hunt game, we chose an approach to the retirement center and its spatial perception. The workshop group, which on this day consisted of more than the usual participants (students from Freiburg, a technology sociologist, and an employee from the development company cooperating with us.), was divided into two small groups. One group went first, identified places where a technical innovation was considered useful, and marked these places with a sticker. The task of the second group was to find the stickers and identify the reasons why they had been put there. This game was great fun for the participants and led to insightful results. In the subsequent discussion, we were able to identify problem areas and prioritize their urgency.

Many post-its pointed out the need for suitable software to place orders. Ordering processes here require too many work steps to be carried out analogously: Meal orders are entered into a list by employees by hand, which is then passed on to the kitchen, where the list has to be evaluated. The organization of orders for care products also takes place in a similarly time-consuming manner. A care worker is assigned to carry order lists to the individual residents and then enter them into an online form and send them off. In addition to criticism of this time-consuming ordering process, there were also complaints about the lack of a telephone system that would allow staff to take calls via headset and Bluetooth so that care processes, which often require the wearing of gloves, do not have to be constantly interrupted. For hygiene reasons, a voice-controlled call answering system would be an advantage here. The discussion about this gap in the care center's infrastructure, which also dealt with the use of an answering machine, brought to light another topic that is also emotionally charged. Does a care worker always have to be available by phone? Can there be certain office hours? How can this be communicated to the residents' relatives, whose demands on caregivers are increasing?

To further improve work processes, a mobile documentation system in the residents' rooms was brought up. Vital signs, drinking protocols, information on bowel movements and positioning are always entered by hand on slips of paper so that these values can be collected and entered into the existing documentation system after care has been provided. This practice harbors too many sources of error. It would be easier to use the documentation program on the move so that information can be entered promptly and on-site. This would also relieve the mental strain on nursing staff. Top priority, however, was given to a dashboard, which could replace the established pegboard system in the nurses' room as a medium for improved communication and organization. The nursing staff were often surprised by their own way of thinking and working during the workshops and were pleased that we had achieved almost tangible results. We followed this up with a design sprint. As part of design thinking, we set the task of modeling initial prototypes. In small groups, the workshop participants created handicrafts that referenced the problem areas recorded.

Although we were able to name a favorite at this point, the abundance of different suggestions for improvement showed that a fundamental discussion of the options was necessary in order to critically evaluate them both in their interaction and in their individual effects.

The problem areas addressed can be roughly divided into two overarching categories: documentation and communication. A lack of infrastructure leads to difficulties in these areas at the care center as a whole. As part of the AI cockpit project, we decided to implement an interactive dashboard for the nurses' room in consultation with nursing staff, scientific staff, and developers. All perspectives were represented at the scientific round-table when discussing the work processes that had been classified as problematic with a direct desire for improvement so that a solution was developed jointly and step by step. This proposal was officially presented once again at the retirement home itself so that everyone involved in the project could have their say. It was particularly important in this process to also consider and include in the argumentation those ideas that we had decided not to implement. We explained why we did not see ordering processes or telephone systems within our area of responsibility and were able to conclusively demonstrate that mobile documentation options fail due to simple infrastructural obstacles. The extent of the effect of this information should not be underestimated. Those who cannot understand decision-making processes, who do not know the path to a certain result, and who are not entirely satisfied with the decisions made are inhibited in their willingness to accept them. The moment in the presentation of our proposed solution was particularly significant when the nursing staff asked us whether we as researchers had hoped for more, whether we were satisfied with this result. This question about how we felt made it clear to us that we had not only built up a good relationship with each other but also that we had not been able to hide our emotional attachment to the care center and its nursing staff. Our desire to carry out a needs analysis in order to optimize work structures quickly and obviously went hand in hand with a personal need and concern.

As a first conclusion, one might say that the participatory research process at the center for the elderly reveals a fundamental phenomenon in the development and implementation of technologies for specific applications in non-technical areas: The challenges and problems that technicians consider to be in need of a solution are not necessarily those identified by the people who will later work with the technology to be developed.

This restriction was and is always to be taken into account when working with the developers of the commissioned technology company. The development team accepted our invitation to a workshop with a scavenger hunt and design sprint because relevance, transparency, and, above all, an understanding of everyday work structures are seen as prerequisites for their own work. The next section presents preliminary methodological considerations for determining requirements from a technical perspective and initial implementation ideas for the dashboard.

8.5.5 Analysis of the Design Thinking Workshop Results Through a Technical Lens and the Technical Implementation of the Dashboard

After conducting human-centered design workshops with all participants from nurses to administrative staff and bystanders the goal was to define a clear way forward. This way had to be approved by everyone affected to meaningfully continue with the implementation stage of the technology. If there is a lack of commitment from those affected the results cannot be as beneficial as they could be. To get the necessary agreement vague ideas had to be clarified, discussed, and depicted. To address fears and prejudices the nurses had to be picked up where they were in their technical adaption and usage of tools. Therefore, a two-step approach was chosen to guide the project participants in the direction of actually using AI in their care facility. The first step is the so-called "enabler" step. In this period, the aim is to enhance the usage of the already present tools and software solutions to increase the general acceptance of mobile devices in the facility and the understanding of the improvement potentials of software to support the staff in their daily work. To

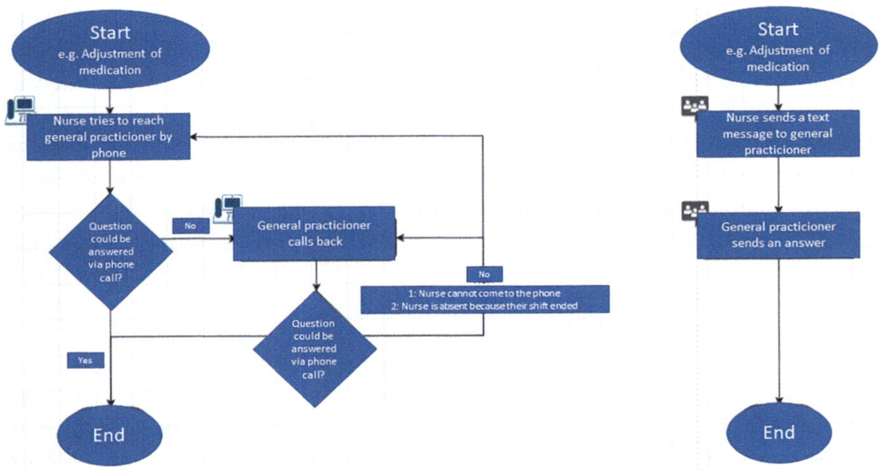

Fig. 8.2 Low hanging fruit: carer-general-practitioner-communication

facilitate this we identified two use cases as so-called "low-hanging fruits" which can be implemented fast and are expected to have an immediate beneficial outcome for the nurses, considering time-saving through process improvements. The two use cases in question are a digitized ordering system for meals and consumable supplies using a simple spreadsheet in Excel, and a more convenient method to communicate with medical personnel outside the facility via an already existing secure messenger system. Both use cases do not contain AI, but digital systems that replace elaborate and time-consuming processes that are currently still carried out analogously on paper (Fig. 8.2).

These use cases will be evaluated with statistical analysis to have a proven enhancement not only a perceived one. In this way, those affected by the technological changes in the facility will be motivated by a sense of achievement and probably become more compliant to support the project in the long run. The next step focuses on the usage of actual AI to further improve in-house processes and to allow the nurses to spend more time actually taking care of their residents than on other tasks like documentation. To achieve this, the technology has to be carefully embedded into their daily work. Because imagining something that is not actually "present" is challenging for everyone. Thus, the focus will first be put on the content that has to be displayed on the dashboard and second on the way how the information is gathered, structured, and transported to the dashboard. This process is centered around the people using the dashboard with multiple feedback- and test loops.

The general user journey, while interacting with the planned system, will be as following: A user can record a message which will then be transcribed by an open source speech to text model specially trained for the care environment into a text message, or the user can directly type in a text message. In the next step, the data will be organized into categories like "important information", "appointments", "events" and "tasks". Eventually, everything will be displayed on a screen in the nurses' room to grant the nurses on duty a good and quick overview of the current status of their unit. In every step, the user should get insights into the process by returning to them what was understood and done as a result of it. This will happen via a commonly used chat interface ("chatbot").

8.6 Acceptance of Technological Innovations

In the context of technological advances, especially in the field of artificial intelligence, acceptance is crucial for the successful deployment and integration of AI systems in various areas, especially in healthcare. Users and stakeholders need to develop trust in AI technologies in order to fully realize their benefits. This requires transparency, data protection, and open communication about how AI is used and what impact it can have on—in our case—working structures in a retirement center. In our project work, the participatory workshops take up the most space because they form the cornerstone for creating acceptance in the use of technology. Depictions of the data flow as shown in Fig. 8.3 were and are discussed with the participants because we consider a basic understanding of the technical processes to be important and, above all, beneficial. If it can be clearly explained which data is processed and how the commitment and cooperation of care staff can be increased. In addition, the reduction of social complexity to machine-processable factors must be carried out very carefully [8]. This reduction, or rather this translation, can be regarded as a key moment in the implementation of technology, to which all those involved in the project must be granted access. This raises further research questions that need to be answered: Who benefits from how much insight at which stages of

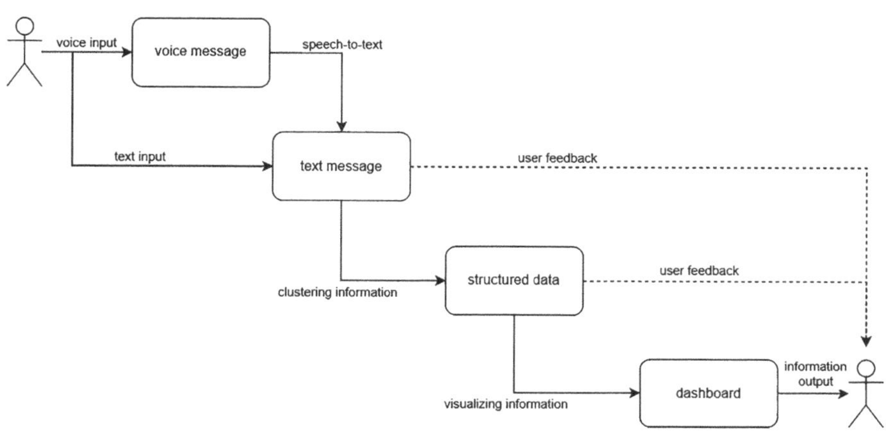

Fig. 8.3 General blocks of the dashboard use case

development? Everyone involved in the project participates for different reasons—for which groups of participants is the developer perspective relevant?

From a cultural anthropological perspective, these "translation processes"—from social/cultural practices to technical infrastructure—are part of research into culturally constructed artificial intelligence systems. At the end of our design sprint, we as researchers designed a results poster together with the nurses involved in the workshops. The workshop participants were asked to recapitulate the work and thought steps to date, to recall how we had started and where we were at this point. In addition to the verbalization and graphic implementation of the steps taken, this visualization had two purposes: Firstly, the nursing staff should be proud of their project work and see what they had achieved. Secondly, this poster, which now hangs in the foyer of the retirement home, is intended for all the other employees who are only marginally informed about what is happening in our AI project.

The aim is to counteract rumors about care robots that are already circulating and fueling fears of losing one's job. The poster provides basic information about our approach and clearly states our objectives. In the next workshop, we want to work with the nursing staff to develop strategies that they can use to explain our joint plans to their colleagues. Communicating the plans to nursing staff is the key to acceptance of the changes. If they are able to talk about their experiences, fears, wishes, and hopes in an understandable way, reservations and inhibitions will be reduced. At this point, we will merely provide help for self-help by showing methods and ways that can be helpful when telling, showing, and explaining (e.g. workshop, lecture, presentation, inspection of an office, role play, etc.). Ultimately, however, all these individual methods for creating acceptance values culminate solely in the suitability of the new technology for everyday use. Only if the dashboard (with its functions and information options) can be smoothly integrated into the everyday work of nursing staff, only if it is practical and useful, will it be accepted. User-friendliness is key here.

8.7 Trust and Technology

When it comes to implementing an AI solution within a care institution it is important to consider trust, as trust is crucial for the acceptance of new technology in a work field, that centers the care of a vulnerable group. But trust is not only a significant component when considering the care workers whose work practice is going to change. Trustful physician-patient relationships are also important for high-quality care and stand in correlation to better health outcomes and more successful therapeutic/care interventions [20]. The AI-based technology is meant to be integrated into the care work and possibly the care interaction itself. Therefore, the AI system also needs to be trust-inducing to the residents [16]. Thus, we have different trust relations to consider in the process of the participatory technology development, that we are working on in the "AI Cockpit" project. First, we will dive into the concept of trust itself within human-human interactions, and then show how and to which extent the previous understanding of trust as a human capacity, can be translated into human–technology interactions within a socio-technical system. Subsequently, we will outline how our interdisciplinary approach might benefit all different trust relations in the process of developing meaningful technology. Our field lab, as already mentioned, is working with an elderly care center, run by a catholic welfare association. It is necessary to highlight because the work we will influence is going to influence the lives of people, who depend on care. Care is considered a fundamental value, ethically and religiously as well, as all humans depend on care either at the beginning of life, towards the end of it, and maybe even throughout it. Care is, therefore, a prerequisite for our existence, not only in the sense of caring about someone in a non-committal way, but the prerequisite is taking care of someone in a sense that is practical and requires labor [5]. The everyday work of care workers consists of responding to individual needs. To recognize the needs of their residents, empathy is required. Empathy, in this case, is the ability to understand the resident's perspective and feelings and respond to this understanding in interpersonal interactions [20]. The practice of responding is, therefore, a condition for care, as a nurse who does not respond to a resident's needs, could not be considered caring [16].

What connects care and trust is the practice of responding. This is especially backed by the recognition, that humans consider a person that they perceive as responding in a caring way as more trustful [16]. Without responsivity, care work would not differ from a mere procedure or a protocol that is being followed [16]. Important to note is, that this is a common fear within the care–technology spectrum, especially the fear of elderly people losing social interactions through i.e. the implementation of social care robots. In conclusion, we understand trust as a responsive phenomenon and a human capability to trust under certain conditions and build relations with others [16]. Fundamental to trust, and why we are talking about trust and not control, is that there is always risk involved. The residents are dependent on the nursing staff, as they cannot perform most tasks by themselves. There are juridical and ethical work standards and rules, but most importantly, a trustful physician-patient relationship is based on trust that the physician has their patient's best interest in mind.

How can this understanding of trust as a responsive phenomenon be translated into human–technology interactions? Following a deeper understanding of human-technology interaction, we could classify robots, machines, or AI systems as 'others' and therefore as responsive. AI systems that are designed to react to specific human needs, could therefore be part of a trust relationship. Central to this point is that the responses given are constructed responsive qualities, that do not suffice to meet the existential complexity of human beings [16]. What essentially differs in human–human, and human–technology interactions is that humans can be thought of as having good intentions, while technology can only be thought of as being developed with a good intention. That makes the developers behind any AI system the 'other' that is considered trustworthy, not the technology itself. Within the ethics guidelines for trustworthy AI, the high-level expert group on artificial intelligence, set up by the European Commission, centralizes trust as well.

> In a context of rapid technological change, we believe it is essential that trust remains the bedrock of societies, communities, economics, and sustainable development. We, therefore, identify Trustworthy AI as our foundational ambition, since human beings and communities will only be able to have confidence in the technology's development and its applications when a clear and comprehensive framework for achieving its trustworthiness is in place [2].

They elaborated on three components, that should be met in AI for it to be considered trustworthy: it should be lawful (complying with law and regulations), ethical (ensuring adherence to ethical principles and values), and robust (both from a technical and social perspective) [2]. AI ethics, as a sub-field of applied ethics, focuses on ethical issues raised by the development, deployment, and use of AI [2]. In our case, the purpose of the ethical reflection is to protect individuals and groups at the most basic level. Fundamental rights such as dignity, freedom, equality and solidarity, citizens' rights, and justice, are all rooted in respect for human dignity, and therefore all AI systems development should follow a dignified human-centric approach [2]. The high-level expert group also listed four explicit ethical principles that must be followed, to ensure Trustworthy AI. These are respect for human autonomy, prevention of harm, fairness, and explicability [2]. All these guides and ethical principles address first and foremost the developers who will design and program these technologies.

By controlling what an AI system can do and in what framework, we as the developing team must ensure that the needs of the workers as well as the residents of the elderly care center are being met, and their rights protected. Regarding the relevance of trust relations in care as well as in developing and using AI systems, our interdisciplinary research and human-centered approach is of great importance. By including the nursing staff that will be using the technology we are developing in every step of the process we ensure that the needs of the people most affected by the AI will be met. By getting to know the care center, the worker's practices, feelings, values, fears, and wishes, we are able to respond in a meaningful and trust-inducing way that takes into account the complexity of human beings. The concept of an 'AI Cockpit' in which end users are supposed to be enabled to have a complete overview to understand and control the AI system is already considering the ethical principles of autonomy, prevention of harm, and explicability, by laying these principles as the grounding condition to any technology being developed. By creating a space in which different skill sets enrich each other while creating something new, we built and continue building an even stronger relationship between researchers, developers, and end users, that is founded in trust. With this interdisciplinary participatory technology development practice, we encourage AI integration acceptance in the very first steps of development.

8.8 Digitized Instead of Automated

> So, at the end of the day, it's cool to change the processes, but you can't change the people. (Transcription Workshop trust in technology, own source)

This statement was made in a workshop on "trust in technology". It has become a central phrase for our work because it shows that all planning, developments and work processes at the retirement center are and must be geared towards the residents. They are the benchmark for all changes. Our needs assessments therefore converge at one point: which restructuring benefits the work routine—be it through more time for the actual care of people, for a conversation or a walk, or through greater satisfaction among staff and carers. These nursing staff, as experts in their day-to-day work, also underpinned our participatory research claim almost as a matter of course:

> Yes, that's our bread and butter. We know what is best placed where and when, where it makes sense. (Transcription Workshop debriefing prototype development, own source)

With the intention of letting the nursing staff speak and decide, to serve as their mouthpiece, we quickly recognized in which areas the need for change is greatest, because

> that's the problem [...] that we basically write [care documentation] to cover ourselves, legally, but it's just bad as a working tool. (Transcription Workshop preparation for prototype development, own source)

The problem of "writing things down", it seems, is quickly solved. We immediately think of Alexa and Siri as conversational agents whose voice-controlled responses in residents' rooms could help the nurses with their documentation tasks. We can think of many ways to get away from writing. There would certainly also be technical solutions for ordering meals that would make it unnecessary to write down the desired meals, e.g. if physically and mentally fit residents could make their own entries on a monitor. In cooperation with the nursing staff, we have come to the conclusion that, despite the simplifications that some technical innovations would bring, there is no need for sophisticated AI-controlled technology. Rather, there is a desire for the fundamental digitization of simple work processes. Cumbersome notes on pieces of paper or the back of one's hand need to be replaced by simpler ways of communicating and organizing work. This kind of digitization creates the basis for the use of artificial intelligence systems, the added value of which is not given under current conditions. AI can only be successfully implemented where sufficient technical infrastructure forms the basis. In view of our predefined project structure, we are therefore only marginally achieving our project goals in this field lab. AI will merely play a role for us in the development of the dashboard where users can feed information and messages into the dashboard via a text-to-speech model in the already existing messenger system. Based on our experience to date, AI can only be used where a certain level of "AI readiness" can be assumed. We are therefore setting ourselves a new project framework: We are comparing the status quo: care 2025 with a future vision of care 2035 and developing various scenarios/stages with different technical levels and solutions. The comprehensibility behind this approach creates acceptance in the nursing home. Impressive AI systems are not suitable at this point.

8.9 A Look into the Future

As part of this research, we also envision the future of elderly care in 2050, considering the long-term impacts of AI-operated tools on the sector. This forward-looking analysis explores how advanced AI technologies could transform elderly care homes, potentially addressing chronic staff shortages and improving care delivery. By projecting current trends and technological advancements, we anticipate a future where AI not only streamlines administrative tasks but also enhances personalized care through predictive analytics and intelligent health monitoring systems. This vision underscores the importance of ongoing research and innovation in AI, highlighting its potential to create sustainable and efficient care environments that can better meet the needs of an aging population. As this part of our research is still a work in progress we are not able to present any results at this point.

8.10 Conclusion

As our research shows, balanced AI integration, focusing on digitizing work processes before implementing AI-controlled systems, can promote acceptance and meaningful adoption of AI in elderly care institutions. This paper highlighted the importance of participatory research in understanding and improving care services, emphasizing the need for collaboration, empathy, and mutual respect between researchers and nursing staff. Participatory research processes are crucial for technology acceptance in non-technical areas, emphasizing the need for aligning developers' and users' perspectives and building trust for successful AI integration in healthcare. Trust is crucial in human-technology interactions, especially in the care sector. Hence, AI systems must adhere to ethical principles to ensure trustworthiness. Since the future of elderly care will surely involve advanced AI technologies that can address staff shortages and enhance care delivery it is crucial to put further research into the participatory implementation approach. The readiness of institutions and current infrastructural limitations, however, may hinder seamless AI integration, and must thus be tackled first. We are aware that the study's findings are based on a single field lab in a specific care home, and can thus hardly be generalized. However, we advocate to further make use of participatory approaches in the implementation of AI. Future research could, for example, focus on scaling AI integration in various elderly care settings, addressing infrastructural challenges, and exploring the long-term impacts of AI on caregiving quality. Additionally, the exploration of the impact of technical innovations on work processes, and further development of participatory research methods in healthcare settings are certainly needed. Our preliminary research findings can guide the development and implementation of AI technologies in elderly care institutions, aiming to improve staff efficiency, enhance care quality, and address the challenges posed by staff shortages in the sector. We emphasize the importance of trust in human-technology interactions, especially in the care sector, and the need for AI systems to be developed to be lawful, ethical, and robust to ensure trustworthiness in their applications in care settings.

References

1. Abbas, R., & Abbas, K. (2023). Socio-technical theory: A review, in *TheoryHub Book*. https://open.ncl.ac.uk/theories/9/socio-technical-theory/
2. AI, H. (2019). High-level expert group on artificial intelligence. *Ethics Guidelines for Trustworthy AI, 6*, 4.
3. Becke, G., Bleses, P., Gundert, H., & Wetjen, A. (2011). *Trendreport ambulante soziale Unterstützungsdienstleistungen im Alter - arbeitswissenschaftliche Perspektiven*, Vol. 177 of *artec-paper*. Bremen: Universität Bremen, Forschungszentrum Nachhaltigkeit (artec).
4. Bieler, P., Cubellis, L., Josties, J., & Klein, A. (2021). Ethnografische theorie ko-laborativ fügen.
5. Biller-Andorno, N., Monteverde, S., Krones, T., & Eichinger, T. (2021). *Medizinethik*. Springer.
6. Bischoff, C., Oehme-Jüngling, K., & Leimgruber, W. (2014). *Methoden der Kulturanthropologie*. Haupt Verlag.
7. Fischer, G., & Herrmann, T. (2011). Socio-technical systems: A meta-design perspective. *International Journal of Sociotechnology and Knowledge Development, 3*(1), 1–33. https://services.igi-global.com/resolvedoi/resolve.aspx?doi=10.4018/jskd.2011010101
8. Gransche, B., & Manzeschke, A. (Eds.). (2020). *Das geteilte Ganze: Horizonte Integrierter Forschung für künftige Mensch-Technik-Verhältnisse*. Wiesbaden: Springer Fachmedien Wiesbaden. http://link.springer.com/10.1007/978-3-658-26342-3
9. Heimerdinger, T., & Tauschek, M. (2020). *Kulturtheoretisch argumentieren: ein Arbeitsbuch*. utb GmbH.
10. Klein, J. (2024). Chronik.
11. Lifshits, I., & Rosenberg, D. (2024). Artificial intelligence in nursing education: A scoping review. *Nurse Education in Practice, 80*, 104148. https://doi.org/10.1016/j.nepr.2024.104148
12. Ma, B., Yang, J., Wong, F. K. Y., Wong, A. K. C., Ma, T., Meng, J., Zhao, Y., Wang, Y., & Lu, Q. (2023). Artificial intelligence in elderly healthcare: A scoping review. *Ageing Research Reviews, 83*, 101808. https://www.sciencedirect.com/science/article/pii/S1568163722002501
13. Mion, L., Latshaw, E., Lin, Y., Migovich, M., Ghosh, R., Khan, N., Sarkar, N., & Tate, J. (2022). Participatory design: An essential process for socially assistive robotic activities in long-term care settings. *Innovation in Aging, 6*, 423–423.
14. Niewöhner, J., Sørensen, E., & Beck, S. (2012). Science and Technology Studies - Wissenschafts- und Technikforschung aus sozial- und kulturanthropologischer Perspektive. *Science and Technology Studies: Eine sozialanthropologische Einführung*. 9–48. transcript Verlag. https://doi.org/10.14361/transcript.9783839421062.intro
15. Raab, J., Pfadenhauer, M., Stegmaier, P., Dreher, J., & Schnettler, B. (2008). *Phänomenologie und Soziologie: theoretische Positionen, aktuelle Problemfelder und empirische Umsetzungen*. Wiesbaden: VS Verl. für Sozialwissenschaften.
16. Schröder, I., Müller, O., Scholl, H., Levy-Tzedek, S., & Kellmeyer, P. (2023). Can robots be trustworthy? Reflections about responsive robots and trust as a human capability. *Ethik in der Medizin, 35*(2), 221–246.
17. St. Antonius (2017). Chronik: Festchronik, 110-jähriges jubiläum altenzentrum st. antonius 1907–2017. *Zeitung des Altenzentrums St. Antonius anlässlich des 110-jährigen Jubiläums*.
18. von Unger, H. (2014). *Partizipative Forschung: Einführung in die Forschungspraxis*. Wiesbaden: Springer Fachmedien Wiesbaden. https://link.springer.com/10.1007/978-3-658-01290-8

19. Waldenberger, F., Naegele, G., Kudo, H., & Matsuda, T. (Eds.). (2022). *Alterung und Pflege als kommunale Aufgabe: Deutsche und japanische Ansätze und Erfahrungen, Dortmunder Beiträge zur Sozialforschung*. Wiesbaden: Springer Fachmedien Wiesbaden. https://link.springer.com/10.1007/978-3-658-36844-9
20. Wu, Q., Jin, Z. & Wang, P. (2022). The relationship between the physician-patient relationship, physician empathy, and patient trust. *Journal of General Internal Medicine*, *37*(6), 1388–1393.

Chapter 9
Using AI to Improve Post-consumer Plastics Recycling for Sustainability in a Smart Environment

Natalie Basedow, Nicole Fangerow, Kathrin Hadasch, Cecilia Colloseus, and Doris Aschenbrenner

Abstract The optimization of plastic waste recycling represents a challenge for sustainable circular economy systems. This chapter explores the potential use of machine learning and robotics applications to improve the recycling rate in existing lightweight packaging sorting facilities in Germany. The research identifies key challenges in the recycling of post-consumer plastics, focusing on the application of AI, machine learning and computer vision. It highlights the importance of open data in creating an intelligent environment conducive to efficient recycling practices. The research also explores the selection of optimal sensors—including RGB (red, green, blue), near infrared (NIR) and RGB depth sensors—to improve the identification and classification of plastic materials. It also discusses the selection process for a suitable gripper mechanism, which is crucial for automating the sorting process, and the journey from laboratory prototyping to the realisation of production-ready systems.

Keywords Recycling · Machine-learning · Automation · Robotics · Computer vision · Post-consumer plastics · Sensors

9.1 Introduction

9.1.1 Current Situation of Post-consumer Plastics in Germany

In this chapter, we present preliminary results of the "RecycleBot" research project at Aalen University, which aims to achieve a higher yield in recycling plants. The amount of plastic waste collected annually via the yellow bin or yellow bag, the German collection system for post-consumer plastics, corresponds to over 2.5

N. Basedow (✉) · N. Fangerow · K. Hadasch · C. Colloseus · D. Aschenbrenner
Hochschule Aalen - Technik und Wirtschaft, Aalen, Germany
e-mail: natalie.basedow@hs-aalen.de; nicole.fangerow@hs-aalen.de; kathrin.hadasch@hs-aalen.de; cecilia.colloseus@hs-aalen.de; doris.aschenbrenner@hs-aalen.de

N. E. M. Khalifa, M. H. N. Taha (eds.), *Empowering AI Applications in Smart Life and Environment*, https://doi.org/10.1007/978-3-031-78038-7_9

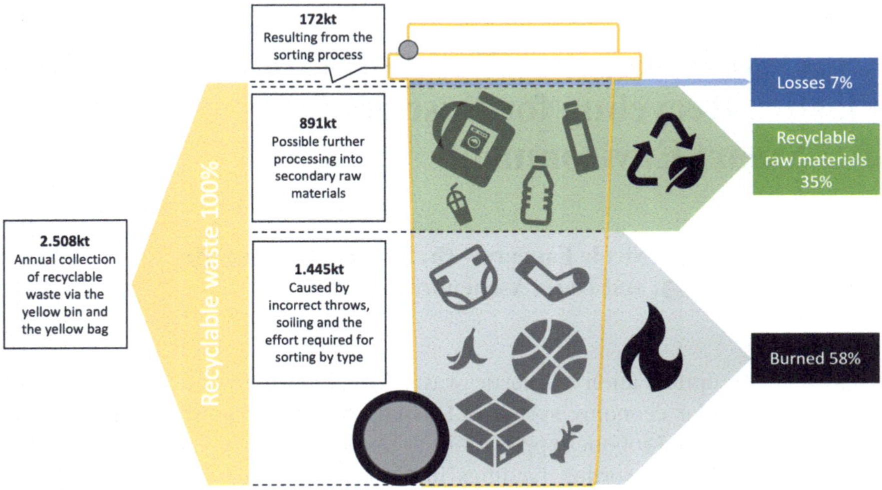

Fig. 9.1 Overview of the percentage recycling of recyclable waste collected annually via the yellow bin and the yellow bag, own illustration based on [8]

million tonnes [8, 10]. Only 35% of this can potentially be recycled into secondary raw materials. Overall, 58% of the waste is burned, and around 7% disappears during the sorting process. An illustration of the current situation of post-consumer plastics in Germany may be found in Fig. 9.1 [8]. The recycling process in Germany begins at home with the correct separation of packaging. One of the main reasons for the high incineration rate of collected plastic waste arises here: On average, around 30% of the contents of a yellow bin or yellow bag are misfits [10]. Misdirected waste must be sorted out, and disposed of separately, which also contaminates recyclable products. Packaging consisting of several materials (mixed plastics and multi-layer) contributes to the problem in terms of recyclability. It cannot be recycled properly as the sorting plant's sensor system cannot recognize which material is involved. These misfits include, for instance, yogurt or cream cups, which are made of plastic, but their lids are usually made of aluminum. "Space-saving" recycling, such as putting yogurt cups inside each other, can also lead to difficulties in the recycling process, as the cups might be made of different plastics and therefore end up in the wrong plastic stream. This results in a decrease of the purity level of the resulting sorted material streams [18].

9.1.1.1 Current Situation of Sorting Facilities

To understand the overall process of post-consumer plastics, an important step is to look at modern sorting facilities, such as MEILO in Gernsheim [53], Germany. The facility is one of the largest in Germany and sorts around 4% of the waste collected annually via the yellow bin or yellow bag. By using state-of-the-art sorting

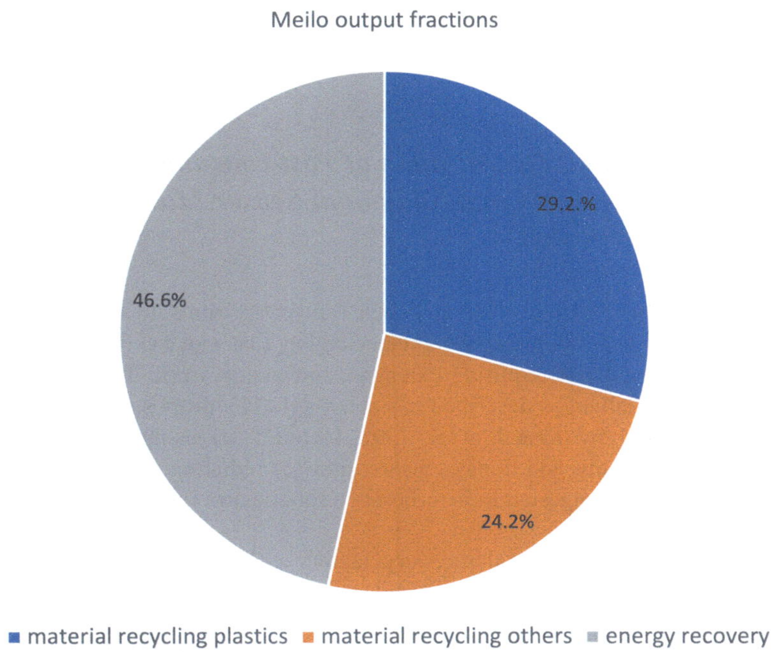

Fig. 9.2 Overview of the percentage of recycling at the MEILO sorting plant, the annual amount of recyclable waste collected via the yellow bin and the yellow bag based on [53]

technology, it can recycle up to 53.4% of the 120,000 tonnes of input per year (see Fig. 9.2). Note that only 29.2% of the material recycled is plastic, and the rest is other materials such as tinplate. One of the challenges facing the RecycleBot research project is how many usable plastics are contained in the remaining 46.6% of energy recovery and could be sorted out profitably.

9.1.1.2 Why Are We Dealing with This Topic?

Under the EU Packaging Directive [20], a minimum of 65% of all packaging waste must be recycled by the end of 2025. Additionally, the recycling rate for plastics should reach 50% by the end of 2025 and 55% by the end of 2030.

To meet these targets, the expansion of light packaging sorting facilities with new technologies could be essential, as the volume of waste tends to increase. Lightweight packaging sorting plants must therefore not only sort larger volumes of waste faster, but also more accurately to meet the requirements of the industry and the specifications of the European Parliament. The challenges of modern sorting facilities, such as MEILO, are that the systems mainly work with mechanical and manual sorting, which means that sorting errors cannot be ruled out. As a result, problems arise, such as space requirements and a lack of money for investment costs, both needed for state-of-the-art technologies such as automated robotic sorting systems.

9.1.2 Our Solution: Optimization of Post-consumer Plastic Sorting Using AI and Additional Sensor Modules for Computer Vision

The RecycleBot research project at Aalen University aims to develop an AI-supported sorting robot for lightweight packaging that can be installed directly in a sorting plant without requiring extensive conversion work. The project takes into account the challenges described in Sect. 9.1.1. The proposed improvements, as partly described by Kroell et al. [39], include: (a) using current sensors, (b) strategically placing additional sensors, and (c) reducing the cost per sensor investment. It is also suggested to incorporate a robotic arm into the sorting process along the material cascade.

Figure 9.3 shows a material recovery factory envisioned by the RecycleBot team. The process starts with an automated step where an NIR sensor separates the materials on the conveyor belts. After the initial default NIR-detection, a second detection and sorting process occurs on each conveyor belt branch. In the first phase, the RecycleBot project will investigate the use of various sensor technologies, including RGB sensors, RGB-NIR sensors, and RGB-depth sensors, in conjunction with a robotic system to facilitate the classification of specific items within a given fraction.

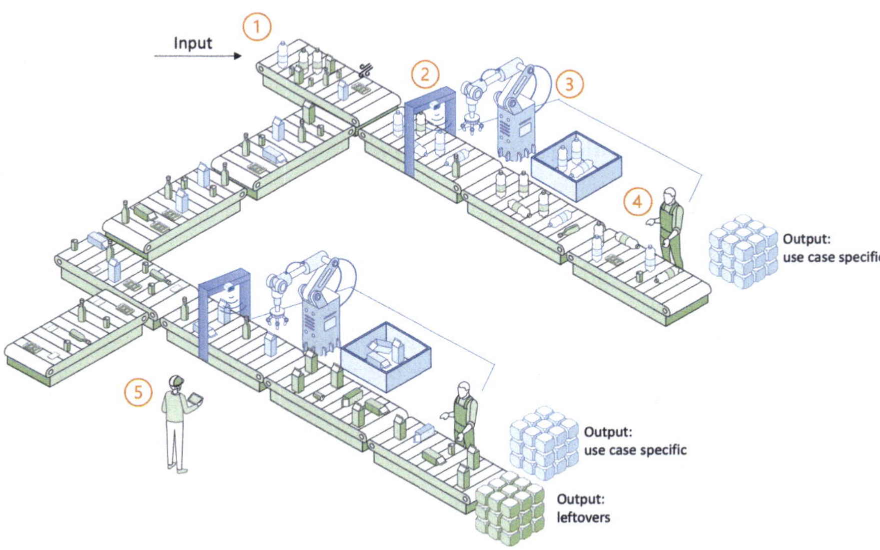

Fig. 9.3 Post consumer plastic sorting using additional sensors and robotic arms

The selection of Near-Infrared (NIR), RGB, combined RGB and NIR, and RGB depth sensors, accompanied by robotic mechanisms for the material sorting process, is primarily driven by the imperative to achieve an optimal balance between cost-effectiveness and safety. Compared to alternatives, such as X-ray systems, which may pose higher operational costs and increased safety concerns, these sensors offer a pragmatic approach to sorting.

In this setup, the use of additional sensors allows for a two-stage focus, which can improve the sorting accuracy. This sequential approach ensures that each sensor operates in its area of expertise and that the robot and its sorting task are a complement to an existing sorting plant. The aim of the RecycleBot project is not to create an environment for robots, but to train them for specific tasks and integrate them into existing sorting facilities to work alongside human workers who do the manual sorting of plastics. The following is a more detailed description of the sorting process in the lightweight packaging plant with additional sensors:

(1) At the start of the conveyor belt, the NIR sorters are responsible for the primary sorting based on the composition of the material. They effectively separate different plastics, such as PET, LDPE, and PP, into the corresponding branches using NIR sensor technology. This technology analyses the infrared light absorption properties of materials to identify polymers.
(2) After the initial near-infrared (NIR) sorting, the materials are fed into the next phase. Additional sorters, consisting of a chosen sensor module and an 6-axis robot arm, are installed along the conveyor belts. These sorters are particularly suitable for further refinements, as, for example, pointed out in Table 9.1.
(3) Specially equipped sorting areas must be available to enable a two-stage sorting process. The system should provide special areas for each sorting section. A transition area should be located directly after the NIR sorters before the additional sorters (robot and additional sensor module) take over the use case-based sorting task.
(4) After the additional automated sorting phase, manual sorting stations would be implemented to handle any exceptions and perform quality checks to ensure the purity of the sorted material. These stations would also serve as a secondary control point for materials that were misclassified during the automated sorting phase. Misclassified materials can be classified by experienced workers and with the help of a plastic scanner. The Plastic Scanner [23, 59] is an open source open data project from TU-Delft, a portable sensor device that can identify the most common types of plastic. The project is currently in the prototyping phase and shows promise.
(5) A control system, known as KI-Cockpit, oversees the monitoring of the current NIR sensors and the recently added detection sensors and robotic arms. The control system gathers and displays data to evaluate the precision and environmental factors of every sorting phase. Figure 9.4 contains potential Key Performance Indicators. The knowledge acquired can be utilized by operators to

Table 9.1 Specialized ML-models for post-consumer plastic sorting based on use cases

Use case	Name	Description
1	Color classification model	The model is trained on a dataset of images featuring plastics of various colors. Example: Sort out white yoghurt pots from the PP fraction
2	Food vs. non-food fraction separation model	Leveraging NIR and RGB visual data, this model tries to distinguish between food-contaminated plastics and those without food residues. Example: The separation of fruit peels and shampoo bottles in the PET fraction
3	Misclassification model	The model detects materials that have been inaccurately sorted. Example: PET bottles or yoghurt pots that have ended up in the residual waste fraction due to multi-layer sleeves, for example, are sorted out

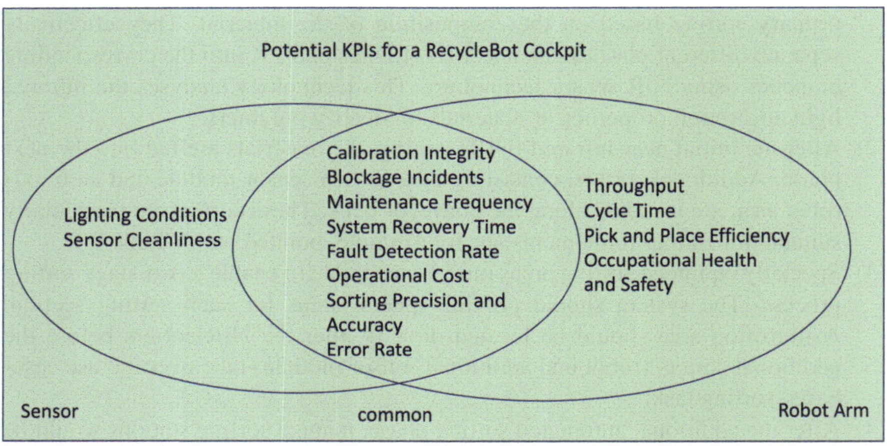

Fig. 9.4 Potential Key Performance Indicators (KPIs) for RecycleBot

adjust the sorting parameters in real-time, address identified issues, and enhance the process for increased throughput and improved material recovery.

9.1.3 *Machine Learning Use Cases for RecycleBot*

From the challenges outlined in Sect. 9.1 we have derived example use cases for the machine learning models as outlined in Table 9.1. These use cases have been conceptualized in a state of ongoing development and are not yet the final use cases of the project.

To optimize the performance of our ML-models, our idea is to apply a modular approach. Instead of training a single monolithic model to handle all types of plastic, we propose a modular approach in which each model specializes in one task, for example, separating white from printed yogurt cups. This allows for targeted optimization and potential replacement of each module without affecting the others. However, as with all ML projects, data is needed to teach algorithms to recognise patterns in different post-consumer plastic items.

9.2 Challenges to Improve Post-consumer Plastics Recycling

9.2.1 Pattern Recognition in a Diverse Environment

9.2.1.1 AI, Machine Learning and Computer Vision

The robotic system discussed, RecycleBot, is designed to identify post-consumer plastic objects on the conveyor belt within the sorting facility and sort them according to a use case (see Table 9.1). To understand the challenges related to this process, it is crucial to have a fundamental understanding of the concepts of artificial intelligence (AI), machine learning (ML), and computer vision (CV).

ML is a subarea of AI and can be seen as a practical application of statistics, focusing more on using computers to statistically estimate complex functions, and less on establishing confidence intervals for these functions [25]. ML allows to address challenges that are too complex to be resolved using predetermined (rule-based) programs developed by humans. A machine learning algorithm is an algorithm that can learn from data and can be broadly categorized as unsupervised and supervised learning algorithms. When it comes to sorting post-consumer plastic, utilizing supervised learning might be the appropriate method in the first iterations, as it involves a typical classification issue, assigning an input image to the output category "yogurt cup" or "no yogurt cup".

Deep learning is a type of machine learning algorithm that uses neural networks with multiple layers to model complex patterns in data and automatically learn hierarchical representations from raw data, capturing features at various levels of abstraction [42]. Computer vision (CV) is a field of study that seeks to develop techniques allowing computers to "see" and understand the content of, for example, digital images or videos. CV can be broadly defined as the process of "translating light into meaning", which may involve understanding geometry by reconstructing the scene or grasping semantics to recognize specific visual elements [22].

Summary ML empowers computers to learn from data, that means to recognize patterns. Deep learning enhances this capability through neural networks, and computer vision utilizes these advancements to interpret visual data from the world. All these areas are interlinked and relevant for a robotic system that must perceive its environment and update its internal representation of this environment.

9.2.1.2 Computer Vision Challenges

To understand the challenges of visual perception for computers, it is important to understand that images are typically represented as a pixel matrix. A pixel matrix refers to a two-dimensional array of pixels that make up a digital image, where each pixel is the smallest unit of the image that represents a particular color or shade [71]. This matrix structure organizes pixels into rows and columns, allowing visual information to be displayed in grid format. Essentially, anything that affects the pixel matrix is a challenge for computer vision software and ML algorithms. Some key challenges are [22]:

1. **Viewpoint challenges/deformation:** Depending on the viewpoint/form of an object, the pixel matrix might dramatically change despite showing the exact same object. A yogurt cup looks different depending on the angle at which the image is taken (see Fig. 9.5).
2. **Illumination:** Depending on the illumination of an image of the exact same scene from the exact same angle, the representation in the pixel matrix changes completely (see Fig. 9.7).
3. **Motion:** The image is blurred. A human might still recognize the object, but for the algorithm, the pixel matrix changed. Pre-knowledge is needed to recognize the object (see Fig. 9.8).
4. **Variations:** An object can have multiple variations. For example, a post-consumer plastic item, such as a yogurt cup (see Fig. 9.6), comes in various versions distinguished by differences in size, shape, color and form.
5. **Loss of information by translating 3D scenes into 2D images**: Converting a three-dimensional scene into a two-dimensional image and attempting its subsequent reconstruction inherently involves substantial information loss due to the projection process, leading to an ill-posed inverse problem characterized by the existence of multiple three-dimensional solutions for a single two-dimensional depiction.

Addressing specific challenges, such as illumination or motion, requires datasets that provide varied examples under different conditions. This enables algorithms to learn more effectively how to handle such variability. It is important to have datasets that are not only large but also rich in diversity and quality to facilitate nuanced learning and adaptation by ML models. Furthermore, the use of different sensors can help balance the challenges but also create new challenges.

In light of potential limitations in data availability or resource constraints, alternative strategies such as transfer learning, data augmentation, and synthetic data generation can emerge as vital components of a comprehensive data strategy. However, they can only be seen as a complement to the foundational necessity of ground-truth datasets.

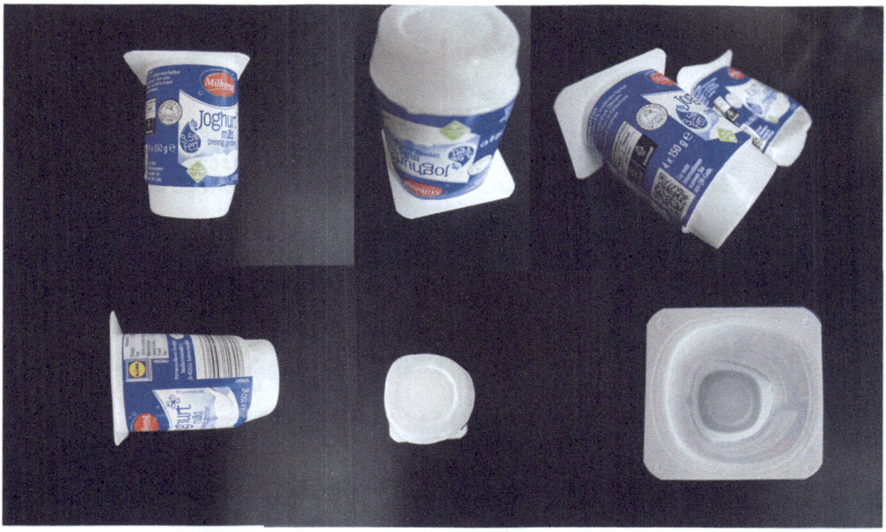

Fig. 9.5 Viewpoint challenge with different perspectives on a yogurt cup

Fig. 9.6 Variation challenge with different types of yogurt cups (random sample)

Fig. 9.7 Illumination challenge

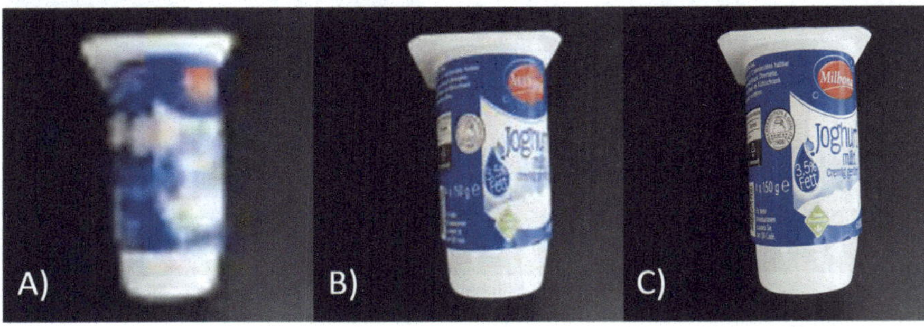

Fig. 9.8 Pixel challenge: (a) Matrix size is 64 × 64. (b) Matrix size is 215 × 215. (c) Matrix size is 1024 × 1024

9.2.1.3 Open Data for a Smart Environment

To address the challenges identified in machine learning and computer vision applications identified in the previous Sect. 9.2.1.2, it can be essential to use a wide range of strategies, tools, and sensors. A common method to overcome some of the obstacles is the use of large, high-quality data sets.

Data sets play a crucial role, as they serve as the foundation for all AI projects. The statement "Without data, there would be no AI" [30] highlights the essential role of data in enabling machines to learn, infer, and make decisions.

The beginning of every machine learning workflow (see Fig. 9.9) involves "data collection", followed by "data preparation" which is a labor-intensive phase, particularly due to the annotation process [7, 36, 56]. Subsequently, the stages of data preparation, model training and evaluation, deployment in production systems, ongoing model monitoring, and the continuous process of model refinement follow.

One common obstacle researchers face when connecting their expertise with the results of machine learning models is the limited availability of open data. According to van Gend and Zuiderwijk [73], the definition of open research data is data that is openly and freely accessible for an extended period, in formats that are open, interoperable, and machine-readable. It should be accompanied by adequate metadata and legally permissible for crawling, reusing, and modifying.

To create a sorting system, which includes a sorting unit consisting of a robotic arm, a sensor unit, and relevant software, it is essential to have data on

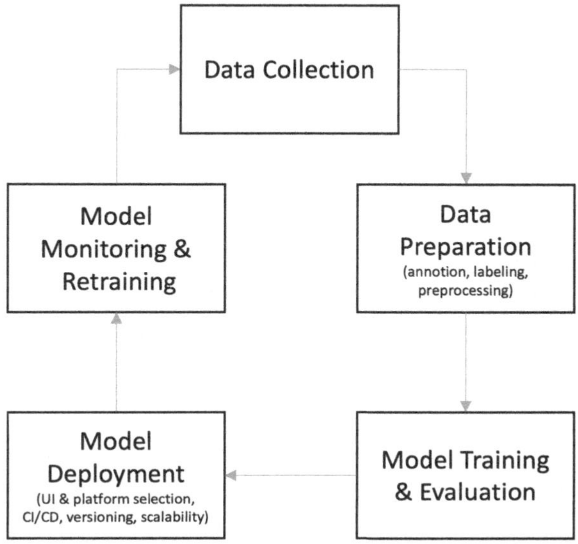

Fig. 9.9 Machine Learning workflow

German post-consumer plastic items that meet the FAIR standards. The FAIR principles emphasize that data should be easily findable, accessible, interoperable, and reusable [75].

Convolutional neural networks (CNNs) have achieved remarkable classification results in RGB datasets related to post-consumer waste, thanks to the use of open access data sets and deep learning techniques [39]. Several RGB datasets on consumer waste have been published in the last 10 years (among other: [6, 9, 28, 38, 41, 48, 61, 69, 72, 74, 79]). We greatly appreciate the sharing of data from researchers. However, none of the datasets address the context of German post-consumer plastics or the specific context of plastics sorting plants dedicated to differentiating output fractions of the sorting process, such as PET, HDPE, LDPE, PP, and PS. A challenge also arises when each research team annotates the data according to their classification problem, which typically involves classifying items as paper, glass, metal, or plastic. This means that, as researches, we can share some of the data, but we may need to repeat the annotation process according to our specific use cases. It is also important to note that most of the datasets differ from the reality of the German material recovery facility.

The availability of open datasets for the selected sensors (RGB, RGB-DEPTH, RGB-NIR Fusion) varies considerably. As mentioned above, there are several open RGB datasets. Until now, we have found a research team from TU-Delft that published their spectroscopic measurements on post-consumer plastics in the near-infrared (NIR) range [23] and "Open Specy" [15], an online tool where users can upload scanned spectra of any materials and with the help of available tools such as smoothing, the input spectrum can be post-processed and then identified using an online reference library. So far we have not found any open datasets with NIR-RGB Fusion or RGB-D data for post-consumer plastic.

9.2.1.4 Machine Learning Models for Waste Detection on the Conveyor Belt

In their review titled "Applications of Convolutional Neural Networks for Intelligent Waste Identification and Recycling" Wu et al. [77] identify ResNet as the most popular model for classification, YOLO for object detection, and Mask R-CNN for segmentation tasks. An in-depth analysis of models trained on conveyor belt datasets, which are of particular interest to the RecycleBot project due to their collection in real-world environments, confirms the trends observed by Wu et al. in the domain of supervised learning.

The ZeroWaste dataset, developed by Bashkirova et al. [6], employs a variety of learning techniques and models to address object detection and segmentation challenges. Initially, it utilizes fully-supervised object detection methods with models such as RetinaNet, Mask R-CNN, and TridentNet (with a Resnet-50 backbone). For semantic segmentation, a baseline is established using the DeepLabV3+ model. Additionally, the dataset incorporates fully-supervised semantic segmentation techniques with the ReCo model, semi-supervised semantic segmentation using the CCT model, and weakly-supervised semantic segmentation through methods like RISE, CAMs, PuzzleCAM, and EPS.

The WARP dataset, authored by Yudin et al. [79], is structured to support supervised detection, classification, and segmentation tasks. It includes various subsets such as WaRP-D, WaRP-C, and WaRP-S, each tailored for different aspects of these tasks. The detection models used encompass YOLOv3, YOLOv5, YOLOX, CenterNet, Faster R-CNN, Dynamic R-CNN, Sparse R-CNN, D-DETR, and TOOD. For classification, models like ViT, DEiT, RepVGG, SWiN, ResNet18, MobileNetv3, DenseNet121, ResXNet, EfficientNet-B5, and ConvNeXt are employed. Additionally, weakly-supervised segmentation techniques are explored using Class Activation Mapping (CAM).

The ReSort-IT dataset, introduced by Koskinopoulou et al. [38], comprises three distinct subsets: Basic Dataset, Synthetic Single Dataset, and Synthetic Complex Dataset. These subsets are designed to facilitate supervised detection, classification, and segmentation tasks on a conveyor belt setting. The primary model used is Mask R-CNN with ResNet-50 for feature extraction, along with four customized implementations.

One of the main challenges identified by the authors [6, 38, 79] is class imbalance, which is inherent in the nature of waste and reality. For example, Bashkirova et al. (ZeroWaste) created ZerowasteAug with augmented data and data from the TACO dataset to address the class imbalance.

A recent study examining transfer learning using the Wadaba dataset [11] demonstrated that the ResNeXt architecture achieved the highest accuracy of 87.44% after being trained for 20 epochs, with an average training time of thirteen minutes and eleven seconds. Implemented on smaller, portable devices, smaller networks such as MobileNetv2, SqueezeNet, and DenseNet offer comparable levels of accuracy. Although AlexNet trains models quickly, it achieved lower accuracy compared to other models. DenseNet, on the other hand, required the longest training time [11]. Transfer learning, a specialized technique within the deep learning field, aims to improve target learners on target domains by transferring the knowledge contained in different but related source domains [82].

9.2.2 *Finding Sensors for Post-consumer Plastics Sorting*

9.2.2.1 RGB (Red, Green, Blue) Sensor

Color is a perception that arises when the visual system is stimulated by electromagnetic waves, commonly referred to as light [24, 50, 62]. Color refers specifically to the perception that results from light within the visible spectrum of the electromagnetic spectrum, with wavelengths ranging from 400 to 700 nm, striking the retina of the human eye [60].

To effectively use color as a visual indicator in image processing, graphics, and computer vision applications, a suitable approach to representing the color signal is essential [60]. Various color specification systems, also known as color models, have been developed to meet this requirement by providing different methods for describing color. A color space specifies precisely the components of the color model. While humans might characterize a color based on its brightness, hue, and saturation, a computer can represent a color through the levels of red, green, and blue phosphor emissions needed to replicate that color [21]. The proposal of a trichromatic color vision that became the basis for the RGB (red-green-blue) color model came from Thomas Young and Hermann Helmholtz in the mid-nineteenth century [12].

The RGB color space can be represented as a cube where the three axes represent red, green, and blue, respectively [12, 21]. In this cube, the bottom corner, where red, green, and blue are all set to 0, represents black, and the top corner, where red, green and blue are all set to 255 (in an 8-bit per channel display system), represents white. RGB is widely used in many computer applications because it does not require any conversion to display information on a screen, making it the default color space for many applications [21, 29].

The computer vision challenges mentioned in Sect. 9.2.1.2 correspond to the difficulties encountered with RGB sensors.

9.2.2.2 Near Infrared (NIR) Sensor

Near-infrared spectroscopy (NIRS) is a spectroscopy in the region of 12,500–4000 cm^{-1} (800–2500 nm) [33, 55, 66] that is often used to characterize materials,

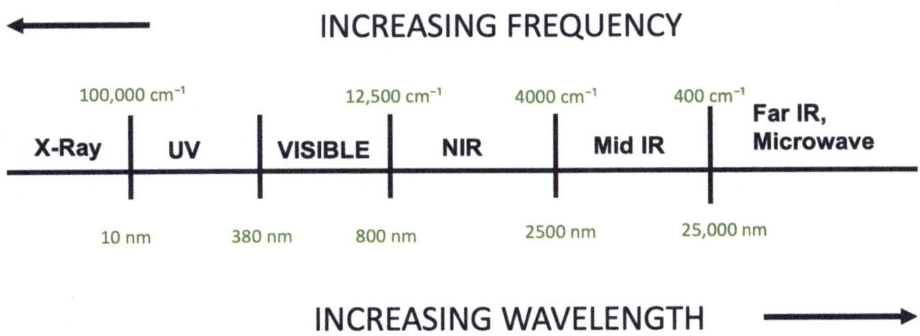

Fig. 9.10 Electromagnetic spectrum overview: From X-ray to microwave, including visible and infrared ranges based on [51]

including plastics. NIR technology utilizes the wavelength signatures of particular polymers to differentiate between them, irrespective of their color, and is utilized in material recovery facilities (MRFs) and plastic recycling facilities [1]. NIR spectroscopy involves absorption, emission, scattering, reflection, and diffuse reflection of light [55] and is considered the most effective technique for sorting [1, 19] in the industry. As shown in Fig. 9.1 RecycleBot is designed to complement existing NIR sensors in MRFs. To propose a sequential solution, it is important to have an understanding of the basics and challenges of NIR spectroscopy.

Figure 9.10 displays an electromagnetic spectrum with various ranges marked, including X-ray, ultraviolet (UV), visible light, near-infrared (NIR), mid-infrared (Mid IR), far-infrared (Far IR), and microwave. Each range is associated with specific wavelengths, measured in nanometers (nm), and wavenumbers, measured in reciprocal centimeters (cm^{-1}). Visible light is highlighted in the spectrum and spans approximately from 380 to 800 nm. The inverse relationship between frequency and wavelength, denoting that as the wavelength increases, the frequency decreases is also illustrated. The NIR section, marked by a hatched pattern, is shown as the region just beyond visible light, extending from about 800 to 2500 nm.

The basic principle of recording a NIR spectrum is that the absorption/transmission of radiation is measured as a function of wavelengths/wavenumber. The molecules in the sample interact with light, whereby certain wavelengths are absorbed and sometimes also transmitted. This absorption leads to an increase in the vibrational energy of specific molecular bonds [55]. A molecule is IR-active if it leads to a change in the dipole moment of the molecule. This change enables the interaction between the molecule and the electromagnetic field of light.

Not all molecular vibrations lead to such a change; those that leave the dipole moment unchanged are "inactive" in IR spectroscopy. These are then often Raman-active, a polarization spectroscopy method [55].

In an IR spectrum, absorption events are displayed as bands. A band corresponds to a specific absorption frequency associated with a molecular vibration. The shape and width of a band can be influenced by various factors, including the molecular environment, the presence of hydrogen bonding, and interactions between molecules. The position of a band in the spectrum indicates the wavelength of the associated vibration, while the intensity (height) of the band correlates with the concentration of absorbing molecules [66].

Spectral band parameters are the position of the band maximum (wavenumber k or wavelength), the intensity of the band (height or area above the baseline), and the band shape (influenced by the environment of the vibrating group). The standard format of an IR spectrum is transmittance T or reflectance R (%) versus wavenumber (cm^{-1}) [55].

Each chemical compound has a unique pattern of absorption bands that depends on the type of bonds present and the molecular structure. A near-infrared spectrum is particularly suitable for identifying functional groups that are characteristic of specific types of plastic. These patterns form the so-called signature spectrum of the compound [66]. The signature spectrum of a substance in the NIR range is a direct consequence of its molecular composition and structure. It enables the identification and quantification of specific components in a sample. This enables fingerprinting of the substances with a comparison of these signature spectra with known reference spectra in order to identify materials or analyze their composition [66].

In the case of NIRS, changes in vibrational modes such as valence vibrations (changes in bond length) and deformation vibrations (changes in bond angle) are considered. Certain vibration modes are excited by absorption. During the subsequent relaxation, light of this energy difference is emitted, which when measured results in the absorption bands. The number of possible vibrational modes of a molecule depends on its size and complexity, with larger molecules having a higher number of specific absorption bands [33, 66].

Two oscillation compositions can be distinguished, particularly in the NIR range. Overtones occur when light of the wavelength is absorbed at a multiple of a fundamental frequency. Molecular vibrations have a fundamental frequency (the so-called fundamental tone) at which they absorb most strongly. Overtones occur at higher frequencies and are usually weaker than the fundamental. Due to the anharmonicity of the molecular potential of a real oscillator, the energy difference between neighboring vibrational states decreases, which enables the excitation of higher vibrational states. These overtones are specific to the chemical structure of the molecules and can be used to characterize substances [55, 66].

Combination vibrations result from the simultaneous excitation of two or more independent vibrational modes of a molecule. In contrast to overtones, where the frequencies are multiples of a single vibration, combination vibrations are sums or differences of the frequencies of different fundamental vibrations. Combination vibrations extend the spectrum of observable bands and provide additional information about the molecular structure [66].

In plastics analysis, NIRS enables the rapid and non-destructive characterization of plastics with regard to their chemical composition. By analyzing the signature spectra, different types of plastic can be distinguished [33].

However, recording a complete spectrum at several wavelengths requires more time. In order to enable fast, robust, and automated in-line evaluation of the spectroscopy data, indices of specific wavelengths can be found in the signal spectra of the plastic types, on the basis of which they can be clearly classified [54].

In addition to the time advantage of the measurement, this drastic data reduction brings advantages in further sensor fusion application development. By reducing the complexity of the raw data, the modeling effort and the computing power required for classification can be greatly reduced.

In Sect. 9.1 some of the general challenges have already been mentioned. The Association of Plastic Recyclers [1] outline two specific issues with NIR sorting from the industry perspective:

(a) **"Shrink sleeve labels"** (Multi-layer): Shrink sleeve labels cover the whole or a relevant part of the bottle and can be made from a different type of plastic. Sometimes, NIR machines cannot see through these labels to identify the plastic type of the bottle. If the label and bottle differ, the bottle could end up in the wrong recycling stream or be considered waste.
(b) **Black and dark colored items:** The reliability of NIR sorting in identifying black plastic bottles or objects is limited. Due to the light absorption by black colorants, NIR sensors often fail to detect black items, as they do not reflect any distinctive signature.

9.2.2.3 Sensor Fusion (NIR and RGB)

A potential scenario for RecycleBot includes the integration of two sensors, namely RGB (see Sect. 9.2.2.1) and NIR (see Sect. 9.2.2.2). By merging the visible and infrared images, it is possible to utilize both the color and texture details from the visible images along with the information provided by the infrared images [46, 68]. Fusion, generally speaking, is the act of combining data from multiple sensors or groups of sensors to create a comprehensive model of the surroundings [31].

The challenge of infrared and visible image fusion is gaining popularity in scientific communities. In their comprehensive systematic review on the use of optical sensors and machine learning algorithms to characterize material flow in mechanical recycling processes from 2000 to 2021, Kroell et al. found that only 15 of 267 (5.6%) studies in their dataset used multiple sensors. The primary factor they point out is the increased technical complexity involved in the integration of data from various sensors [39].

Creating an effective data representation and structure that can integrate information from multiple sources is a major challenge because the data collected by these sensors is diverse, complex, erroneous, and voluminous [70] and even the most advanced sensors exhibit some level of inaccuracy [4].

In RecycleBot we face at least two fusion challenges with our central hardware components: (a) State estimation (combining position, orientation, and velocity) for the robotic arm to pick and place post-consumer plastics items. (b) Object recognition (combining NIR and RGB images) to make the robot arm pick an item defined in Table 9.1.

Challenge 1: State Estimation Methods

Classical signal processing techniques such as the Kalman filter [35, 57] have established the foundational theories behind data fusion technology, which have been expanded upon by a diverse range of approaches including statistical inference [64], Dempster-Shafer theory [65], and fuzzy logic [78], significantly advancing the field of information fusion technology [70].

The Kalman filter is a state estimation technique. The state estimation technique is a method to determine the state of a system based on measured observations [17]. In robotics, this would for example be to estimate the position and orientation of the robot, since the robot is moving, this requires a permanent update of the prediction and the update step. The state of a robot comprises various variables, such as position, orientation, and velocity, which, when identified, completely define the robot's movement throughout time. Understanding the importance of state estimation requires understanding the characteristics of sensors, and sensors inherently possess limited accuracy, resulting in uncertainties in all measurements obtained from them [4]. While certain sensors excel at measuring particular parameters, even the most advanced sensors exhibit some level of inaccuracy [4]. When integrating multiple sensor readings to form a state estimation, it is crucial to consider and manage all associated uncertainties [4]. In the context of the Kalman filter, data fusion refers to the process of combining predicted state information with new observational data to produce an updated estimate that is more accurate than either source of information alone.

In order to address the main challenges faced by the traditional Kalman filter, scholars have devised remedies by combining machine learning methods with the Kalman filter [3, 44, 70]. The key concerns include system modeling (whether theoretical or experimental) and parameter identification [3]. This means that data fusion involves combining different methods.

The modeling and design of state estimators for pick-and-place robotic arms is a central challenge in the research area of robotics. Pick-and-place robots are engineered to be capable of grasping components, relocating them in a particular direction (using translational or rotational motions), and accurately placing them at a specified location [16].

Challenge 2: NIR and RGB Image Fusion Methods

Image fusion techniques can be broadly categorized into spatial domain fusion methods, transform domain fusion methods, and deep learning methods [36, 44, 46]. Spatial domain fusion methods [46] involve direct manipulation of pixel values within images to synthesize a new image that combines the desired features of each input image. This method works by evaluating individual pixels across multiple images, using algorithms to select or combine pixel values based on predefined criteria to produce a result that ideally captures the optimal characteristics of each source image. Spatial domain techniques, such as the simple average method, involve the combination of images by calculating the average of pixels [36] (Fig. 9.11).

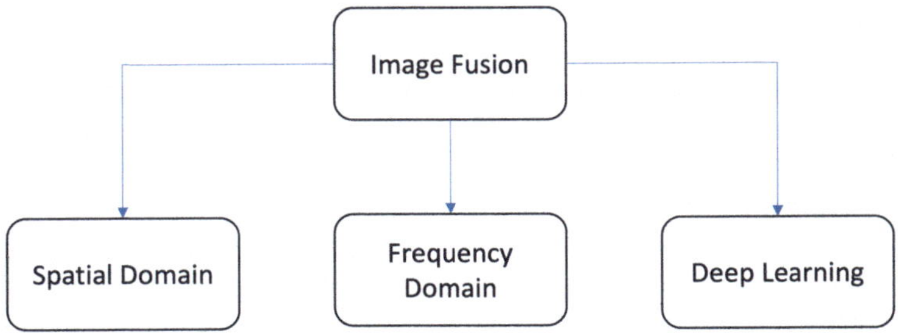

Fig. 9.11 Image fusion techniques, own illustration

Transform domain fusion methods [46], conversely, require an initial conversion of images from their spatial representation into a frequency domain, utilizing mathematical transformations such as the Fourier Transform. This conversion facilitates the differentiation and manipulation of image components on the basis of their frequency characteristics. Following the fusion process in the frequency domain, an inverse transformation is applied to revert the synthesized image back to its spatial form.

Deep learning methods, as described in Sect. 9.2.1.1, are a type of machine learning algorithm that uses neural networks with multiple layers to model complex patterns in data and automatically learn hierarchical representations from raw data, capturing features at various levels of abstraction [42]. Generally speaking, deep learning methods are used to combine different images into a single complete image. Several papers focus on using deep learning methods as fusion methods. Han and Jung [26] propose the deep selective fusion of VIS and NIR images using unsupervised U-Net. Mei and Jung [52] propose deep fusion of RGB and NIR paired images under low light conditions using convolutional neural networks. Zhou and Jung [81] propose multi-spectral fusion of RGB and NIR images using weighted least squares (WLS) and alternating guidance. Soroush and Baleghi [68] introduce a fusion technique that relies on modified visual saliency points. To create a superior quality fused image that accurately captures visual details of both NIR and RGB images, the method uses the pixel intensities and gradients of the images [68]. Salience is a visual characteristic that distinguishes an object from its surroundings [76]. The visual saliency detection model simulates the human visual system to perceive the scene, and has been widely used in many vision tasks [13]. For a more generic review of infrared and visible image fusion methods, see [49].

However, it should be noted that deep learning methods do not solve all of the challenges of infrared and visible image fusion. In the field, we encounter several obstacles that we still need to solve:

1. **Cost:** Higher costs compared to standard RGB systems (approximately €20,000 vs. €5500)

2. **Hardware synchronization:** Hardware triggers to synchronize the cameras increased complexity and costs.
3. **Special lighting systems:** Special lighting systems are required to cover a broader area to ensure visibility
4. **Adaptation of the ML pipeline:** IR+RGB systems produce special image formats that differ from standard 3-channel RGB formats, leading to incompatibilities with existing AI pipelines and labeling tools.
5. **Additional labeling effort:** The different input requires more effort in labeling the data, making the overall process more time-consuming and labor intensive.
6. **Calibration mechanisms:** The differing functionalities and capture ranges of the IR and RGB sensors require individually tailored calibration processes.
7. **Advanced algorithms for data processing and analysis:** Complex information resulting from the combined data streams requires advanced algorithms for effective interpretation

9.2.2.4 RGB-Depth Sensor

RGB-D images combine RGB (red, green, blue) color data with depth data, resulting in a more comprehensive representation of a scene. They include both color information captured by standard cameras and distance information captured by depth sensors, providing both the appearance (color and texture) and the shape (geometry and relative positioning) of the scene elements [34]. Each pixel in this grid has values for the colors red, green, and blue, ranging from 0 to 255, and an additional numerical value to each pixel that represents the distance from the object to the camera, the depth, resulting in four values per pixel (RGB-D). Depth data is valuable for computer vision applications because it enables robots to measure their environment more accurately, leading to a better understanding of the scene. In industrial contexts, algorithmic architectures that integrate state-of-the-art computer vision and machine learning models, such as Yolactedge [43], use RGB-D data for accurate garbage detection and spatial localization [47].

General challenges of RGB-D consumer cameras [34]:

1. **Holes:** The holes in the depth map are a common challenge when working with RGB depth cameras, as described in various studies. These occlusions occur when an object is only visible from one perspective, making it impossible to record it in the depth map.
2. **Edge erosion:** Another major problem is the blurring of edges. Sharp edges are usually not clearly defined in the depth map, which can cause problems when processing the data further.
3. **Ambient lighting:** Ambient light can be a problem, particularly for cameras that use active lighting [37], which is the use of a controlled light source that is an integral part of the camera system to improve depth perception and image quality.

4. **Motion:** RGB depth cameras are intended for use in dynamic environments. However, rapid movement between shots can result in significant artifacts on the depth map.
5. **Multiple reflections:** A particular problem arises when multiple reflections arrive at the camera, for example, through glass or reflective surfaces. Filtering out the correct depth information from these multiple reflections is a very active problem in the further development of 3D cameras [47].

9.2.3 Finding the Appropriate Gripper to Automate the Sorting Process

The appropriate handling technology generally depends on the characteristics of the workpiece (Fig. 9.12), which include the properties and behavior. In practice, the best gripping technology is often selected depending on the application and the associated requirements for the operating principle. In addition to the most commonly used mechanical or pneumatic operating principles, there are electromagnetic and positive locking operating principles. Mechanical grippers are suitable solutions for a wide range of gripping processes, as a high holding force and fast gripping times characterize them. If a specific application is required, alternative operating principles are used, for example, vacuum grippers when it comes to sensitive component surfaces, such as glass panes [27].

The first step in selecting a suitable gripper was to determine the characteristics of the workpiece and the requirements of the grippers. As shown in Fig. 9.13, the parameters of the gripping objects are wide-ranging, which means that the waste objects are subject to damage and differ in each case. For this reason, the gripper selection was based on the manufacturer's data on grippers and sorting systems.

During the analyses of the gripper selection, various gripping methods were found to be used in current sorting systems for waste separation, including compressed air nozzles, industrial vacuum suction grippers, and, in some cases, 2-finger grippers [2]. However, each of these methods presented difficulties in our specific application. The biggest challenge for the proven robotic systems for waste

Feature		Behavior	
Geometrical	Physical	Resting behavior	Conveying behavior
• Dimensions • Shape • Size • Significant form elements • Symmetries	• Hardness • Mass • Material • Surface structure • Centre of gravity • Stiffness	• Hanging ability • Orientation • Stability • Stackability	• Sliding behavior • Rolling behavior • Stability

Fig. 9.12 Workpiece features according to Lotter [45]

Possible parameters of post-consumer plastics

Shape	Curved, cylindrical, flat, oval, rectangular
Material	Impermeable, mouldable, rigid
Surface condition	Cracked, creased, grooved, smooth
Appearance	Countamination due to content residues
Mass	Lightweight (up to 70 gram)
Temperature	Outdoor and room temperature (0°C-24°C)
Gripping direction	Vertical, different levels
Type of handling	Grip, lift, hold, release
Available surface	Varies depending on the property
Cycle time	At least 80 picks/min

Fig. 9.13 Possible parameters of post-consumer plastics, own illustration

sorting lies in the characteristics of gripping non-standardized objects. Hereby it is meant that all objects to be grabbed have different parameters and properties, for example, due to damage that occurs during the collection process of the yellow bag or the yellow bin. Therefore, we focused intensively on identifying the most suitable gripping method for our RecycleBot. By analyzing the different gripper mechanisms mentioned, it was possible to determine whether the combination of individual gripper mechanisms is promising [2]. Extensive market research into combination grippers revealed that there are currently two different grippers that may be suitable, both of which have a similar design and characteristics. Both grippers are intended for use in the food industry, logistics, or for automated systems to handle small and non-uniform objects. They have different numbers of flexible fingers arranged in a circle. A vacuum gripper is mounted in the center of each circle to support the fingers in their handling.

Due to the limited selection of combination grippers and the fact that their properties, such as the choice of the suction pad, cannot be customized at will, the next step was to take a closer look at vacuum grippers to develop a new gripper if necessary (Fig. 9.14).

Vacuum grippers for the packaging sector are available in various sizes and shapes for all kinds of materials. To limit the market research in the field of vacuum grippers, the manufacturers explicitly searched for packaging grippers and grippers for plastic objects and films. The suction pads discovered all have similar designs and properties.

The leading supplier of suction pads for the packaging industry is Schmalz GmbH, with 24 different designs, each with additional variations due to their characteristics. The designs can be oval or round, with diameters from 7 to 95 mm

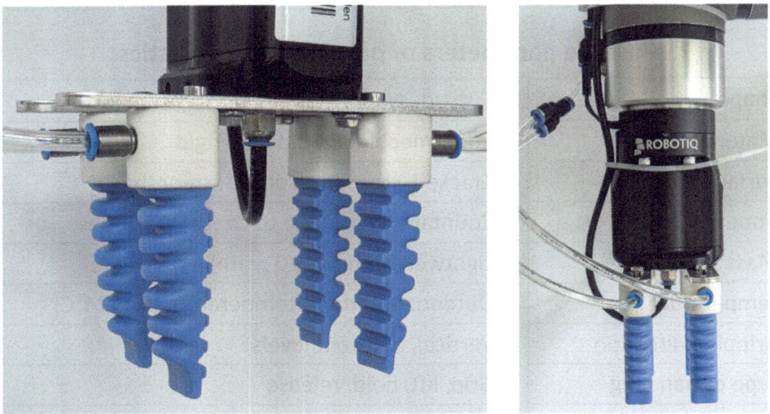

Fig. 9.14 Current gripper in use in the Aalen University laboratory

Fig. 9.15 Selection of grippers, own illustration

and several folds from 1.5 to 4.5. Partially equipped with a flexible sealing lip, the suction pads can handle flat and even objects (1.5 to 2.5 folds) up to very uneven products (3.5 to 4.5 folds) [63].

Piab Vakuumtechnik distinguishes six different types of suction pads for the packaging industry. The difference lies in the design. While Schmalz lists both oval and round grippers, Piab only offers round versions. The other features are identical, such as the number of folds and possible diameters, as well as a flexible sealing lip in some cases [58]. In addition, a few suppliers offering vacuum grippers specifically for the packaging sector could be found. One was the "suction pad 4.5 bellows for the packaging industry, MVP series" from Coval Vakuumtechnik GmbH, available in diameters 20–50 mm. Like some previous grippers, it has a flexible sealing lip [14]. The vacuum gripper from SMC Deutschland GmbH, "Vacuum cup, 5.5-stage bellows with guide attachment -ZP3P-JT", which has an additional fold, has almost identical properties [67].

For the first series of tests, vacuum grippers, shown in Fig. 9.15, were selected. The grippers tested for their suitability for handling post-consumer waste were

Specified designation	Size [mm]	Number of folds	Sealing lip	Material	Material hardness [Shore A]	Holding force F_H [N]	Special properties according to manufacturer
FestoD40	Ø40	1,5	Nein	VMQ	60 ± 5	58	robust, reliable
PiabD40	Ø40	2	Ja	SI[1] TPE[2]	50[1] 87[2]	23,5	for surfaces that are uneven and rough
Schmalz Grey D40	Ø40	1,5	Ja	EDPM	45	8,8	for thin flexible objects
Schmalz Green Orange D40	Ø40	3,5	Ja	SI	30[1] 55[2]	40	for thin flexible objects
Schmalz Green Orange D30	Ø30	3,5	Ja	SI	30[1] 55[2]	24	for thin flexible objects
Schmalz Green D30	Ø30	4,5	Ja	SI	55	12,8	for particularly uneven workpieces

[1] Material or degree of hardness of the sealing lip
[2] Material or degree of hardness of the base body

Fig. 9.16 Features of the selected grippers

initially limited to vacuum grippers based on market research and the fact that functioning technologies also work with them. Primarily, suction cups were chosen which, according to the manufacturer, are intended for the packaging industry. These comprise a robust body to which a soft sealing lip is attached, which can adapt to packaging deformations. Two diameters were selected for adequate comparison, each with different and partly identical construction characteristics. The exact gripper properties are shown in Fig. 9.16.

9.2.4 Establishing the Experimental Groundwork: From Laboratory Prototyping to Production Realization

Robots are already used in recycling plants today to carry out the sorting process at high speed (up to 80 picks per minute). Although such systems fulfill their purpose, they are associated with considerable costs and are often not feasible. In addition, failures (mechanical or electrical) are connected to a standstill of the entire sorting system. Our test setups are designed to simulate realistic conditions and test the gripping methods in various scenarios. A variable-speed conveyor belt, a camera system for precise recognition of recyclable materials, and a robot arm with an interchangeable gripper form the basis of our experiments. These structured experiments enable us to gain comprehensive insights into the performance of the various gripping methods.

Based on an initial series of tests at Aalen University, which originated from a research project and was performed with the setup shown in Fig. 9.17, the first results were obtained for the selection of suitable grippers. The evaluation of the test series shows that the grippers should be vacuum grippers with at least 3.5 folds and a flexible sealing lip. The material hardness grades of the sealing lip and the base

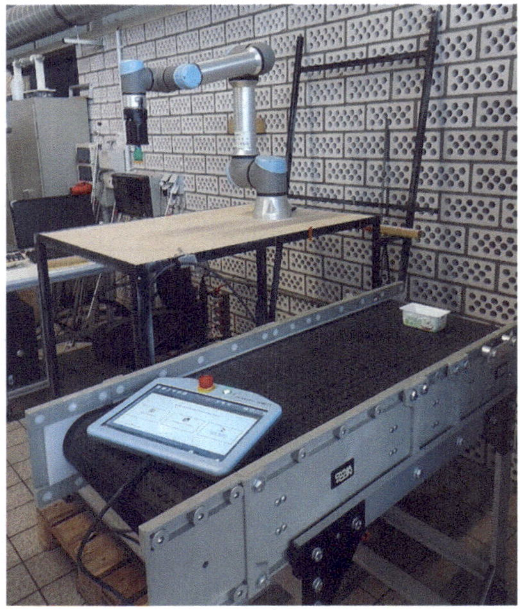

Fig. 9.17 Laboratory set-up at Aalen University

body, in contrast, should differ in that the base body should be significantly harder than the sealing lip. It was also found that smaller diameters (Ø 30 millimeters instead of Ø 40 millimeters) are more suitable as they can be positioned more precisely. As the results of the research work are not yet sufficient to decide on an exact gripper, further test series are planned in the form of student projects.

9.3 Conclusions and Future Work

The current chapter investigates the optimization of post-consumer plastic sorting using machine learning and sensor technologies. The analysis focuses on the situation of post-consumer plastics in Germany, proposing solutions involving machine learning and additional sensor modules for computer vision. Machine learning models are evaluated for their efficacy in waste detection on conveyor belts, considering the challenges posed by pattern recognition in diverse environments. Specific sensor technologies such as RGB, NIR, sensor fusion (NIR and RGB), and RGB-depth sensors are explored for their potential to improve sorting accuracy. The development of appropriate gripper mechanisms to automate the sorting process and the establishment of experimental groundwork from laboratory prototyping to production realization are also discussed.

Future research into optimising the sorting of post-consumer plastics through the RecycleBot project will involve an ongoing, iterative investigation of the operational context of recycling facilities. This will include visiting sorting cabins and working with workers who manually sort waste and have to solve complex tasks. This collaboration provides valuable expertise and possible insights into the intended robot-human interactions, which is crucial for the design of systems in the field.

The evaluation of different ML models for sorting tasks will be a focus. This will involve experimenting with both existing and new datasets to identify the most effective machine learning approaches. Expanding these datasets with more diverse and real-world samples from the German context will be essential for training context-aware models. The application of transfer learning on carefully curated datasets for fine-tuning models represents a possibility to explore enhancing AI efficiency in resource-constrained environments. Given the limited availability of open data for German post-consumer plastics [5] we propose implementing an AI policy that prioritizes data-centric approaches in the machine learning life-cycle to address this challenge [32, 40, 80].

Efforts will also be directed towards optimising gripper mechanisms to ensure precise and efficient handling of multi-materials. Collaborations will be established with researchers in the field to leverage their expertise and integrate the latest advances into the project. These efforts aim to improve the overall performance and reliability of sorting systems, ultimately contributing to more efficient and effective recycling processes.

References

1. APR. (2018). *The Association of Plastic Recyclers*. https://plasticsrecycling.org/images/Design-Guidance-Tests/APR-RES-SORT-2-NIR-sorting-resource.pdf
2. Aschenbrenner, D., Colloseus, C., Khoury, R., & Fangerow, N. (2023). Robot-assisted automated sorting techniques for plastic recycling. *Procedia CIRP*, *120*, 1232–1237. https://www.sciencedirect.com/science/article/pii/S2212827123008867
3. Bai, Y., Yan, B., Zhou, C., Su, T., & Jin, X. (2023). State of art on state estimation: Kalman filter driven by machine learning. *Annual Reviews in Control*, *56*, 100909. https://www.sciencedirect.com/science/article/pii/S1367578823000731
4. Barfoot, T. D. (2017). *State estimation for robotics*. Cambridge: Cambridge University Press. https://www.cambridge.org/core/books/state-estimation-for-robotics/AC0E0AC229C55203B3C8F106BCB61F48
5. Basedow, N., Hadasch, K., Dawoud, M., Colloseus, C., Taha, I., & Aschenbrenner, D. (2024). Open data sources for post-consumer plastic sorting: What we have and what we still need. *Procedia CIRP*, *122*, 1042–1047.
6. Bashkirova, D., Abdelfattah, M., Zhu, Z., Akl, J., Alladkani, F., Hu, P., Ablavsky, V., Calli, B., Bargal, S. A., & Saenko, K. (2022). ZeroWaste Dataset: Towards deformable object segmentation in cluttered scenes. arXiv:2106.02740 [cs]. http://arxiv.org/abs/2106.02740
7. Benenson, R., Popov, S., & Ferrari, V. (2019). Large-scale interactive object segmentation with human annotators. arXiv:1903.10830 [cs]. http://arxiv.org/abs/1903.10830
8. Billmayer, L. (2023). *Gelbe Tonne: Wie viel wirklich recycelt wird | ZDFheute*. http://zdfheute-stories-scroll.zdf.de/gelbe-tonne-recycling/
9. Bobulski, J., & Kubanek, M. (2021). Deep learning for plastic waste classification system. *Applied Computational Intelligence and Soft Computing*, *2021*, 6626948.
10. BVSE. (2022). *Knapp vorbei ist auch daneben: Wie Fehlwürfe in der Gelben Tonne oder dem Gelben Sack das Recycling behindern*. https://www.bvse.de/sachverstand-bvse-recycling/themen-ereignisse/8237-knapp-vorbei-ist-auch-daneben-wie-fehlwuerfe-in-der-gelben-tonne-oder-dem-gelben-sack-das-recycling-behindern.html

11. Chazhoor, A. A. P., Ho, E. S., Gao, B., & Woo, W. L. (2022). Deep transfer learning benchmark for plastic waste classification. *Intelligence & Robotics*, *2*(1), 1–19.
12. ColoRotate. (2024). *Color theory | ColoRotate*. http://learn.colorotate.org/color-models/
13. Cong, R., Lei, J., Fu, H., Cheng, M.-M., Lin, W., & Huang, Q. (2019). Review of visual saliency detection with comprehensive information. *IEEE Transactions on Circuits and Systems for Video Technology*, *29*(10), 2941–2959. arXiv:1803.03391 [cs]. http://arxiv.org/abs/1803.03391
14. Coval. (2024). *Coval - Sauggreifer 4,5 Faltenbalg für die Verpackungsindustrie, Reihe MVP*. https://www.coval-germany.com/Produkte/sauggreifer-4-5-faltenbalg-fur-die-verpackungsindustrie-reihe-mvp-5078.htm
15. Cowger, W., Steinmetz, Z., Gray, A., Munno, K., Lynch, J., Hapich, H., Primpke, S., De Frond, H., Rochman, C., & Herodotou, O. (2021). Microplastic spectral classification needs an open source community: Open specy to the rescue! *Analytical Chemistry*, *93*(21), 7543–7548. https://pubs.acs.org/doi/10.1021/acs.analchem.1c00123
16. Dandago, K., Mohammed, A., Ubadike, O., Zango, M., Hassan, A., Muhammad, I., & Yahaya, J. U. (2021). Modelling and design of state estimator for a pick and place robotic arm. *FUOYE Journal of Engineering and Technology*, *6*, 375.
17. Dehghanpour, K., Wang, Z., Wang, J., Yuan, Y., & Bu, F. (2019). A survey on state estimation techniques and challenges in smart distribution systems. *IEEE Transactions on Smart Grid*, *10*(2), 2312–2322. Conference Name: IEEE Transactions on Smart Grid. https://ieeexplore.ieee.org/document/8466598
18. Eberl, T. (2023). *Plastikmüll reduzieren: Erprobte Schritte gegen Verpackungsabfall im Haushalt: Grundwissen zu Verpackungen, Recycling, Mikroplastik und Umweltverschmutzung sowie ein Praxisbeispiel für die Plastikreduzierung in einem Privathaushalt*, tredition. Google-Books-ID: 59DbEAAAQBAJ.
19. Eichhorn, S. (2022). *Basics of NIRS and how it is used in plastic recycling*. https://www.solidscanner.com/en/basics-and-limitations-of-nirs-nirs-and-how-it-is-used-in-plastic-recycling/
20. EUR-Lex. (2018). *Richtlinie 94/62/EG des Europäischen Parlaments und des Rates vom 20. Dezember 1994 über Verpackungen und Verpackungsabfälle*. Legislative Body: OP_DATPRO. http://data.europa.eu/eli/dir/1994/62/2018-07-04/deu
21. Ford, A., & Roberts A. (1998). *Colour space conversions* (Vol. 657, pp. 1–31). London: Westminster University.
22. Geiger, A. (2023). *Computer Vision | Universität Tübingen*. https://uni-tuebingen.de/fakultaeten/mathematisch-naturwissenschaftliche-fakultaet/fachbereiche/informatik/lehrstuehle/autonomous-vision/lectures/computer-vision/
23. GitHub-Plastic-Scanner. (2022). *GitHub - Plastic-Scanner/data: Collection of dataset from different boards and spectrometers*. https://github.com/Plastic-Scanner/data
24. Gonzalez, R. C., & Woods, R. E. (1992). *Digital image processing*. Addison-Wesley. Google-Books-ID: C_FRAAAAMAAJ.
25. Goodfellow, Y. B., & Courville, A. (2016). *Deep learning*. https://www.deeplearningbook.org/
26. Han, Q., & Jung, C. (2022). Deep selective fusion of visible and near-infrared images using unsupervised U-net. *IEEE Transactions on Neural Networks and Learning Systems*, 1–12. Conference Name: IEEE Transactions on Neural Networks and Learning Systems. https://ieeexplore.ieee.org/document/9697423
27. Hesse, S., & Malisa, V. (2016), Taschenbuch Robotik? Montage? Handhabung, in Stefan, H. & Viktorio, M. (Eds.), *Taschenbuch Robotik - Montage - Handhabung* (pp. 1–11). Carl Hanser Verlag GmbH & Co. KG. https://www.hanser-elibrary.com/doi/10.3139/9783446445499.fm
28. Hong, J., Fulton, M. S., & Sattar, J. (2020). *TrashCan 1.0 an instance-segmentation labeled dataset of trash observations*. Accepted: 2020-07-23T18:22:58Z. http://conservancy.umn.edu/handle/11299/214865
29. Ibraheem, N. A., Hasan, M. M., Khan, R. Z., & Mishra, P. K. (2012). Understanding color models: A review. *ARPN Journal of Science and Technology*, *2*(3), 265–275.
30. Institute, O. D. (2023). *What do we mean by 'without data, there is no AI'?*. https://theodi.org/news-and-events/blog/what-do-we-mean-by-without-data-there-is-no-ai/

31. ISO-23150. (2021). *ISO 23150:2021(en), Road vehicles — Data communication between sensors and data fusion unit for automated driving functions — Logical interface*. https://www.iso.org/obp/ui/fr/#iso:std:iso:23150:ed-1:v1:en:term:3.1.7
32. Jarrahi, M. H., Memariani, A., & Guha, S. (2023). The principles of data-centric AI. *Communications of the ACM*, *66*(8), 84–92.
33. Jr, J. W., & Weyer, L. (2007). *Practical guide to interpretive near-infrared spectroscopy*. Boca Raton: CRC Press.
34. Kadambi, A., Bhandari, A., & Raskar, R. (2014). 3D depth cameras in vision: Benefits and limitations of the hardware: With an emphasis on the first- and second-generation kinect models, in Shao, L., Han, J., Kohli, P., & Zhang, Z. (Eds.), *Computer vision and machine learning with RGB-D sensors* (pp. 3–26). Series Title: Advances in computer vision and pattern recognition. Cham: Springer International Publishing. https://link.springer.com/10.1007/978-3-319-08651-4_1
35. Kalman, R. E. (1960). The seminal Kalman filter paper (1960), *82*, 35–45. https://www.cs.unc.edu/~welch/kalman/kalmanPaper.html
36. Kaur, H., Koundal, D., & Kadyan, V. (2021). Image fusion techniques: A survey. *Archives of Computational Methods in Engineering*, *28*(7), 4425–4447. https://doi.org/10.1007/s11831-021-09540-7
37. Kong, D., Zhang, Y., & Dai, W. (2021). Direct near-infrared-depth visual SLAM with active lighting. *IEEE Robotics and Automation Letters*, *6*, 7057–7064.
38. Koskinopoulou, M., Raptopoulos, F., Papadopoulos, G., Mavrakis, N., & Maniadakis, M. (2021). *Robotic waste sorting technology: Toward a vision-based categorization system for the industrial robotic separation of recyclable waste*. https://ieeexplore.ieee.org/document/9395690
39. Kroell, N., Chen, X., Greiff, K., & Feil, A. (2022). Optical sensors and machine learning algorithms in sensor-based material flow characterization for mechanical recycling processes: A systematic literature review. *Waste Management*, *149*, 259–290. https://www.sciencedirect.com/science/article/pii/S0956053X22002628
40. Kumar, S., Datta, S., Singh, V., Singh, S. K., & Sharma, R. (2024). Opportunities and challenges in data-centric AI. *IEEE Access*, *12*, 33173–33189. https://doi.org/10.1109/ACCESS.2024.3369417
41. Kumsetty, N. V., Bhat Nekkare, A., Kamath, S., & Kumar M. A. (2022). *TrashBox: Trash detection and classification using quantum transfer learning*. https://ieeexplore.ieee.org/abstract/document/9770922
42. LeCun, Y., Bengio, Y., & Hinton, G. (2015). Deep learning. *Nature*, *521*(7553), 436–444. Publisher: Nature Publishing Group. https://www.nature.com/articles/nature14539
43. Liu, H., Rivera Soto, R. A., Xiao, F., & Jae Lee, Y. (2021). YolactEdge: Real-time instance segmentation on the edge, in *2021 IEEE International Conference on Robotics and Automation (ICRA)* (pp. 9579–9585). ISSN: 2577-087X. https://ieeexplore.ieee.org/document/9561858
44. Liu, Q., Luan, G., Wang, F., Peng, B., & Hu, D. (2021). Multi-focus image fusion algorithm based on unsupervised deep learning, in *2021 International Conference on Computer Information Science and Artificial Intelligence (CISAI)* (pp. 362–366). https://ieeexplore.ieee.org/document/9718997
45. Lotter, B., & Wiendahl, H.-P. (Eds.). (2012). *Montage in der industriellen Produktion: Ein Handbuch für die Praxis*. Berlin: Springer Berlin Heidelberg. https://link.springer.com/10.1007/978-3-642-29061-9
46. Luo, Y., & Luo, Z. (2023). Infrared and visible image fusion: Methods, datasets, applications, and prospects. *Applied Sciences*, *13*(19), 10891. Number: 19 Publisher: Multidisciplinary Digital Publishing Institute. https://www.mdpi.com/2076-3417/13/19/10891
47. Lv, Z., Chen, T., Cai, Z., & Chen, Z. (2023). Machine learning-based garbage detection and 3D spatial localization for intelligent robotic grasp. *Applied Sciences*, *13*(18), 10018. Number: 18 Publisher: Multidisciplinary Digital Publishing Institute. https://www.mdpi.com/2076-3417/13/18/10018

48. Lynch, S. (2018). OpenLitterMap.com – Open data on plastic pollution with blockchain rewards (Littercoin). *Open Geospatial Data, Software and Standards*, *3*(1), 1–10. Number: 1 Publisher: SpringerOpen. https://opengeospatialdata.springeropen.com/articles/10.1186/s40965-018-0050-y
49. Ma, J., Ma, Y., & Li, C. (2019). Infrared and visible image fusion methods and applications: A survey. *Information Fusion*, *45*, 153–178. https://www.sciencedirect.com/science/article/pii/S1566253517307972
50. MacDonald, L. (1999). Using color effectively in computer graphics. *IEEE Computer Graphics and Applications*, *19*(4), 20–35. Conference Name: IEEE Computer Graphics and Applications. https://ieeexplore.ieee.org/document/773961
51. Materials, A. (2022). *AZO materials*. https://www.azom.com/images/Article_Images/ImageForArticle_19837_16055024942l5494.png
52. Mei, L., & Jung, C. (2021). Deep fusion of RGB and NIR paired images using convolutional neural networks, in *2020 25th International Conference on Pattern Recognition (ICPR)* (pp. 6802–6803). ISSN: 1051-4651. https://ieeexplore.ieee.org/abstract/document/9412411
53. MEILO. (2024). *MEILO Gesellschaft zur Rückgewinnung sortierter Werkstoffe mbH & Co. KG - MEILO Gesellschaft zur Rückgewinnung sortierter Werkstoffe mbH & Co. Kg*. https://www.meilo-gernsheim.de/leistungen/hochwertiger-output
54. Moroni, M., Mei, A., Leonardi, A., Lupo, E., & Marca, F. L. (2015). PET and PVC separation with hyperspectral imagery. *Sensors*, *15*(1), 2205–2227. Number: 1 Publisher: Multidisciplinary Digital Publishing Institute. https://www.mdpi.com/1424-8220/15/1/2205
55. Ozaki, Y., Huck, C. W., & Beć, K. B. (2018). Chapter 2 - Near-IR spectroscopy and its applications, in Gupta, V. P. (Ed.), *Molecular and laser spectroscopy* (pp. 11–38). Elsevier. https://www.sciencedirect.com/science/article/pii/B9780128498835000024
56. Pande, B., Padamwar, K., Bhattacharya, S., Roshan, S., & Bhamare, M. (2022). A review of image annotation tools for object detection, in *2022 International Conference on Applied Artificial Intelligence and Computing (ICAAIC)* (pp. 976–982).
57. Pei, Y., Biswas, S., Fussell, D. S., & Pingali, K. (2019). *An elementary introduction to Kalman filtering*. arXiv:1710.04055 [cs, eess]. http://arxiv.org/abs/1710.04055
58. PIAB. (2024). *Round suction cups*. https://www.piab.com/suction-cups-and-soft-grippers/round-suction-cups/
59. PlasticScanner. (2022). *Plastic scanner*. https://plasticscanner.com/
60. Plataniotis, K. N., & Venetsanopoulos, A. N. (2000). *Color image processing and applications, Digital signal processing*. Berlin, Heidelberg: Springer. https://link.springer.com/10.1007/978-3-662-04186-4
61. Proença, P. F., & Simões, P. (2020). TACO: Trash annotations in context for litter detection. arXiv:2003.06975 [cs]. http://arxiv.org/abs/2003.06975
62. Robertson, P., & Schonhut, J. (1999). Color in computer graphics. *IEEE Computer Graphics and Applications*, *19*(4), 18–19. Conference Name: IEEE Computer Graphics and Applications. https://ieeexplore.ieee.org/document/773960
63. Schmalz. (2024). *Sauggreifer für die Verpackungsindustrie | Schmalz*. https://www.schmalz.com/de-de/vakuumtechnik-fuer-die-automation/vakuum-komponenten/vakuum-sauggreifer/sauggreifer-fuer-die-verpackungsindustrie/
64. Sen, B. (2020). *GU4204: Statistical Inference*. [Online]. Available: https://sites.stat.columbia.edu/bodhi/Talks/Lecture-Notes-Sp-2020.pdf
65. Sentz, K., & Ferson, S. (2002). *Combination of evidence in Dempster-Shafer theory*, Technical Report SAND2002-0835, 800792. https://www.osti.gov/servlets/purl/800792/
66. Siesler, H. W. (2001). Introduction, in *Near-infrared spectroscopy* (pp. 1–10). John Wiley & Sons, Ltd. Section: 1 _eprint: https://onlinelibrary.wiley.com/doi/pdf/10.1002/9783527612666.ch01. https://onlinelibrary.wiley.com/doi/abs/10.1002/9783527612666.ch01
67. SMC. (2024). *5,5-stufiger Faltenbalg mit Führungsbefestigung und Adapter - ZP3P-JT online kaufen | SMC Deutschland*. https://www.smc.eu/de-de/produkte/5-5-stufiger-faltenbalg-mit-fuehrungsbefestigung-und-adapter-zp3p-jt~163886~cfg

68. Soroush, R., & Baleghi, Y. (2023). NIR/RGB image fusion for scene classification using deep neural networks. *The Visual Computer*, *39*(7), 2725–2739. https://doi.org/10.1007/s00371-022-02488-0
69. Sosa Garcia, J., & Odone, F. (2017). “Hands on” visual recognition for visually impaired users. *ACM Transactions on Accessible Computing*, *10*, 1–30.
70. Tang, Q., Liang, J., & Zhu, F. (2023). A comparative review on multi-modal sensors fusion based on deep learning. *Signal Processing*, *213*, 109165. https://www.sciencedirect.com/science/article/pii/S0165168423002396
71. Themes, U. F. O. (2016). *Digital imaging characteristics*. https://radiologykey.com/digital-imaging-characteristics/
72. Thung, G., & Yang, M. (2016). *Classification of trash for recyclability status*. https://www.semanticscholar.org/paper/Classification-of-Trash-for-Recyclability-Status-Thung-Yang/c9081108292401 1c73fea6252f42b01af9076f28
73. van Gend, T., & Zuiderwijk, A. (2022). Open research data: A case study into institutional and infrastructural arrangements to stimulate open research data sharing and reuse. *Journal of Librarianship and Information Science*, p. 09610006221101200. Publisher: SAGE Publications Ltd. https://doi.org/10.1177/09610006221101200
74. Wang, T., Cai, Y., Liang, L., & Ye, D. (2020). A multi-level approach to waste object segmentation. *Sensors*, *20*(14), 3816. Number: 14 Publisher: Multidisciplinary Digital Publishing Institute. https://www.mdpi.com/1424-8220/20/14/3816
75. Wilkinson, M. D., Dumontier, M., Aalbersberg, I. J., Appleton, G., Axton, M., Baak, A., Blomberg, N., Boiten, J.-W., da Silva Santos, L. B., Bourne, P. E., Bouwman, J., Brookes, A. J., Clark, T., Crosas, M., Dillo, I., Dumon, O., Edmunds, S., Evelo, C. T., Finkers, R., Gonzalez-Beltran, A., Gray, A. J., Groth, P., Goble, C., Grethe, J. S., Heringa, J., ’t Hoen, P. A., Hooft, R., Kuhn, T., Kok, R., Kok, J., Lusher, S. J., Martone, M. E., Mons, A., Packer, A. L., Persson, B., Rocca-Serra, P., Roos, M., van Schaik, R., Sansone, S.-A., Schultes, E., Sengstag, T., Slater, T., Strawn, G., Swertz, M. A., Thompson, M., van der Lei, J., van Mulligen, E., Velterop, J., Waagmeester, A., Wittenburg, P., Wolstencroft, K., Zhao, J., & Mons, B. (2016). *The FAIR Guiding Principles for scientific data management and stewardship. Sci Data*, *3*, 160018. https://www.ncbi.nlm.nih.gov/pmc/articles/PMC4792175/
76. Wong, B. (2010). Salience. *Nature Methods*, *7*(10), 773–773. https://www.nature.com/articles/nmeth1010-773
77. Wu, T.-W., Zhang, H., Peng, W., Lü, F., & He, P.-J. (2023). Applications of convolutional neural networks for intelligent waste identification and recycling: A review. *Resources, Conservation and Recycling*, *190*, 106813. https://www.sciencedirect.com/science/article/pii/S0921344922006450
78. Yen, J. (1999). Fuzzy logic-a modern perspective. *IEEE Transactions on Knowledge and Data Engineering*, *11*(1), 153–165. Conference Name: IEEE Transactions on Knowledge and Data Engineering. https://ieeexplore.ieee.org/document/755624
79. Yudin, D., Zakharenko, N., Smetanin, A., Filonov, R., Kichik, M., Kuznetsov, V., Larichev, D., Gudov, E., Budennyy, S., & Panov, A. (2024). Hierarchical waste detection with weakly supervised segmentation in images from recycling plants. *Engineering Applications of Artificial Intelligence*, *128*, 107542. https://www.sciencedirect.com/science/article/pii/S0952197623017268
80. Zha, D., Bhat, Z. P., Lai, K.-H., Yang, F., Jiang, Z., Zhong, S., & Hu, X. (2023). *Data-centric artificial intelligence: A survey*. Preprint. arXiv:2303.10158.
81. Zhou, K., & Jung, C. (2020). Multispectral fusion of RGB and NIR images using weighted least squares and alternating guidance, in *ICASSP 2020 - 2020 IEEE International Conference on Acoustics, Speech and Signal Processing (ICASSP)* (pp. 1489–1493). ISSN: 2379-190X. https://ieeexplore.ieee.org/document/9054182
82. Zhuang, F., Qi, Z., Duan, K., Xi, D., Zhu, Y., Zhu, H., Xiong, H., & He, Q. (2020). A comprehensive survey on transfer learning. *Proceedings of the IEEE*, *109*(1), 43–76.